Mormon Women Have Their Say

Mormon Women Have Their Say

Essays from the Claremont Oral History Collection

Edited by
Claudia L. Bushman and Caroline Kline

GREG KOFFORD BOOKS
SALT LAKE CITY, 2013

Cover design by Loyd Ericson

Cover painting, "Wave Womb," by Galen Dara (www.galendara.com)

Published in the USA.

Greg Kofford Books
P.O. Box 1362
Draper, UT 84020
www.gregkofford.com

2017 16 15 14 13 5 4 3 2 1

Library of Congress Cataloging-in-Publication Data

Mormon women have their say : essays from the Claremont Oral History Collection / edited by Claudia L. Bushman and Caroline Kline.
pages cm
Includes bibliographical references and index.
ISBN 978-1-58958-494-5 (pbk.)
1. Mormon women--United States--Attitudes. 2. Women in the Mormon Church. I. Bushman, Claudia L., editor of compilation. II. Kline, Caroline (Caroline Esther), editor of compilation. III. Claremont Graduate School. Oral History Program, sponsoring body.
BX8643.W66M67 2013
289.3082--dc23

2012049780

"My voice unto all."

"Thy time shall be given to writing, and to learning much."

Doctrine and Covenants 25:16, 8

To learn more about or become involved with
the Claremont Oral History Project, visit
http://claremontmormonstudies.org/oral-histories

Contents

Foreword

Tammi J. Schneider

Women's voices, so common in domestic spaces, are rarely heard in the history books discussing the role of women in religious institutions and in the history of religions and their associated theologies and practices. This volume, a collection of essays based on the pioneering Claremont Mormon Women's Oral History Project overturns this and produces a volume where women's voices are not only heard but are the main focus. The essays cover a large range of women's experiences, grouped under the categories of Life Cycle, Life as a Latter-day Saint, and Relationships with the Institutional Church.

The root of this project is solidly planted in the tradition of Mormonism and Claremont Graduate University. There is a long tradition of Mormon women chronicling their lives through diaries. Mormon women have also been groundbreakers in social movements. The Mormon focus on providing for oneself and others, through such institutions as the Relief Society, make a firm foundation for Mormon women to lay a bold trail for other groups to follow. Thus, while this volume focuses specifically on the unique tradition and practices specific to Mormons, the data for the project (women's oral histories) and the approach (examining women's lived experiences) are those with universal appeal and potential for application well beyond Mormon women.

It is also not surprising that such a project and volume would originate from Claremont Graduate University (CGU). CGU is home to the first Women's Studies in Religion program in the United States. For more than twenty years, CGU Religion faculty and their students have been asking questions previously considered unimportant, highlighting the significant role women have had in the construction of religion in the broadest sense and in how it was conducted in the past.

The focus on the past is not merely an academic exercise, but it raises the profile of what women are doing today in the numerous spheres of religion, lifting the hopes of what women can and will do in the future.

CGU also has the first Mormon Studies Program outside the state of Utah. The reason for this is the recognition in Claremont that Mormonism must be treated as a religion just as worthy of academic study as other religious traditions. While Mormon scholars have participated for years in the most prestigious institutions of the academy—and some have examined history and literature of the Mormon religion—studying Mormonism as a religion alongside others is a new venture for the academy. Thus, it is particularly exciting that at the beginning of this journey the focus is not on the traditional forms of treating a religion, namely men and their role in the institutions of the religious structure and its theology, but on the lived experiences of women: how they incorporate the teachings and lifestyle of the Church and how religion feels from different women's unique personal vantage point.

This volume, even with a focus on women, still lifts up some of the important issues that must be examined in an academic study of religion in general and Mormonism in particular. Issues found in many religious traditions include: fertility, revelation, personal devotion, agency, and patriarchy. The volume also includes topics unique to Mormonism: how Mormons approach topics such as singlehood, adversity, missions, a Heavenly Mother, and the Relief Society. As a result, the volume provides a blueprint on how to situate a study on women's lived experiences within the general realm of Women's Studies and yet still retain the unique perspective of a specific religious tradition.

This volume as a blueprint is significant in light of the impact that the Mormon Women's Oral History Project has had upon CGU and its next stage. The unique approach of this project—examining religion through the personal oral histories of women—has sparked a larger project, The Claremont Women's Living History Project, whose goal is to record, store, and create a database of women's religious oral histories from numerous religious traditions. This project grows directly from the Mormon Women's Oral History Project and seeks to follow the path of examining religion and women through recording the lives of women who lived it. By incorporating other religious traditions, the hope is that the similarities and differences between women's lives in relation to their religions will help scholars understand the various traditions of their own religions as well as to further broaden the data for doing work in comparative religion.

This volume is a timely and much-needed contribution to the academic fields of Religion, Women's Studies, and Mormon Studies. While the volume and the project from which it grows are clearly an academic contribution, they also contain another feature widely promoted in Claremont: research that matters. The project combines the best of academic rigor with a passion for the impact this study and the data set from which it flows has on those people living the tradition. As the many oral histories attest, religion is not simply a matter of what someone says or does periodically but the rules and traditions that shape a person's life and the lives of her family and those around her. It is therefore not a purely academic matter of distant people whose lives are far removed from today and are interesting artifacts of time. These oral histories belong to living people and demonstrate how religion plays a role in their grappling with all that we face today.

Tammi J. Schneider
Dean, School of Arts, Humanities, and Religion
Claremont Graduate University

Introduction

Claudia L. Bushman

I

Throughout the tangled past of the Church of Jesus Christ of Latter-day Saints, women have been active and vocal participants. Their journals and diaries, primarily from the nineteenth century, have been plumbed for evidence of their experience and attitudes. Less is known and written about *contemporary* Mormon women. LDS women today still live in a patriarchal society. What is it like for them? How do they respond to the Church they have joined or inherited? Can they make space for their interests? How do they envision their contemporary role in the Church? What are the issues that define their lives? How do they experience their family relations? How have Mormon principles shaped their lives? What is the basis of their faith and loyalty? Do they think for themselves? To what extent do they speak out? The Claremont Oral History Project on Mormon Women in the Twentieth and Twenty-First Centuries, on which this book was based, was organized to help address such questions.

The Claremont Oral History Project is a response to a grant from the Singer Foundation to do "something for women." An oral history program was settled on because we considered that it would be beneficial to many women: students would learn to manage a new program, the women interviewed would review their lives and create a written account for themselves and their families, and our scholars would benefit from a trove of signed and dated primary sources to work on now and into the future. The program has proved valuable to all those groups and has been of interest to other Mormons and members of the general public who have listened to and applauded the presentations of the papers coming out of the project. Already the voices of Mormon women have been amplified.

Begun in 2009 and carried out by the graduate students in the Claremont Graduate University School of Religion and by women from the Latter-day Saint community, the collection now numbers more than 160 completed, transcribed, and digitized interviews with more in the process of transcription and editing.

While written accounts of Mormon women's lives have been encouraged and valued for the almost 200 years of the Church's history, those from eminent women have, for the most part, been privileged. The stories of female leaders and the wives of male leaders, along with faith-promoting accounts of pioneer heroism, have been used to teach faith and inspire religious principles in the rising generation. Recently the stories of interesting dissidents have documented their involvement in Mormon culture.

The Claremont Oral History Project has collected stories from a wide group of Mormon women. Those interviewed for the project—we call them our narrators—are chosen not at random, but by growing outward in all directions from the original student nucleus. Some women are chosen by the interviewers, some by committees or because they have had interesting lives, some, wanting to tell their stories, volunteer, and some write and submit their own stories. No one knows all these women. In choosing our narrators, our only requirements have been their female gender, a significant connection to the LDS Church, and a willingness to tell their stories. They do not need to be of any particular age, activity in the Church, marital condition, or ethnic group. They range from their teens to their nineties, with widely differing educational achievement, marital status, number of children, and faithfulness. We have interviewed beauty queens, CEO's, converts, Relief Society presidents, inactives, bishops' wives, high school drop-outs, PhDs, and women on welfare. We have women returned from Church missions and divorcees, temple workers and excommunicants. This project records the experiences of LDS women in their homes and family lives, their church lives, and their work lives, in their roles as homemakers, students, missionaries, career women, single women, converts, and disaffected members. We have many frank voices. These signed and dated statements, currently amounting to 2,500 single-spaced pages, are a rich source at the moment of their creation and will continue to increase in value. I think that they are pure gold.

Our narrators see in advance a single page of general questions. Our effort has been to record what they say in response. They are asked biographical questions and for comments about current Mormon women's issues and experience. If they can carry on a monologue without prompting, we are happy to record that. We do not want to lead our narrators. We do not require them to make certain strong statements. We want to record their stories as they wish to tell them. If the narrator has nothing to say about some subject, that is fine. If there are certain topics that the interviewer would like more information on, she may ask, "Do you want to say anything more about that?" but she doesn't probe. This is not a tight interview. Our guiding principle is to be open. Our interviewers try to be warm, interested, and approving. They listen to our narrators and maybe nod occasionally. Interviewers sometimes cannot resist offering comments, but this is the narrator's story, not a conversation. If people offer to talk about some other topics, good. We like episodes, stories, attitudes, anecdotes, experiences. Narrators are reminded that they will be free to take out anything that on second thought they wish omitted. They will also be able to add, rearrange, and expand down the line. They have the final say.

As they type, transcribers edit the recording a little, smoothing out repetitions, grammatical errors, false starts, and whatever else they find distracting. Narrators do not want to hear themselves making mistakes. All questions and interviewer comments are edited out. We try to provide clean versions of what the narrators said for them to look over and edit. Considerable labor goes into completing these transcriptions. This is demanding work.

As the project began, Claremont students continually discussed the process, working through the policies and questions. Procedures were adjusted as the finished interviews rolled in. Reviewed and finalized documents were numbered and added to the collection. At the time of the May 1, 2010, Oral History Tea, the project had completed fifty-three interviews toward the projected goal of one hundred. At the time of the February 5, 2011, conference, *Women's Lives, Women's Voices: Agency in the Lives of Mormon Women*, the project had completed one hundred and seventeen interviews; a new goal to reach two hundred interviews was agreed on.

These recorded stories combine the private lives of women with their lived religion and Church experience. Their stories feed into and illuminate the broader narrative of LDS history and belief. The accounts expand and soften the more rigid assumptions about private life and religion, bringing an additional and valuable dimension to the

Mormon story. The stories of these women, marked by subtlety and nuance, defy the stereotypes. Many of these narrators would ordinarily be silent. They may have had things to say but would have been unlikely to say them because they did not understand the value of their own stories. This project preserves and perpetuates their voices and memories. The silent majority speaks in these records.

This project was begun in Southern California and soon expanded to the western states. The voices now reflect the broader United States, and workers are taking on the global Church. So far, we have interviews from ten other countries. Translations complicate the process, but we soldier on.

For now, the collected materials are used for projects by the people who have created and recorded them. The materials are not yet open to the public. Eventually the body of material will be added to the collections of professionally managed archives and opened for the wider use of scholars. The specific individual interview material belongs equally to the narrators of the stories and the project.

This ongoing project has no natural ending point, and we are always willing to broaden the group. Individuals can contribute their own first-person stories in written form. Organizers can recruit interviewers and narrators and set about creating their own local cells and projects. We invite groups to keep in touch and ask that copies of their documents and interviews in online form be sent to us to be included in our larger project.

We have happily seen positive social consequences of the oral history work and the creation of this book. The students have racked up numerous items for their professional résumés. Our narrators have seen more value in their own stories. They have seen opportunities for speaking up and expanding their personal spaces. Some, having found their voices, keep writing. Women with secrets have felt more disposed to own them than to hide them. The range of the acceptable has been expanded, and a sense of community and sisterhood has grown.

II

Our aim has been to produce a product that can be put to multiple ends by multiple minds. This publication of topical essays is the first to explore the riches of the collection in print. A group of young scholars and others who have used the interviews as sources for presentations and papers, have written these essays. Several of them plan to write theses and dissertations based on the collection. They have studied the interviews, looking for light and knowledge on a range of possible beliefs and actions. They have valued the frank paragraphs, the painful episodes, the life lessons learned, along with the humanity that they find in the writings of their sisters.

Just what do they have to work with? They have long statements, most between fifteen and thirty-five single-spaced pages, of what women had to say at that particular moment on many different topics. This is an open-ended effort, a net to catch whatever topic was thrown out in the hope of gathering in an abundance of valuable and interesting material. We do not aim to prove anything about what Mormon women think or have to say. Everything here is suggestive. We work with an extensive sample of mostly oral communications in written form, which show a range of responses on a number of issues. This book represents experience transferred into language through the limited views of many narrators and essayists.

Mormonism is a culturally abundant topic, full of supernatural events, but real to those who have experienced them. There are magical objects, events out of time and place, a separate religious language. This vital and fertile tradition allows free speaking and individual thinking on all issues. The doctrine of free agency allows people to make their own decisions about what they think and what paths they should pursue. People who have been through that process can describe those experiences. Some receive what they feel is divine direction and revelation. They feel their prayers have been answered. They have had rich experiences and have rich things to say, intensely personal accounts that come from deep wells of experience.

What can be found in these documents? Everything. I find more individual thinking and less conformity than I would expect. People speak openly. They know the rote answers, but they say other things. I see lots of doctrinal creation as people make sense out of their traditional beliefs and their experiences. I see lots of free agency, dependence on divine sources, and bypassing marital and structural authority. I see defiantly strong women who have overcome early guilt. There is lots of pain, lots of triumph, and many specific answers to contemporary questions by women who have been there.

Writing our own stories empowers us. Many of these narrators do not ordinarily speak out. This project preserves and perpetuates their voices and memories. The silent majority goes on record. What they say is only a representation of what is in their minds, not the impossibly elusive truth. Yet with all the limitations, these stories illuminate their worlds. We have to get such stories down. If we want to live forever in the minds and annals of the earth, if we want other women to be represented into the future, we have to leave a record.

This present volume of essays is by writers who have worked over the interviews thematically and comparatively, aiming to interpret and make sense of them. Our essayists here, familiar with the Mormon tradition, have been told to give context to their quotations from the collection, and they have chosen varied settings. They have organized the material through the lenses of history, LDS Church doctrine, mythology, feminist theory, personal experience, the work of other historians, and even through current events. Each topic could be viewed through other lenses. Each writer could have chosen from dozens of other topics or dozens of other interviews. We see this collection as an inexhaustible source of illumination.

These interviews can be mined in the future for answers to questions still unformulated. We expect that future scholars will use them to understand our present. We hope that the written records we produce will prove useful to the narrators and their families. We hope that the available pot of interviews will grow much, much larger. We hope that there will be multigenerational records: grandmother, mother, and daughter. We hope that these ongoing records, which are very much of their own date and place, will reflect changing attitudes in the Church.

What are the dangers of this kind of information gathering? Oral historians have been criticized for taking advantage of their subjects because the relationship between them is unequal: the interviewer may steal the narrator's story for her own purposes. We have tried to make this a more equal partnership by creating the collection so that the primary end of the project is to preserve the voices of the narrators rather than the conclusions of scholars writing about them. Scholarship resulting from study of the interviews is secondary to preserving the documents as spoken and approved by the narrators. The project is also made more equal by including the interviewers themselves and their relatives as narrators. Many of our narrators have gone on to interview others. We are all in this together. We consider it a privilege rather than an exploitation to be part of the program. Many of the narrator-interviewer pairs are acquainted as equals and feel comfortable together, sharing a basic trust.

We are respectful of our narrators. They may say whatever they want to say and we will record it. They may say anything they wish to say and we will not question it. They may choose to remove parts of the interviews and we honor the request. We try to provide an accurate, if tidied up, account of what they have said and what they would like to have said. We refer to our interviews by number and edit quotations to avoid identification. All names in this volume are pseudonyms.

We hope that readers of this volume will enjoy these glimpses into Mormon women's lives. These essays and the interviews that they deal with are our gift to the women who were interviewed, to their families, and to the future.

Acknowledgments

As always we acknowledge the fruitful donation of the Singer Foundation, administered by Dianne Callister, as the founding gesture of this project. We thank Tammi J. Schneider for her generous foreword. We appreciate the help and ongoing support of the Mormon Studies Council at Claremont Graduate University and the Howard W. Hunter Chair of Mormon Studies, now held by Patrick Q. Mason. We thank Lisa Thomas Clayton for administering the Claremont Oral History Project in California and David Golding for formatting and digitizing the entire collection for easy use. He has refined the gold. We appreciate the permission that the Society for Mormon Philosophy and Theology gave to publish Amy Hoyt's paper, originally published in another form in *Element*. We thank Greg Kofford and Loyd Ericson for seeing the value of these women's voices and publishing them.

I particularly thank Caroline Kline for her assiduous and thoughtful work as co-editor of this volume. Although she had plenty of other things to do, she took on heavy responsibilities for seeing this project to fruition.

Greatest appreciation goes to all past, present, and future collaborators and participants in this project for the community they have created and will continue to create.

Claudia L. Bushman
October 2012
New York City

Part One

Life Cycle

Chapter One

Self and Other

Caroline Kline

In 1975, Mormon poet Carol Lynn Pearson published a poem entitled "Millie's Mother's Red Dress." In this poem she describes a woman whose self-sacrifice and self-abnegation were so extreme that she ultimately taught her family "that a woman doesn't / Even exist except to give." As she lies dying she tells her daughter Millie:

> I always thought
> That a good woman never takes her turn
> That she's just for doing for somebody else.
> . . . Always keep
> Everybody else's wants tended and make sure
> Yours are at the bottom of the heap.
>
> . . .
>
> Oh Millie, Millie, it was no good—
> For you—For him. Don't you see?
> I did the worst of wrongs.
> I asked nothing—for me!

Her last words to her daughter Millie are, "Do me the honor, Millie, / Of not following in my footsteps. / Promise me that."[1]

Pearson's poem highlights a dangerous type of self-sacrifice, a self-sacrifice that is so extreme that it leads to near self-obliteration. While Pearson's poem focuses on a Mormon woman practicing extreme self-denial, feminist theologians and scholars for decades have noted the tendency women have in general toward this kind of self-abnegation. Christian theology has traditionally placed pride or selfishness as humankind's greatest moral failing, but in the 1960s, feminist theologian

1. Carol Lynn Pearson, "Millie's Mother's Red Dress," *Exponent II*, October, 1975.

Valerie Saiving postulated that, in fact, this paradigm generally fits men better than women. She posited that women's greatest sin is actually the opposite—"the underdevelopment or negation of Self," or in other words, living for and through others and continually sacrificing one's own wants and needs for others. Saiving writes, "a woman can give too much of herself, so that nothing remains of her own uniqueness; she can become merely an emptiness, almost a zero, without value to herself, to her fellow men."[2]

Later feminist ethicists like Sarah Hoagland suggest that this paradigm of selfish versus selfless, or pride versus self-sacrifice is not the lens through which we should view our relationships or ourselves. She sees it as inadequate and advocates stepping away from this language of self-sacrifice, since it presupposes that an individual's needs or desires are naturally in conflict with others' needs and desires. She explains, "the selfish/selfless dichotomy does not accurately categorize our actions. . . . Concern for ourselves does not imply disregarding the needs of others."[3]

Hoagland goes on to say that in order to move away from the self-sacrifice/selfish paradigm, one must obtain the self-understanding that our actions are deliberate choices to engage which benefit both self and other. She states that when we help a friend move or fix her furniture, we tend to view these acts as a sacrifice. However, she proposes that instead we "regard choosing to do something as creation." She explains that choosing to help someone else

> involve[s] a choice between two or more things to do, and we will have reasons for any choice we make. . . . We can regard our choosing to interact as part of how we engage in this living. Such choices are matters of focus, not sacrifice. That I attend certain things and not others, that I focus here and not there, is part of how I create value. Far from sacrificing myself, or part of myself, I am creating.[4]

---

2. Valerie Saiving, "The Human Condition," *Womanspirit Rising*, ed. Judith Plaskow and Carol Christ (New York: HarperOne, 1992), 35.

3. Sarah Hoagland, *Lesbian Ethics: Toward New Values* (Palo Alto: Institute of Lesbian Studies, 1989), 88. It is important to note that Hoagland's ideas and insights arise from and are situated within the lesbian community, a community that has rejected hetero-patriarchal power structures. However, I believe that many of her ideas can illuminate women's lives and choices, whether women locate themselves in hetero-patriarchal communities or not.

4. Ibid., 91.

Hoagland sees this emphasis on creation and choice, rather than self-sacrifice, as a source of power for women—one that leads to female agency. For Hoagland, this female agency then begins to be a process of engagement and creation, as women regard their choices, not as sacrifices, but rather as opportunities to create something meaningful. Whether the choice is to teach high school rather than go into law, whether it is to stay home with children or open up a bookstore, or whether it is to spend time with a friend or read an inspiring book, these choices are opportunities to create meaning in a person's life. Hoagland's paradigm of finding engagement and meaning in our choices is premised on the idea that self-understanding is essential. A person must understand her limits, her desires, and the meaning she wishes to create in her life. She must also have the self-understanding to know when it is time to change course in her life.

In short, Saiving and Hoagland give us two different paradigms through which to view women's choices. Saiving's paradigm is based on the idea that women are in particular danger of privileging others' needs and desires to such an extent that they nearly erase themselves as humans. Implicit in Saiving's framework is the idea that the self is separate (maybe even opposed) from the other—that in paying attention to the needs of the other, one is in danger of neglecting or harming the needs of the self. Hoagland, on the other hand, finds this framework inadequate, arguing that the self and the other are not necessarily opposed. A person is not necessarily harming the other when she focuses on her own needs, and she is not necessarily harming herself when she focuses on the needs of others. Hoagland also argues that considering our choices as opportunities for creation is more fruitful than seeing them as self-sacrifice or selfishness. Ultimately, Hoagland's framework occupies a flexible middle space between the extremes of selfishness and self-sacrifice.

As I examined oral histories from the Claremont Mormon Women Oral History Project, I explored how these differing concepts play out in the lives of Mormon women. Do Mormon women tend toward an extreme self-sacrifice for the good of their families or their communities, in accordance with Saiving's ideas? Or, as Hoagland suggests, do women regard their choices to care for themselves and others as creation and engagement? Do they listen to both their own needs and the needs of others, and not necessarily see them as conflicting? How do motherhood, career, and family relationships fit into this paradigm?

In this paper, I have organized anecdotes from these oral histories into three main sections: a) self-sacrifice, in which I explore anecdotes that highlight the sort of self-denial or self-abnegation that Saiving warns against; b) beyond self-sacrifice, in which I explore the ways women take a flexible and nuanced approach, like Hoagland, to issues of work and stay-at-home motherhood, as well as the ways they view their choices as opportunities to create meaning in their lives; and c) embracing the whole self, in which I analyze the ways women abandon the idea that concern for the self is selfish, as their rich senses of self-understanding lead them to leave behind people and thought patterns that diminish or abuse them.[5]

Self-Sacrifice

While the majority of oral histories do not display the kind of self-obliterating self-sacrifice that Saiving describes women being particularly susceptible to, there are moments in the lives of some Mormon women interviewed that show glimpses of self-abnegation—a willingness to sacrifice their own good, their own interests, and sometimes, their own selves in order to please others. These moments appear most often when the women describe relationships with their parents or with their spouses.

The following anecdote is one such example. Connie describes her own self disappearing in the early part of her marriage in the late 1950s as she tried to meld her life with her new husband's:

> I was living the life I had always been told to look forward to.... And yet, I had this sense that I was disappearing. I had felt that upon marriage a woman should give up her life and become part of her husband's life. They were to share everything, spend time together. I was willing to give up my own interests and life which were not that great, but I found that my husband had little interest in sharing his life. He had no time for me.... He was plainly bored by our occasional Sunday outings.... We had little to discuss. I began to feel that I only existed in his mind and that he very seldom thought about

5. These categories are fluid. An anecdote might fall into any one of these three categories depending on what aspect of the anecdote one is emphasizing.

> me. I went to an occasional student party with him and found myself completely ignored, looked through, although that would not have been the case when I was a single student myself. . . . Even at church I felt that I had lost status by becoming a married woman instead of a single student.
>
> What to do. I did a lot of thrashing around. What I eventually did do was to go back to school. . . . These classes helped me a lot as they gave me something to think about, books to read, places to go. I was much more cheerful. But I still spent a lot of time crying.[6]

This passage reflects Connie's willingness to give up her interests and goals in order to submerge her life into her husband's, only to find that she was not welcome there. Her sense of herself as invisible or disappearing mirrors Saiving's ideas about self-sacrificing women—those who stifle their desires to be separate individuals but instead become emptiness or zeros. She was only able to remove herself from this mind frame by giving herself a new sense of purpose as she pursued her own goals and interests through classes. Her final statement, that she still spent a lot of time crying, reflects the difficulty and pain of this transition, as she learned the necessity of nourishing her own self and growing, independent of her husband.

The following anecdote likewise gives us glimpses into the minds of Mormon women as they deal with ideas of female self-sacrifice. Laurel, a woman with a strong sense of self, saw other Mormon women around her being damaged by their interpretations of certain messages that were being promulgated in LDS Church culture during the 1980s. Unlike the previous example, in which self-obliteration occurs as the result of internal ideas about the fusing of two people in marriage, these women in this next example experience self-obliteration because of external injunctions from certain Mormon leaders to devote themselves wholly to the home. As Laurel states,

> In the 1980s there was a big area [women's] conference in the Rose Bowl. . . . There were three men who spoke, and two women. The [speakers] all emphasized . . . motherhood. Wifehood. Home, home, home. I was singing in the big choir that was performing that day and I was listening to the young women around and they were crying. . . . They said they weren't doing enough . . .

---

6. Claremont Mormon Women's Oral History Collection, Library of the Claremont Colleges, Claremont, CA, hereafter COHC, #012 (2009), 12–13.

> The young women were saying, "I'm not a good enough wife and mother." One especially who had been working on a weight problem had been going to a gym some distance from her home. . . . She said, "I have to drive quite a long distance, leaving my family for several hours. They're well taken care of, but I'm away from them." She cried and cried, saying she'd have to give it up. So I started writing down all of these things . . . . I shot off a letter to Barbara Smith, the general Relief Society president, saying that instead of being uplifted by the conference, the women around me had fallen into a pit of depression. I also said, "I brought my daughter to the conference, expecting to have women's problems talked about. But all we heard was that we must submerge our own personalities to be faithful wives and mothers." She wrote back, saying, "After all, isn't this what we'll be doing in the eternities?" I wrote back saying, "So the men go off and create the worlds and we're home taking care of all of the multitude of kids." She wrote back a very nice letter after that. I had kind of jolted her a little bit. . . . She explained that this was what we concentrated on but there were so many more aspects to life. So I wondered why they had not mentioned those aspects in the women's conference. After that, my daughter pretty well departed from the Church.[7]

This passage reflects two very different images of Mormon women's self-conceptions. On the one hand, we see the crying young women who were ready to unhappily sacrifice outside pursuits they felt enhanced their lives in order to follow the injunctions of their Mormon leaders to focus on the home. On the other hand, we see Laurel who is absolutely confident that the needs of women which go beyond the home are important and lead to self development in healthy ways. Her sense of self is so strong and her belief that women should have the freedom to develop beyond the home is so secure that she is willing to write the general Relief Society president a letter asking her to account for these messages. Unlike the previous example, in which the narrator discovers for herself a way to transcend this unhealthy self-abnegating dynamic, we see in this example an outside person, Laurel, attempting to shepherd young women toward a different perspective—one that honors female development on a multitude of levels.

While the previous examples highlight self-abnegating conceptions of women's roles that lead to stunted and limited senses of self,

7. COHC, #009 (2009), 12.

the oral history of Julie features a self-sacrificing mentality that is not gendered. Rather, the narrator attributes her mentality to messages of Christian love and forgiveness that led her to tolerate abusive treatment from her family members for years.

> The biggest crisis moment of my life was when I realized I could no longer maintain a close relationship with extended family members whom I could not trust. I had to let go of all relationships that were damaging my spiritual and mental health. [There was one particularly painful betrayal]. . . . I absolutely knew I could not be the same person any more. I could not be the same scared me and become the healthy happy individual I wanted to be. I wasn't safe physically, mentally, or emotionally with my family members. I had to move out of target range.
>
> I was home alone when all the pain, fear, and sadness I had stuffed inside came out. I was alone on the floor in my bedroom, spread eagle clawing at the ground much like I had as a child. I allowed myself to feel how bad I felt about all the pain in my family of origin. I realized that no matter how much I loved and forgave these family members, I had to let them go. I had to become a different person who was able to say, "I cannot maintain relationships with anyone who doesn't treat me with kindness and respect." It was an extremely painful yet freeing decision. Once I allowed myself to feel, to really feel the pain, I was able to get to the other side. I had been stuck for fifty years thinking it was okay to let people abuse me because the Gospel taught me to love and forgive. I have learned that I don't have to let go of my love for them but I must not allow abusers in my life for my own safety and well-being. I can never place myself or my posterity in harm's way again. That was a changing moment in my life.[8]

This passage highlights the pull Julie feels between protecting herself and maintaining relationships with her family. She had been operating under a self-sacrificial love, one that was damaging to the "healthy happy individual" she wanted to be. But a crisis moment forces her to realize that her well being must take precedence in this kind of abusive situation, that boundaries must be established to protect herself and her children. We see in this passage a pivotal moment in which the narrator realizes that she has a duty not only to love others, but also to love and protect herself. She is able to move herself away from a self-sacrificial love, as

8. COHC, #070 (2010), 6–7.

she learns that she can still follow Christian dictates to love and forgive without putting herself in situations where she would be further abused.

Each one of these passages showcases moments (sometimes years) of women sacrificing their own well-being, their own sense of self, and their own needs in order to care for or love those around them. These are choices of a self-obliterating self-sacrifice that do not expand their beings. Rather this dynamic leads these women to collapse in on themselves, much like Valerie Saiving's depiction of sacrificial love.

It must be noted, however, that in every one of these anecdotes, we also see escape. Self-abnegation is not an equilibrium that can be perpetually maintained. There is always a trajectory out of this mind frame; these women describe leaving it behind through the pursuit of their own goals, through the realization of the importance of their own selves, or through outside women taking action to stop this dynamic and shepherding other women beyond it.

Moving Away from the Self-Sacrifice Paradigm

While there are moments in these oral histories that highlight self-abnegating love, I found that Hoagland's paradigm regarding the choice to engage with others as a form of creation, rather than self-sacrifice, was generally more useful in evaluating both the thoughts and the actions of Mormon women who were navigating between their own needs and the needs of others. The nuanced and flexible quality of Hoagland's paradigm—that in helping others, one wasn't necessarily denying the self, and that in focusing on one's self, one wasn't necessarily hurting the other—was a view that came out in many of the histories.

Motherhood and career choices were two main topics that brought out fluidity and flexibility of Mormon women's thoughts on their choices regarding how to engage in the world and nurture both self and other. Despite the Proclamation on the family's assertion that individual adaptation to the prescribed gender roles according to circumstance is acceptable,[9] there is, I would argue, a narrative (not the only narrative, but a narrative) in Mormon culture that the choice to work is a selfish decision for mothers who are not in desperate financial straits,

---

9. "The Family: A Proclamation to the World," read by President Gordon B. Hinckley as part of his message at the General Relief Society Meeting held September 23, 1995, in Salt Lake City, Utah.

while choosing to stay home is a selfless decision for mothers. A 2007 article in the Church magazine *Ensign* titled, "Mother, Come Home," exemplifies this particular narrative as the author, a woman, talks about giving up a high-powered career to be a stay-at-home mom.[10] In it, she creates a stark opposition between the two choices. Being a stay-at-home mom is rewarding in deeply human ways as she leads a life full of compassion and kindness, whereas having a high-powered career is about the clothes, the power, impressing people, and bringing home a large paycheck. One can see the opposition the author is creating as she says that since becoming a full-time stay-at-home mom she has "worn clothes covered in peanut butter smears instead of power suits; cleaned my home each day instead of enjoyed a penthouse view from my office; bandaged 'owies' and encouraged piano practice instead of handing out performance reviews; and enjoyed hugs and kisses instead of stock options as my compensation plan."[11] In short, the message emerges that stay-at-home motherhood is about devoting oneself to the other, and working in her chosen field is about the self and the superficial.[12]

The rhetorical strategy of the article—to paint these two decisions into these two different selfish/selfless camps—leaves little room for nuanced points about how women can be motivated by the righteous desire to use their God-given abilities and talents to contribute meaningfully to the world through working. Some families and children might be better off for having a mother who is happily and productively engaged in activities outside the home, or the choice to stay at home with children might actually give women time and freedom to pursue other interests and passions that they would otherwise be unable to pursue if they were working. The stark categories the author establishes—selfish actions and selfless actions—mirror the overarching framework of Saiving, who likewise views women's actions through this dichotomous paradigm. The article does not reflect the flexibility

10. Shauna Bird Dunn, "Mother, Come Home," *Ensign*, April 2007, 9–13.

11. Ibid., 12–13.

12. Interestingly, while the author creates this dichotomy between the selflessness/meaningfulness of stay-at-home mothering and the superficiality of pursuing a corporate career, she does mention that she worked full-time when some of her children were small, because she felt spiritual confirmation that this was the best decision for her family. So even though her rhetoric creates this opposition, her lived experience is clearly more nuanced.

that Hoagland describes, as she advocates women viewing their life choices, not as opportunities for selfishness or selflessness, but rather as opportunities for creation.

In the oral histories, these kinds of nuances revolving around the development of the self and the other often emerged as the interviewers asked questions about home and work in their lives. There was a theme of women often taking a flexible approach to these questions, revealing a tendency to veer away from austere ideas about women's duties to self-sacrifice through focus on the home. Perhaps this reluctance to take a hard line on the issue of working mothers is due to other narratives present in Mormon culture that encourage female achievement outside the home. President Gordon B. Hinckley himself created a counterpoint to the selfish working mother narrative when he said to the young women in 2001, "The whole gamut of human endeavor is now open to women. There is not anything that you cannot do if you will set your mind to it. You can include in the dream of the woman you would like to be a picture of one qualified to serve society and make a significant contribution to the world of which she will be a part."[13] Hinckley's characterization of career as "serving society" stands in direct contrast to other Mormon narratives that define careers for mothers as serving the self. In accordance with the variety of narratives present in Mormon culture about work and motherhood, I found that while women often voiced support for the *principle* that families and motherhood were supremely important, they were wary of *prescribing* what form that principle should take.

Principle as Opposed to Prescription

The oral history of Elizabeth is a classic example of this flexibility. The narrator points to her view about the importance of family and motherhood by stating that staying at home was personally the correct decision for her, but she also indicates an openness toward other paths:

> For me it was the right decision to be home with my children. I am fortunate to be in a position where I could make that decision. I have friends [however] who have been much better mothers for

13. Gordon B. Hinckley, "How Can I Become the Woman of Whom I Can Dream?" *Ensign*, May 2001, 93.

> having work to be engaged in, to be active in careers or jobs. I trust women to do what's right for themselves.[14]

We can see here an unwillingness to take a hard stand about the universal correctness of women choosing to stay at home with their children. As Hoagland suggests, Elizabeth regards other women pursuing their goals and passions outside the home as not necessarily opposed to the best interests of their families. Her last sentence about trusting women to do what's right for themselves indicates an unwillingness to state a prescription for how individual mothers should make these decisions.

Holly likewise shows a fluidity of thought on the topic of mothers, work, and obligations to nurture both self and other, while at the same time affirming the importance of the principle of family.

> I do think that it's extremely important to nurture the next generation . . . whether they are your own children, or other people's children, whether they are young or teens or also young adults. I see no virtue in staying home if you're not using your time well to nurture your children or others, none at all. (In fact it seems selfish when there is so much that needs to be done in the world, so much suffering to care for, so much truth to be discovered, so much beauty to be shared, so very much to be done to make things better.) But children can be nurtured in a wide variety of ways. I stayed home when they were home, mostly, but I saw no reason to be there when they were in school, so I wasn't! Everyone's circumstances are different, so I think it's very important to talk about nurturing the next generation, but not to preach the details of what this means for individuals. I think the idea shouldn't be home vs. work, but to go deeper into what the real issue is, and that, I think, is that children should be very well cared for. Then we should each figure out the details given our own circumstances.[15]

Holly actually turns the selfish working mother narrative on its head by stating that staying at home is actually the selfish choice if one's time isn't spent well. She sees a need for nurturing the next generation to extend beyond the walls of the home, and affirms women who choose to contribute to their worlds and communities and future generations in this way. Like the previous narrator, Holly steps back from hard and

14. COHC, #019 (2009), 7.
15. COHC, #051 (2010), 34.

fast prescriptions for women, and she instead focuses on women having the personal obligation to figure out the best way for them to contribute to their communities, their families, and future generations.

Anne's oral history gives us a vivid recounting of a woman's attempt to live up to the prescribed ideal of mothers staying in the home and the ultimate realization that it just was not the best choice for her family. She discusses her sister's decision to quit her full-time job in order to be home with her small children. She tries desperately to make this work financially through taking odd jobs. Anne recounts this story:

> So she was trying to work this job in the middle of the night. She worked another part-time job on weekends. She was constantly trying to find ways to make ends meet. . . . Then in 2000, when her youngest was two, she invented her product. They got their company started in 2001. And all during that time . . . she was again working full time, and she had a nanny who would come in and care for her kids. She was completely ok with doing that. This is the interesting thing about my sister—she did try to conform to the stay-at-home motherhood ideal, but she was also completely willing to set it aside when she felt it was right to be working.[16]

This woman's story once again highlights a fluidity and flexibility when it comes to women working, despite making serious attempts to live up to the prescribed ideal. For this family, it turned out that what was best for the mother's health and sanity—working full-time—was also best for the family at large. As Hoagland suggests in her framework, this is an example of a woman's choice that benefits both self and other simultaneously. Her story is also notable in that it highlights a woman who is ultimately willing to be guided by her family circumstances and her personal convictions about the rightness of this path in making this decision to work full-time again.

While nuance and flexibility came out in several women's discussions about the benefits to the self and to the family that might come about from women working, other women emphasized flexibility in a slightly different way. They adhered to a "seasons of life" idea, stating the notion that young children should ideally have mothers in the home, but that as soon as they were in school, there was absolutely room to

16. COHC, #026 (2010), 15.

pursue personal dreams and desires. Geraldine provides a good example of this kind of thinking in her oral history:

> I also think that women need to develop all their talents. They need to go forward. But I think that, for those that have children, that that's the primary calling for them while the children are young. . . . [My daughter, who has a small child and is interested in entering the world of politics] said, "Mother! I just live a few blocks from Barack Obama! We both went to the same law school, and he's President of the United States!" I said, "[Daughter,] it's not your time, but your time will come."[17]

Most Mormon women interviewed subscribed to the principle that the family is extraordinarily important. However, many supported a flexibility and fluidity in how women interpret this principle. Often, as Hoagland suggests, they did not see the needs of the family as being at odds with the needs of the self and could see that families might indeed be better off for having an engaged mother who participated in pursuits outside the home. Others affirmed the importance of women pursuing personal goals and talents but preferred women to focus on those pursuits when the kids were in school. All in all, there was a reluctance to aver a universal prescription that a woman cares best for her family by staying at home.

Choice as Creation

Hoagland's injunction to view the way we choose to spend our time as creation and set aside the dichotomy of self-sacrifice and selfishness is a perspective that we see echoed in the thoughts of many Mormon women in their oral histories. Whether they choose to contribute to the world through career, motherhood, or both, these women see their actions and choices as God-given opportunities to create meaning in their lives and develop personally.

Kerri provides the perspective of a single woman who affirms her path as a career woman as a God-given opportunity to develop herself and create meaning in her life:

> Both home and work have a significant role to play in a woman's life. However, it's an individual matter. I truly believe that there are

17. COHC, #073 (2010), 11–12.

> some women that are called to be mothers in this life. That is their calling. That is their life mission. I believe some women are to work. I believe that's one of my life's missions, to work. I don't know all of the reasons why. A lot of it has to do with my personal growth and development.... I believe both roles have eternal significance, mothering skills and work skills will be needed eternally from women. Why would the Lord give us talents if he didn't want us to grow and utilize these talents? I think both are important, and one should not be diminished by the other, one should not be thought of as lesser. Too often we have heard in the Church that the most important thing you can do is be a mother. Well, for those of us sitting in the audience who aren't mothers, who are working and have contributing careers, it makes you feel like what you are doing is not meaningful or of significant eternal value. I understand the concept of motherhood, but I have a strong testimony that I'm following a path that was very important to me, so I don't like it diminished.[18]

Clearly, this is a woman who is uncomfortable with any intimation that working is a superficial pursuit without true meaning. She affirms that both choices about how to spend one's time both create value and significance in a person's life and contribute to a person's development. Such reflections mirror Hoagland's emphasis on creating meaning in our lives through our choices to engage—whether that is in the workplace or the home.

Other women staunchly defend the good that can come from choosing to devote oneself to a profession, even while mothering at the same time. Kimberly sees meaning, growth, and good for both the individual and the community through women working:

> Clearly women from the beginning of the time have been extraordinary creatures who had special skills who were remarkable women in the sciences, the industries or in medicine. They were destined to do great things. One of our daughters is one of those special women who is supposed to seek higher education in addition to raising a family. Because we have such long lives, we are going to live into our nineties. We have plenty of time to do career and child rearing.... [T]he world would be a sorry place if we didn't have women in the workforce. They are an important part of how our world operates.[19]

18. COHC, #038 (2009), 7.
19. COHC, #055 (2010), 6–7.

Kimberly locates decisions to pursue career in a cosmology that destines women to do great things in the world as well as in the home. She sees her daughter as having a divine mandate to pursue both motherhood and higher education; and as Hoagland suggests, she does not regard these simultaneous pursuits as mutually exclusive or damaging to self or other.

Laura gives us a glimpse of the psychology of a woman learning to embrace Hoagland's ideas about choice as creation.

> About the time I was in my early thirties I remember questioning for the first time, "was this all I was meant to do?" I wondered if I had wasted my life by making the decision to have children and be home with them. I was probably depressed for a good year. I felt useless and underutilized. I felt like I was a woman who had potential and I wasn't using it somehow. [My husband] was a little frustrated and didn't know what to say or do. He told me to go back to school or work if that's what I needed to do, he was very supportive. I didn't feel held back by [my husband]. I felt like maybe God or the Church had maybe held me back. . . . [T]hen [he] said something to me that was a pivotal question. He said he thought that that [life as a stay-at-home mom] was what I had wanted. It was a cold water in the face kind of moment. . . . [H]e walked out, and I just thought, this is what I wanted. I had to dig deep and go back to what I had felt when I made those decisions. I really [felt] it had nothing to do with the Church or with [my husband], it came from me. There was something in me that had felt that, and I wasn't being true to it by [not] recognizing that choice.
>
> That didn't make my life completely easier, I still felt inadequate at times, but I didn't feel useless for being a woman anymore. I just needed to adjust and find my strengths within what I wanted. I couldn't rely on an outside source to give me commendation.[20]

After doubting her choice to be a stay-at-home mom and wondering if she was not contributing to the world in a meaningful way, this woman describes a moment in which she decides to own her choice to stay at home. The decision to be a stay-at-home mom was not something that has diminished her opportunities, but rather something that has created an opportunity to engage with the world in a meaningful and important way.

---

20. COHC, #056 (2010), 14–15.

Hoagland says, "What we choose is what we've decided to create."[21] The women quoted above display a tendency to view their choices in the same way. Whether they stay at home with children, contribute to their communities through career, or do both, these women ultimately view their choices not through the lens of what they sacrifice, but rather, through the lens of what they gain by their various choices to engage and create meaning in their lives.

Embracing the Whole Self

A central tenet of Hoagland's ethic is that self-understanding is essential for women to develop agency based on choice as creation. They must, according to Hoagland, be able to see their own needs, goals, limits, strengths, and weaknesses. A number of women interviewed in the oral history project mentioned major turning points in their lives as being moments in which they saw and embraced themselves as whole and healthy individuals, willing to insist on their own worth and the validity of their own truth and experience.

In these stories we see women, like those Hoagland modeled, moving beyond the idea that a concern for the self is selfish. Not only have these women moved away from a self-sacrificing mind frame that leads to an erasure of self, but they also move away from a self-doubt dynamic that leads to a crippling of self. We also see them own their choices and their beliefs, as they insist on the meaning they have created in their lives and insist on the respect of others who might not give it to them.

Self-doubt to Self-acceptance

Paula's oral history reveals a woman who has decided to accept and appreciate herself, leaving behind self-doubt that had characterized her thoughts in the first half of her life. As she says,

> Today, I would characterize my Church relationship as pre-age forty and after-age forty. . . . I like the attitude I've acquired after turning forty. My attitude is that I'm OK the way I am. Before I was forty, I had a lot of angst about being good enough. Am I going to qualify for the celestial kingdom? Am I charitable enough? Am I reading the

21. Hoagland, *Lesbian Ethics: Toward New Values*, 92.

> scriptures? Am I doing my genealogy? Am I checking off all my little checkboxes of all the things I'm supposed to do to gain salvation? Am I teaching the children well enough?
>
> After forty I decided that what I am is good enough. It was very freeing. I wish I had come to that realization much, much earlier. I don't remember anything specifically happening to make that change. I just remember thinking at one point that it's time to be OK with who I am right now. Maybe it had to do with going to school, I don't know. Maybe it had to do with accomplishing things myself—big things—and being successful at it, which made me more confident in myself.[22]

This woman attributes growing confidence as potentially being a key factor in leaving behind a self-doubt dynamic and instead embracing herself as sufficient and whole. This passage also points to a religious evolution in which this narrator learns to rest confident in God's love and leave aside those "checklist" worries that had previously guided her behavior and self-assessment. The passage reflects a self-understanding of her own value and wholeness that Hoagland sees as necessary for women to move forward with agency in their lives.

Joanne, a narrator in her sixties, likewise touches on the subject of confidence and self-doubt as she describes self-doubt and angst in women of her generation—qualities which she does not see as much of in women of her daughter's generation. She sees these younger mothers deciding to stay home with children, or deciding to remain in the work force, and feeling good about their decisions.

> One young woman, married a couple of years, expecting her first baby, is an excellent engineer. She is not going to work any more. She has not even hesitated about her future. I see her and her sisters as looking at where their lives are and what will happen. Some keep working, some do not. I see this deep joy in them, even in the midst of problems. I would like to encourage this kind of focus in them to be able to say this is who I am and what I do. They are not apologetic. We women are gradually making a little more headway toward that end.[23]

Joanne describes these younger women as having a confidence, a wholeness of self, and a joy in their choices that was lacking in many

---

22. COHC, #029 (2009), 12.
23. COHC, #062 (2010), 16.

women in her generation. She sees these young women deciding that whatever their choices in regards to motherhood or professions, they are justified. Perhaps this feeling of peace, with whatever road mothers choose, could be attributed to the variety of narratives Mormon women have now about their life paths. While the narrative of the selfish working mother does still exist in Mormon culture, other narratives like the one President Hinckley mentioned in 2001 also have validity.

Finding Wholeness through Ending the Toxic Relationship

While the above passages highlight an internal process of women embracing themselves, their lives, and their choices with wholeness, joy, and confidence, other oral histories recount women embracing their wholeness, truth, and authenticity in the face of confrontation with the other. Jacqueline's oral history reveals a woman who after years of accommodating her abuser for the sake of her mother, embraces her voice, refuses to be manipulated, and finds freedom in her rejection of the man who was so damaging to her. This passage showcases a situation in which the self and the other cannot be simultaneously accommodated; Jacqueline ultimately draws boundaries in order to liberate herself from a toxic relationship:

> When I was ten years old my Stepdad sexually molested me and it continued for at least six years and overshadowed our relationship pretty much forever. It overshadowed how he treated my husband, it overshadowed how he treated my mother, and it finally resulted in him disowning me. I forgave him. I went through the whole forgiveness process. But after my mother died in 1994 he wanted me to tell him that what had happened was ok. He wanted me to acknowledge that my Mother approved and I knew she did not. I would not say what he wanted me to say. It was the final blow. I would not let him influence me. . . . I did not need him nor did I need that toxic relationship in my life. And so that crisis actually led to a wonderful thing in my life: "freedom." Rejecting this brought freedom. . . . I didn't have to tip toe around like I was walking on egg shells. . . . I became my own person.[24]

This woman displays an enormous capacity to forgive and sacrifice for the sake of her mother. Ultimately, however, Jacqueline describes

24. COHC, #027 (2009), 7–8.

refusing to be manipulated and dragged down by her abuser any longer when certain lines were crossed. This passage highlights a rich sense of self-understanding—a self-understanding Hoagland sees as essential for women to move forward with power and agency as the narrator realizes that to accede to her abuser's wishes was to deny her own truth and tarnish the memory of her mother.

A theme of freedom, of liberation, runs through these passages about the emergence of a whole and healthy self. Embracing their choices to shed limiting outside expectations or toxic relationships gives these women the freedom to embrace themselves in a new and healthy way.

Conclusion

In conclusion, we do find traces of an extreme self-sacrificing dynamic, like Saiving describes, among some of the Mormon women interviewed. These women recounted moments in their lives in which they felt themselves disappearing or endangered. However, there is always an outward trajectory, always an impulse to leave this state that they know cannot be sustained and that poses a threat to their beings.

More common than recollections of self-sacrifice, however, were anecdotes and stories that reflect a balance and intertwining of self and other. Hoagland's paradigm of choice as creation is reflected in the ideas of many of the narrators, as they took a flexible "principles over prescription" approach to work and motherhood issues. This approach valued the well-being of both the woman and the well-being of those around her, and it saw meaning and creation in the various ways women engage with the world.

Finally, these oral histories also capture moments of whole and healthy selves emerging, of selves that are confident in their life choices, of selves unwilling to be manipulated by others or crushed by self-doubt. This emergence of the whole and healthy self mirrors Hoagland's paradigm of a self that understands its own limits, draws boundaries when it needs to, and also seeks engagement with others that enlivens and enriches all involved.

An overarching theme of this paper is about finding or restoring a healthy self, one that resides in that optimal space of caring for oneself and caring for those around it. While most Mormon women interviewed easily fall into patterns of interaction in which relationship/communing with the other is highly valued, some oral histories, as we see here, give us glimpses of how these women also place importance on the autonomous separate self—which in moments of crisis or conflict rises up, establishes boundaries, and protects itself from irredeemable harm. "I became my own person," Jacqueline asserts, as she cuts ties with her abuser and refuses to be manipulated by him anymore. This anecdote gives us a glimpse of a moment that appears in the lives of many different Mormon women—a moment in which a woman restores optimal balance between self and other, between autonomy and relationality, as she embraces her agency and moves forward into a new healthier, happier era of her life.

Chapter Two

Fertility

Sherrie L. M. Gavin

The conventional Western conception of the nuclear family is well entrenched in Mormon society, where the traditional, stereotypical, and culturally-defined family is described as a wife and husband who have been sealed in a temple marriage ceremony and have vowed to "multiply and replenish the earth." This latter phrase is institutionally interpreted as the act of having children born "within the bonds of matrimony," making fertility a primary component of Mormon dogma and overall Mormon culture.[1]

This policy of having children is perceived within the institutional Church as a commandment rather than a choice. Recently, Boyd K. Packer, President of the Quorum of the Twelve Apostles, reminded Church members that the "first commandment" given to Eve and Adam was to "multiply and replenish the earth." In Mormon theology, this commandment to bear and raise children is one of humankind's central tenets of mortality.[2] The women interviewed in the Claremont Oral History Project felt this command. Yet the cultural and personal expectations in regard to individual fertility choices reflected a sense of conflicting institutional advice, as well as varying attitudes toward fertility as choice or divine assignment.[3] This essay seeks to address this

1. "The Family: A Proclamation to the World," *Ensign*, Nov. 2010, 129.

2. Boyd K. Packer, "Counsel to Young Men," *Ensign*, May 2009, 52.

3. Claremont Mormon Women's Oral History Collection, Library of the Claremont Colleges, Claremont, CA, hereafter COHC, #021 (2009), 5; #029 (2009), 10; #033 (2009), 13; #036 (2009), 9; #050 (2010), 16; #053 (2010), 12; #069 (2010), 14; #093 (2010), 8; #109 (2011), 2; #117 (2011), 9; all of these specifically quote "multiply and replenish" in discussion of family planning.

conflict by looking at the experiences and attitudes of the women of the Claremont Oral History Project.

The women interviewed in the project generally felt a degree of autonomy in the choice of fertility management and family size. However, the advice of LDS Church leaders and actual reproductive capability led to a state of individual reproductive sovereignty. Each woman had a personal, unmatched experience. Whether mild or profound, fleeting or lasting, each woman and her experience were individual. The term reproductive was used as it described the choice to engage in birth control, fertility treatments, childbearing, and overall fertility management. Sovereignty is a dual-purpose descriptive. It first describes a relationship perceived by many of the women who felt their fertility and fertility impressions were connected in a type of individual spiritual experience with the Divine, one that trumped institutional prescriptions. The term is equally used to describe the autonomous, sometimes isolated experience that many of the women expressed in regard to fertility issues.

This sense of individual reproductive sovereignty was manifested in various ways: through moments of loneliness and seclusion, in eventual compliance with reproductive (in)ability, with indignation in regard to unsolicited fertility advice, and through satisfaction with their individual fertility capability and family size. This essay seeks to examine individual reproductive sovereignty in Mormon women through a chronological comparison of periodic Church declarations to the experiences and responses of the women interviewed. These women were born between 1915 and 1981, and for the purposes of this paper I considered reproductive periods to be when the respondents were between the ages of twenty and forty—which means the very earliest reproductive period considered for these begins in 1935.[4]

Generational Attitudes: The Early Years

Generational attitudes reflected a change in the position of Mormon women regarding fertility and birth control, but did not always suggest compliance with Church policy. Although the 1930s reflected a decrease in birth rates—likely in reaction to the economic issues of the period—there was still a sense that Mormon women should have

4. COHC, #045 born in 1915; COHC, #032, 1922; COHC, #015, 1925; COHC #001, #003, #011, 1926; COHC #065, 1927; COHC #009, #043, 1929.

as many children as possible.[5] Rudger Clawson articulated this attitude when he said, "woman is so constituted that, ordinarily, she is capable of bearing, during the years of her greatest strength and physical vigor, from eight to ten children."[6] Though this statement was published in *The Relief Society Magazine* in 1916, when he was a general member of the Quorum of Twelve Apostles, Clawson served as the President of the Quorum of Twelve Apostles from 1921 until 1943. As a result, it is presumed that attitudes like his were influential in the period of his general authority church positions, therefore, in the first part of the twentieth century.[7]

Even more influential were Joseph F. Smith's anti-birth control statements. He taught that wives and husbands who "agree to limit their offspring to two or three, and practice devices to accomplish this purpose . . . are guilty of iniquity which eventually must be punished."[8] As President of the Church from 1901–1918, Smith left a large collection of writings, which were, and continue to be, regularly quoted in the Church's General Conferences. President Smith led the Church during a period of increased industrialization; he was the last to have more than one living wife during his tenure as President of the Church and one of the last to have children by more than one woman. This, and the social climate of Smith's hometown, Salt Lake City, may have influenced his attitudes toward women and children. Like most major American cities, Salt Lake City grew in urbanization in the first decades of the twentieth century, increasing what was perceived as detrimental societal problems having specific negative effects on Mormon youth. Taking aim at the "indifference and neglect of parents," the *Improvement Era* magazine throughout the 1920s attacked the perceived lackluster performance of mothers and fathers who neglected to properly parent their offspring.[9] The increased focus on proper parenting, as well as Clawson's earlier

5. Melissa Proctor, "Bodies, Babies and Birth Control," *Dialogue: A Journal of Mormon Thought* 36, no. 3 (Fall 2003): 159–175.

6. Rudger Clawson, *Relief Society Magazine* 3, no. 7 (July 1916): 365.

7. Richard S. Van Wagoner, *Mormon Polygamy: A History* (Salt Lake City: Signature Books, 1989), 119.

8. Joseph F. Smith, *Relief Society Magazine* 3, no. 7 (July 1916): 367–68.

9. Richard Ian Kimball, *Sports In Zion* (Bloomington: University of Illinois Press, 2003), 30–31; "Editor's Table-True Love," *Improvement Era*, 14 July 1911, 829.

admonitions about specific family size, evolved into a cultural ideology regarding the expected size of devout Mormon families.

Anti-birth control statements from the institutional Church quieted in the 1930s, again as a likely reflection of the economic slump prevalent in the period. Although the Church reiterated its anti-birth control policy in the 1940s, the women of reproductive age in this period shared in their oral histories a general sense of personal choice in regard to reproductive options—even as the institutional Church admonished them to have as many children as possible.[10] These women demonstrated independent reproductive sovereignty, a fertility attitude that traverses the various generations of women interviewed.

For example, Grace, born in 1915, said,

> I have always felt, as the Church teaches, that it is appropriate to have as many children as your health and circumstances can handle. It is an individual decision. I believe in birth control. I think that is entirely up to the husband and wife.[11]

Heidi, born in 1927, echoed some of Grace's sentiments:

> I've never heard the Church come out and condone the use of contraceptives—but I don't think I've heard them say one way or the other. I have always had the feeling that the Church embraces the idea that we should have all the children that we can. My belief is that a couple should decide that for themselves, but love the children with whom they are blessed. The Church has a good point with populating the Church, but health conditions especially should be taken into consideration. You know what you can take, and how to do your best. You should use your own good judgment.[12]

Both Grace and Heidi felt that fertility choices were to be made by individuals rather than by institutional assignment. Grace noted her perception that the Church encouraged women to have as many children as possible, an ideological concept that was reflected by the majority of the women interviewed. This was also reflective of counsel that

10. Lester Bush, "Birth Control among the Mormons," *Dialogue: A Journal of Mormon Thought* 10, no. 2 (1976): 20. John A. Widstoe, "Should Birth Control be Practiced?" *Improvement Era*, Dec 1942, 831.

11. COHC, #045 (2010), 10.

12. COHC, #065 (2010), 14.

came from the LDS Church leaders for the majority of the twentieth century, though in different gradients.

Institutional instruction in regard to fertility management, birth control, and family size quieted in the post-World War II baby boom phase, but warmed up again starting in the late 1950s.[13] Alexandra, born in 1927, told of her experience.

> When I was first married during the 1950s, birth control pills were just beginning to be used. Birth control wasn't always successful and sometimes caused blood clots. It seemed to me that every Sunday on the editorial page of the *Church News* there was an article reminding people that birth control was not approved, only the rhythm system [was allowed]. My first children were born in 1951, 1952, 1953, 1954, and after that my obstetrician said that I really ought to consider using birth control. The change in emphasis came, I think, about when Elder Nelson first joined the Quorum of the Twelve [in 1984]. Being a doctor, he had more understanding of women's health. The former leaders were mostly very elderly men. I have connected that only in my own mind. I think the *Church News* birth control editorials stopped about then.[14]

Alexandra's first fertility years were at the forefront of the age of modern contraceptive development, a decade when religion and law were often joined in opposition to any form of birth control. The birth control pill became available in the United States in 1957 but was ambiguously labeled as a treatment for "menstrual disorders" with a side effect of, among other things, contraception. Finally, in 1960 the birth control pill was allowed to be advertised openly as contraception.[15] As Alexandra states, the LDS Church was active in relaying its own policy in opposition to birth control in the years surrounding the development of the pill—yet it is important to note that Alexandra perceived the Church's anti-birth control warnings as editorials, rather than edicts. Even though these editorials were printed in the Church-owned *Church News*, Alexandra discerned that the advice from "mostly elderly

---

13. Proctor, "Bodies, Babies and Birth Control," 166.

14. COHC, #003 (2009), 18.

15. R. Christian Johnson, "Feminism, Philanthropy and Science in the Development of the Oral Contraceptive Pill," *Pharmacy in History* 19, no. 2 (1977): 63–78.

men" was not necessarily applicable to her or others because it was an opinion found among editorial articles.

Reproductive Choice and the Ability to Care for Children

A more common consideration regarding fertility management was the capacity of the individual woman to appropriately care for the children in her immediate care. This was reflected in all of the women, regardless of age and was the primary consideration for most of the women limiting their family size. They generally shared a sense of independence in making fertility choices based on their emotional, financial, and personal temperament capacities in regard to the number of children they felt they could successfully parent. Most of the women also reported that the decision to limit or expand family size was shared or influenced by their husbands.

Georgia, born in 1935, tells her story:

> I had four, and they are two and three years apart, all of them. That's how it happened. It was all that I could handle. I decided that four was enough, and I had my tubes tied. I talked to my stake president about it when I did it. I said, "Am I doing anything really wrong to do that? This is all I can really deal with." So, I had an OK there, and I never thought I was doing anything wrong. I did use birth control; that didn't bother me either, and it didn't bother me that my daughters did.[16]

Georgia and her husband made a choice that was independent of the stance of most LDS Church authorities at that time. In doing this, Georgia limited her reproductive capabilities, yet was satisfied that she was well in compliance with her temperament for parenting. With her stake president's approval, she gained a sense of spiritual sovereignty regarding her choice to obtain permanent birth control.

In competition with the concept of independent reproductive sovereignty was Bruce R. McConkie's *Mormon Doctrine*, published in 1958. In this book, McConkie repeated a warning from 1917 by Joseph F. Smith that users of birth control were "guilty of gross wickedness."[17] McConkie's book was never an official publication of the Church—

16. COHC, #095 (2010), 9.
17. Bruce R. McConkie, *Mormon Doctrine* (Salt Lake City: Bookcraft, 1958), 81.

and although subsequent editions were edited to correct and soften McConkie's hard line of doctrinal interpretation, the continued popularity of the book (until the cessation of publication in 2010) confirmed its place, and its associated attitudes, in Mormon culture.[18] There was little sense, however, that the women interviewed felt that birth control, regardless of the period of fertility, was "gross wickedness." Rather, there was repeated emphasis on responsible parenting and the ability to appropriately care for a child, as was related by Marianne, born in 1949:

> I know the family is the foundation of the Church, but the Church doesn't dictate how many children you should have. Children are precious and need to come into homes where they are wanted and will be taken care of physically, emotionally and spiritually.[19]

For Marianne, children are to be born into families where they are "wanted" and, as a result, these wanted children will be well cared for. She uses the term "precious" to describe the value of children, an expression that is common in Mormon culture. Spencer W. Kimball was one of the first to use the term in relation to children, when, as President of the Church, he said, "We move forward to see that our children are taught and trained and controlled, since they are the most precious possession we have."[20]

Conflicting Messages

Apparently unaware of its growing benefits in infertility treatment, Kimball labeled the birth control pill as parallel to abortion, citing these two practices as "subvert[ing] the right way."[21] The longstanding position

18. Dennis B. Horne and David H. Garner, *Bruce R. McConkie: Highlights From His Life & Teachings, Eborn Books Mormon Classics Series, Volume 6* (Salt Lake City: Eborn Books, 2000), 63–64; Peggy Fletcher Stack, "Landmark 'Mormon Doctrine' Goes Out of Print," *The Salt Lake Tribune*, May 21, 2010.

19. COHC, #083 (2010), 13.

20. Spencer. W. Kimball, "Seeking Eternal Riches," *Ensign*, May 1976, 107.

21. Spencer W. Kimball, "The Blessings and Responsibilities of Womanhood," *Ensign*, March 1976, 70. No mention of developments and use of the pill to aid healthy pregnancy are noted in any Church work I have been able to find. In October 2011, Elder Neil L. Andersen in his talk titled "Children" repeated a phrase more common to the twenty-first century that "When to have a child and how many children to have are private decisions to be made between a husband and wife and the Lord." *Liahona*, November 2011, 9–16. The absence

of the institutional Church is that an abortion is in conflict with overall Mormon ideology. There is some leeway, however, in cases where the woman "is seriously endangered or where the pregnancy was caused by rape and produces serious emotional trauma in the mother."[22] Kimball's thoughts on birth control and abortion as subverting the right way are in harmony with a common Mormon concept that children are foreordained for particular families. This concept was not emphasized by the participants of the Oral History Project.[23] Rather, some conveyed a sense of interference, unwarranted advice, and overall conflicting messages from Church leadership in regard to fertility choices. Such was the experience of Lillian, born in 1949, who demonstrates:

> Prior to our wedding, we received conflicting counsel. First, our Bishop cautioned against the use of birth control and counseled us to let children come when they will (as he and his wife had problems getting pregnant, then lost a child and finally had successfully had only one living child at that time of our temple recommend interviews). Then our Stake President advised us to prayerfully seek a safe method of birth control (his wife having given birth to 7 children very close together). He thought it wise to consider your wife's health in choosing your form of birth control. After moving to California following the birth of our first child, our new bishop was a medical doctor. He strongly recommended the use of the birth control pill stating that statistically it was much safer on a woman's body than pregnancy. The differences in these opinions was striking. I was never willing to use the pill, and we made our own decisions about having our family.[24]

Though Lillian does not state if she sought religious counsel in regard to fertility management, it is clear that she perceived the advice she received from her local Church leaders as influenced by their personal

---

of the phrase "birth control" is of importance in comparison to earlier fertility-focused Church speeches.

22. First Presidency (Spencer W. Kimball, N. Eldon Tanner, Marion G. Romney), Priesthood Bulletin, Feb. 1973, 1–2.

23. Spencer W. Kimball, *Report of the Annual Conference of the Church of Jesus Christ of Latter-day Saints*, April 1960, 83–86. None of the women in the COHC mentioned a sense of foreordination in reference to family size. Some said they felt inspired or directed spiritually to have an additional, or final child, but none declared a sense of foreordination for their particular family size.

24. COHC, #034 (2009), 9.

experiences. She candidly labels the advice of her leaders as "opinions," rather than as spiritual recommendations or religiously inspired admonitions. She also applies a sense of practicality in stating that she was "unwilling" to use the pill, yet was active in negotiating a family size of four children.[25] Rather than making choices based on the contradictory advice from Church leaders, Lillian made fertility choices that were suited to her and her husband. (Note how she uses "we.") For Lillian, these contradictions, rather than clouding her fertility decision-making, created a clarity wherein she gained independent reproductive sovereignty.

Personal Choice and Partnership with God

Though the LDS Church remained steadfast in its official policy in regard to abstaining from birth control, the women of childbearing age in the 1970s and '80s expressed an increased sense that the decision of family size was to be a joint decision between a prayerful wife and husband. Laurie, Catherine, and Emily (all born between 1958 and 1961) are examples:

> My understanding of what the Church teaches is that it's up to the couple, through prayer, to figure out or determine how many children they're going to have.[26]

> I believe that we're taught to "multiply and replenish the earth." But, I believe that it is up to each of us as couples to decide how many children we should have. I believe that we should be prayerful about it and seek the counsel of Heavenly Father, but to have as many children as we can handle physically and emotionally. If some couples feel like they can't handle a family of six or seven or eight children, then their family with two or three children is perfect for them.[27]

> I think that the Church's teaching is to have the number of kids that you can handle. And it's not "multiply and replenish the earth" at the expense of yourself emotionally, mentally, physically. I think the Church's views are changing. Are we still commanded to multiply

25. Ibid., 4.
26. COHC, #036 (2009), 9.
27. COHC, #093 (2010), 8.

and replenish the earth? Yes, but I think within reason, and it's up to you and your husband.[28]

Even though the majority of women leaned toward the belief that family size was a choice, and that the evaluation of family numbers was to be resolved privately between wife and husband, there was still a sense that a large family was preferred—or even required. Emily's observation was that Mormon couples were to "have the number of kids you can handle." This belief, shared among many of the respondents, referred not to a *minimum* number of children, but was perceived to be in relation to the *maximum* number of children the couple was able to support. The ideology associated with having the largest family possible in the post-war era is principally attributed to Spencer W. Kimball, who preached of the ills associated with "fewer children," and labeled mothers as "partners with God, as well as with their own husbands, first in giving birth to the Lord's spirit children and then in rearing those children so they will serve the Lord and keep his commandments."[29]

In partnering women with God in a spiritual relationship that could only be forged in righteous childbirth,[30] Kimball reinforced a conceptual relationship for Mormon women that can be compared to the Catholic concept of Mary, as the "Mother of God."[31] By deifying the act of bearing children in the same terms that Orthodox Christianity venerated Saint Mary, Kimball aligned motherhood as the most revered status that pious Latter-day Saint women should endeavor to achieve. In this, motherhood was not only required of Mormon women, it was a sacred calling, one where women were partnered with God. This idea of placing motherhood in equal relationship to divinity was not new in Mormon theology—Mormon women in the 1970s were reminded that the American Equal Rights Amendment only aimed to give women a degree of equality and partnership with mortal men, whereas the act of

28. COHC, #021 (2009), 5.

29. Spencer W. Kimball, "Voices of the Past, of the Present, of the Future," *Ensign*, June 1971, 16–19; "Privileges and Responsibilities of Sisters" *Ensign*, November 1978, 102–6.

30. Conception must occur post-marriage, in a marriage that was solemnized in a Mormon temple sealing ceremony.

31. Jaroslav Pelikan, *Mary Through the Centuries* (New Haven, Conn.: Yale University Press, 1998), 55.

childbirth partnered women with God.[32] Still, the position of Mormon motherhood as partner to divinity gained momentum after Kimball's statement and is commonly used in institutional Church rhetoric today. Interestingly, this elevated partnership of mothers and deity is absent in the 1995 "The Family: A Proclamation to the World," which suggests some reticence to the partnering of childbearing women with God. That relationship could be seen as disempowering men.[33]

In combination of spiritual, institutional, practical and personal interpretation, Carol, born in 1950, suggests a three-part team is needed for childbirth:

> I believe that a husband/wife/God team creates a child and that each member of that team is involved in deciding how many children come to join a couple's family.[34]

Miscarriage

It becomes clear that LDS Church authorities advocate large families when considering general anti-birth control sentiments, the position of motherhood partnered with deity, and the perception that couples should have a self-determined maximum number of children. In 2012, Elder Dallin H. Oaks reminded church members that "From the perspective of the plan of salvation, one of the most serious abuses of children is to deny them birth," citing an international trend in decreased birthrate.[35] A year earlier, Elder Neil A. Andersen reminded Church members that oppositional "voices in the world today marginalize the importance of having children or suggest delaying or limiting children in a family." Andersen's speech included numerical details

---

32. Victorian era masculinity ideology included the positioning of women as naturally more spiritual than men. Kimball took this a step further and "partnered" motherhood with God. E. Anthony Rotundo, "Learning about Manhood: gender ideals and the middle-class family in nineteenth century America" in *Manliness and Morality*, eds. J.A. Mangun and James Walvin (Manchester: Manchester University Press, 1987), 45; Orrin Hatch, *Understanding the Equal Rights Amendment: Myths and Realities* (Conservative Press, January 1976).

33. Gordon B. Hinckley, "Stand Strong against the Wiles of the World," *Ensign*, November 1995, 98–101.

34. COHC, #117 (2011), 9–10.

35. Dallin H. Oaks, "Protect the Children," *Ensign*, November 2012, 43–46.

for four families. These families had seven children, five children, seven children again, and lastly, two children. The couple with just two children, labeled as infertile, gained their children through adoption.[36] The message in this example approves infertility as an acceptable reason to have a small family. Otherwise, five to seven children were Andersen's examples of preferential family size. This evidence suggests that from an institutional LDS Church perspective, independent reproductive sovereignty is acceptable for couples who choose to have large families or for those with infertility issues who have small families.

As already noted, a primary concern associated with having a large family for many was the capacity to properly care for children, including children with special needs. Brenda, born in 1956, came to grips with this concern:

> As I understand it the Lord wants us to provide bodies for his spirit children. It is our privilege and responsibility to bring as many children into our homes as we can reasonably look after. We have a stewardship to raise children once we have them. We will have to answer for how we treat our children. It is a personal decision for each couple to make regarding the number of children they bring into their family. Any parent knows it is not easy to raise children and it can take a lot more faith to have number six than it did to have number one. This is to be worked out with the Lord and each married couple with the understanding that the Lord never asks us to do easy stuff, but if we do what he asks, diligently, we will reap happiness. We all have limits and we must use wisdom in all things. When I was 40, I was pregnant with our 8th child. I knew I was close to exhausted and felt that if there was anything wrong with this child I would be seriously challenged, considering I had seven other children to care for. I spoke to the Lord about this and asked that the child be whole as I couldn't give more than basic care. Shortly after that prayer I had a miscarriage. Our youngest was still breastfeeding so it was not hard to transfer my nurturing feelings to her.[37]

For Brenda, having a large family was a "privilege and responsibility." This was grounded in her belief that mothering was not easy, and that it was a personal decision for each couple as to the number of children they believed they could successfully parent. As a proviso, she also

36. Neil A. Andersen, "Children," *Ensign*, November 2011, 9–16.
37. COHC, #110 (2011), 14.

notes that "we all have limits." Aware that pregnant women over the age of forty are statistically more likely to have children with chromosomal abnormalities, Brenda sought reprieve through prayer—not necessarily to lose the child, but to ask that there would not be "anything wrong." Her words suggest that her miscarriage was a result of this prayer, and in transferring her "nurturing feelings" to her youngest child, she was able to successfully manage her emotions in regard to the failed pregnancy. Brenda was also able to rationalize her miscarriage as a blessing, rather than a curse from God, wherein she was permitted absolution from the trial of raising a child with "serious challenges" in addition to her ongoing duty to raise seven healthy children. In what she perceived was a spiritually sovereign state, she sought a personal pardon and intervention from God. It is interesting that she does not mention that she sought any input, or received any support from her husband in regard to her prayer and later miscarriage, which further emphasizes her degree of individual reproductive sovereignty regarding her miscarriage.

Not all women felt Brenda's degree of religious reprieve when experiencing miscarriage. Estimates for pregnancies that end in miscarriage range from ten percent to much higher, which places miscarriage as a prominent theme in association with overall fertility.[38] Out of about one hundred fifty oral histories, the term "miscarriage" was used forty-three times. Certainly miscarriage was a presence in the lives of the women interviewed.

There is no official LDS policy or doctrine about miscarried fetuses, though Church leaders have commented on abortion. Both miscarriage and abortion generate questions about the status of the fetus. Does it have a spirit? Will parents be able to raise miscarried fetuses in the next life? Recent comments by Church leaders have emphasized that abortion is a serious sin that ends human life.[39] Such statements raise the

38. Kate Parsons, "Feminist Reflections on Miscarriage, in Light of Abortion," *International Journal of Feminist Approaches to Bioethics* (Spring 2010): 1–22.

39. Elder Russell M. Nelson stated that induced (unnatural) abortion is an act that forces mortal death of an unborn child. It is often presumed that the aborted child, per Nelson, had a spirit associated with its rudimentary "23 chromosomes from the father and 23 from the mother." This is supported by Kimball's statement on abortion which is that "It is a crime next to murder itself to destroy and abort the fetus." Russell M. Nelson, "Abortion: An Assault on the Defenseless," *Ensign*, October 2008, 18; Spencer W. Kimball, "Fortify Your Homes Against Evil," *Ensign*, May 1979, 6.

question of whether a spirit is associated with each fetus. While there is no authoritative LDS stance on this issue, many Mormon women who have miscarried choose to believe that their unborn children did have spirits. Others do not report reflecting on this. Consider these examples of miscarriage and the roles that the fetus's spirit and personal spirituality play (or do not play) as these women reflected on these difficult moments. Connie, born in 1934, tells her story:

> I was maybe three months pregnant, not sure that I was ready and willing to have another baby. I was sick, dragging around, miserable. Unable to cope. One day the pains began. I had never had a miscarriage before so didn't know what to expect. I called the doctor who said to lie down and see what happened. I called [my husband], but he was not interested. Alone and in such terrible pain, I finally figured out that I was having a baby. For several hours my poor body tried to expel that fetus and eventually succeeded. The doctor had told me to save whatever came out in a jar in the refrigerator so it could be checked. I realized later that he wanted to see if there was a real fetus or not. I could see that there was, but regret that I did not look at it more closely. My primal self emerged violently after the event. Not sure that I even wanted a baby, still my hormones flashed and flared in response to the loss. I sobbed and howled, unable to stop myself, for hours. The family looked at me with alarm and distaste, but I did not care. I eventually got hold of myself again.[40]

Connie omits the mention of any spirit she could have deemed assigned by God to reside with the fetus; she does not relay the experience in any degree of piousness. For her, the experience was wholly human, even labeling her emotions as a result of "hormones." Her independent reproductive sovereignty was defined by her physical and emotional isolation of the experience; neither her husband nor her doctor were present, and the resulting rush of emotions served to further detach her miscarriage from her family. For Connie, any spiritual association with her miscarriage and the lost fetus is absent in her retelling.

For Penelope, born in 1945, her Mormon life and understanding played more of a role in her experience.

> I got pregnant. After a couple of months the doctor put me on bed rest. I spent almost a month in bed with the Relief Society and

---

40. COHC, #012 (2009), 21.

> friends helping with meals, childcare, and house cleaning. Finally I was able to get out of bed, but after 3 more weeks at a doctor's appointment I was told there was no heartbeat. [My husband] was out of town and I don't think he understood, I don't think men do, and not only the emotional feelings but also the physical part because of hormones. I had great friends, who helped so much. Many shared their experiences of having a miscarriage. I learned that so many women have experienced that feeling of loss. I know I couldn't complain too much because I had four healthy children, but it still was a real feeling of personal agony when I was told there was no life. The doctor was LDS and said this was Heavenly Father's way and I knew it all in my brain, but I remember going and sitting in the car; I had four kids to get home to and probably somewhere to be, but I couldn't move. I felt such pain and agony.[41]

Penelope notes that her miscarriage was "Heavenly Father's way," but neglects to elaborate further on what this means to her. This is her only acknowledgment of spirituality in respect to her miscarriage, but noted that friends who likewise experienced miscarriages had "helped so much." Though it is clear that Penelope desired to have a child at the end of the pregnancy, there is no mention of perceived assignment of a spirit to her fetus. Rather, Penelope is more focused on this sense of communal, feminine empathy in dealing with her miscarriage, virtually disregarding any spirituality that could have been associated with her loss.

Ginger, born in 1952, was acutely aware of the relationship between fetus and spirit, yet offers a new ideological interpretation regarding the spiritual aspect of miscarriage.

> With my miscarriages, I don't know about raising them in the next life. I am not sure that they formed into a child. So I don't know. I believe that they had life. But to me, I never saw a baby—I saw broke away tissue. I thought that spirit came in my daughter [who was born after two miscarriages]. That she was trying to come [before], but she didn't come. Everyone has their way of adjusting to it. So she is trying to come, and I am the vessel for that and Heavenly Father, He will work it out.[42]

Ginger's attitude in regard to her miscarriages represents a general shift in the assignment of a spiritual life to a fetus. Disregarding state-

41. COHC, #039 (2009), 9.

42. COHC, #122 (2011), 10–11.

ments by Church authorities that associated a fetus with human life (and by implication, a fixed spirit), Ginger believed that her naturally aborted fetuses were attempts by a spirit that would eventuate into the full-term pregnancy and live birth of her daughter—rather than spirit children who would not eventuate as mortal beings.[43] In her understanding that Heavenly Father would "work it out," her independent reproductive sovereignty is aligned with an attitude of spiritual independence that is driven by her connection to the Divine—a connection which led her to believe that the spirit form of her daughter would become a mortal being.

Jean, born in 1959, was surer of the future of her miscarried fetuses.

> I continued to have miscarriages, and still had no answers, but at least now [having joined the Church in my 20s], I knew that one day I would have an opportunity to raise them.[44]

Her attitude reflects a part of Mormon theology that teaches that children who die in infancy will be allowed to develop and mature in the millennial period following the Second Coming of Christ. This is based on scriptures in the Doctrine and Covenants, which state that "all children who die before they arrive at the years of accountability are saved in the celestial kingdom of heaven" (D&C 137:10) and that, in the millennial period, "children shall grow up until they become old" (D&C 63:51). This concept has been addressed several times in Church history, usually pointing to the occasion when Joseph Smith told a mother of a lifeless child that, following the resurrection of Christ, the child would be fully restored to his young age at the time of mortal death and she would have the privilege of nurturing her child to maturity at that time.[45]

Doctrinal references such as this are always made in relationship to a child or children. There is no wording that suggests that this concept includes embryos and fetuses in every stage of prenatal development. This is an important, yet undetermined doctrinal point from a fertility perspective. In the era of abortion, some LDS Church leaders have as-

43. The Phrase "Spirit Children" is common in LDS rhetoric and is used to describe the belief that children are spiritual beings waiting to gain mortality through birth. See Mary F. Foulger, "Motherhood and the Family," *Ensign*, November 1980, 105.

44. COHC, #108 (2011), 14.

45. Bruce R. McConkie, "Salvation of Little Children," *Ensign*, April 1977, 7.

signed some degree of personhood or spiritual value to aborted fetuses as the determining argument against abortion. However, by failing to seek or announce additional revelation in regard to the spiritual value of miscarried fetuses, the Church has provoked questions that have no answers—questions such as if a woman who was unmarried (or whose marriage was not solemnized in a temple sealing ceremony) were to miscarry, would she bear a religious obligation to ensure that the fetus is part of a temple sealing ceremony? If a miscarriage occurred in a failed marriage, will divorced spouses be required to raise the unborn fetus together in the millennium? And, if abortion is acceptable in cases of rape, do the fetuses of rape victims not have spirits? These questions and others continue to develop as a result of the murky doctrine regarding the soul of a fetus and are an ongoing burden laid upon fertile women as the vessels of naturally or unnaturally terminated pregnancies.

Gail, born in 1972, wrestles with such questions:

> I fell pregnant again 3 months after the first miscarriage, but to my dismay, experienced irregular spot bleeding. An ultrasound at 9 weeks showed the baby moving and growing, to the approval of the doctor, but still I was not 100% convinced. The continued spot bleed fuelled my anxiety that something was not right. Two days before my next check up I rang the doctor from work and scheduled an emergency appointment during my lunch break—another one of those "nightmare" days forever etched in my memory. The doctor did an examination then sent me for an ultrasound which confirmed the baby had passed away—or in lovely medical lingo, was not viable. I was 14 weeks pregnant but the baby only measured 10 weeks. I've never felt lonelier than lying on the stenographer's table with no one else around.
>
> Often miscarriage is termed "nature's way" and because many women experience miscarriage, it's thought to be not such a big deal. Compared to what some mothers have to experience, it probably isn't, and comparatively I drew the better end of a raw deal. But to this day, I can still become emotional about losing that baby. It made me question why women have to experience such pain and sorrow with procreation in general. Why would such a loving Father in heaven want this for us? And of course, I know the answer, but it doesn't have to make sense. I don't know if I will get to raise these two babies in the eternities. There seems to be no definitive answer in Church doctrine that I have found, but I hold onto my feeling that Heavenly Father

> wouldn't allow these babies to be created for nothing; he wouldn't let mothers be torn apart mentally, emotionally and physically and not allow us to be connected to that child in the life here after. I hope and pray that that is the case.[46]

To be clear, all of the women described varying degrees of loss—mostly very deeply felt—as a result of failed pregnancies. Some, like Gail, still felt sadness in recollection of their miscarriages for years after the events. And while it is clear that the idea of raising children in the millennium was a healing theory for Jean (who, herself, suffered numerous miscarriages), wherein she felt surety that she would have that opportunity, the differences in the doctrinal assumptions in regard to miscarriage reveal a spiritual chasm that increases the sense of emotional isolation some Mormon women carry. Without definitive spiritual answers, Gail "hopes and prays" that her feelings, rather than Church doctrine, are spiritually correct. In the end, she resolves, through prayer, her sense of loss and trusts that unknown spiritual answers will culminate in a healing solution for her in the hereafter.

Infertility

> I struggled with infertility and didn't have [my daughter] until we had been married 8 years. I had miscarriages before and had a miscarriage after her. But we were very private about that. So the perception, the "rap on the hallway," was that I was too busy being the career woman to do the right thing and that was very hurtful. It was very hard to realize that there were people making value judgments upon which there was no basis.[47]

Miscarriage is often paired with infertility, as was the case for Sami, born in 1956. Infertility and the inability to produce a family become defining factors for married Mormon women without children because of the prominent admonition to "multiply and replenish the earth." Seeming to shadow the Talmud in Jewish tradition, where there are three partners in the creation of a human being (mother, father, and God), there is a similar Mormon cultural assumption that the absence of children is equivalent to the absence of appropriate levels of religi-

46. COHC, #114 (2011), 7.
47. COHC, #031 (2010), 8.

osity.[48] Sami and other respondents who dealt with infertility—either personally, or through the experience of their daughters—all noted the presence of imperceptive judgments in regard to the very personal struggle of infertility. Ardeth Greene Kapp, perhaps the best-known married, childless, Mormon woman, wrote that insensitive Church members often associate childlessness with unrighteousness, apathy, and incompatibility. She wrote:

> [Eventually] came the day my young husband was called to be a bishop and I was finally convinced that our not having children was not because of our unrighteousness. Some don't understand that. A good man in the ward who had desired that position came to him privately with strong emotion and said, "What right do you have to be a bishop, and what do you know about helping a family? Don't ever expect me or my family to come to you for anything!" In time my husband helped that man's family through a serious crisis, and through it we forged a lasting bond of love with them.
>
> [Those dealing with infertility] have undoubtedly had similar experiences. If you haven't, you will.[49]

It is presumed that Kapp is speaking with genuine humility. However, while she presents an empathetic resource for those dealing with infertility, she does not suggest reprimand for those who make aloof and even obtuse judgments regarding the fertility of others. In this, she still allows ample space for the continuation of infertility-inspired presumptions which suggest that a degree of divine reproach is still an accepted label for those who deal with infertility.

The pervasive idea that fertility equals righteousness is an ideology cultivated through the institutional LDS Church. Elder Andersen's speech describing the couple that healed their infertility through adoption is an example. Further, the April 2011 *Ensign* attempted to address infertility with an article titled "Faith and Infertility."[50] Like Andersen's illustration, all of the couples in the print edition of the *Ensign* were eventually successful in becoming parents. The electronic version of the *Ensign* included additional stories of childless couples that were unsuccessful in their attempts to become parents, but those are outnumbered

48. Aaron L. Mackler, "An Expanded Partnership with God? In Vitro Fertilization and Jewish Ethics," *The Journal of Religious Ethics*, 25, no. 2 (1997): 277.

49. Ardeth G. Kapp, "Just the Two of Us For Now," *Ensign*, February 1989, 20–24.

50. Melissa Merrill, "Faith and Infertility," *Ensign*, April 2011, 25–29.

by the stories of those who were eventually able to become parents.[51] By including only the infertile couples who eventually became parents for the print version, the infertile couples who have been unable to become parents are sequestered to a secondary link only available in an electronic source. In this, the inference is that unsuccessful infertile couples are systematically concealed by the institutional LDS Church.

As previously discussed, there is the idea in Mormon culture that purposefully restricted family size is a symbol of selfishness, and therefore, unrighteousness. Because of this, willingly or unwillingly childless couples are often associated with selfishness and unrighteousness.[52] This misperception becomes a social and doctrinal issue for Mormon women at large. It is clear in examples through this essay that the LDS Church has an expectation of fertility for its female members. When Mormon women are unwilling or unable to perform to the level of fertility taught through the institutional Church, the result is that these women are often treated as suspect.

Conclusion

While there are underlying currents in Mormon culture that associate selfishness with small family size, none of the women of the Oral History Project associated the number of children with righteousness, and in cases where the women knew of other women who experienced infertility, empathy was always expressed.[53] The overwhelming majority of the respondents said that fertility management and the number of children in a family were decisions to be made between wife and husband and sometimes God. Although this mirrors the contemporary Church's official policy in regard to family size, additional rhetoric suggests ongoing pressure for Mormon women to have large families.

This attitude contrasts with the degree of individual reproductive sovereignty expressed by the women of the Oral History Project. It seems that in spite of (or because of) the Church's non-definitive stance on unborn children and family size, these women, for the most

---

51. Merrill, et al. "Faith and Infertility Expanded-An *Ensign* Online Exclusive," http://www.lds.org/ensign/2011/04/faith-and-infertility-expanded (accessed August 31, 2012).

52. Spencer W. Kimball, "Glimpses of Heaven," *Ensign*, December, 1971, 36–39.

53. COHC #060 and #062 are examples.

part, across generations, took a view of fertility that was less prescriptive, more flexible, and more individual than many statements made by LDS Church authorities.

Their perspectives were culturally influenced by the Church, but not defined by it. As such, the application of individual reproductive sovereignty as a whole for these women can be described as inspired, but not defined, by Mormon culture. Just as Mormon doctrine teaches that by partaking of the forbidden fruit Eve and Adam were given the responsibility to make choices and to "multiply and replenish," the women of the Oral History Project generally felt at liberty to make fertility choices that were best suited to their individual circumstances, bounded by the belief in the importance of children and child-rearing.

Chapter Three

Singlehood

Elizabeth J. Mott

Is it possible to emphasize a theology based on eternal kinship relationships without alienating unmarried LDS Church members (or married Church members, for that matter)? Forty-seven percent of the respondents in a 2011 survey of 3,000 Mormons who had left the faith indicated that women's issues were a "significant" reason for their decision. Among female respondents, that percentage increased to sixty-three percent, and to seventy percent for single Mormon women.[1] These numbers suggest that unmarried Mormon women may not always feel valued in their local congregations.

This family-focused feature of religious life is not unique to Mormonism. Across denominations in the United States, women and especially men who are married with children are significantly more likely to participate in churches.[2] However, Mormonism's theology of marriage is unique. According to Richard Bushman, even though the family practices of Mormons and their Evangelical Christian neighbors appear similar on the surface, the impact of this unique LDS theology on young Mormon women and men distinguishes them from their Evangelical counterparts. Bushman explains that temple marriage rep-

---

1. See the newspaper account of Neylan McBaine's FAIR conference presentation in Peggy Fletcher Stack, "LDS apologetics tackle same-sex attraction, women's issues," *The Salt Lake Tribune*, August 2, 2012, http://www.sltrib.com/sltrib/lifestyle/54619090-80/women-sex-lds-mormon.html.csp?page=1 (accessed August 2, 2012).

2. Church adherence in the United States has been positively correlated with being married and having children; unmarried and childless individuals are significantly less likely to attend and participate in churches. See Robert Wuthnow, *After the Baby Boomers: How Twenty- and Thirty-Somethings Are Shaping the Future of American Religion* (Princeton: Princeton University Press, 2007).

resents Mormon parents' highest hopes for their children. For if their young adult children are sealed to spouses in a temple, this "implies [that] the children have lived the rigorous Mormon lifestyle, have chosen a worthy Mormon mate, and are willing to enter into the demanding covenants of the temple endowment." With the organization of a new family through the sealing ordinance, a temple marriage "perpetuates the Mormon way of life." Like a great chain, families continue indefinitely into the eternities. "The implication of the eternal marriage revelation is that although other institutional forms, including the Church, might disappear, the family will endure." It is "the foundation of heavenly society."[3]

Such lofty significance of married life can inspire couples to endure its mundane realities. Bushman points out, though, that this theology can also discourage young Church members—usually women—who desire to follow the pattern but cannot find a partner:

> However inspiring for young couples, the doctrine sometimes troubles single adults. Mormon girls grow up with the expectation that marriage to a worthy Mormon man is the highest form of a good life. What are they to make of themselves if at age thirty-five they are still unmarried? Some Mormon girls fail to prepare for a career in the expectation of an early marriage. Even those with serious careers and many achievements wonder about their state as single women. Such uncertainties, common to single women of every belief, are magnified by the doctrine of eternal marriage.[4]

Whether they would find this fact comforting or disconcerting, single Mormon women might be interested to know that their experience accords with a larger sociological trend in marriage. The percentage of American adults who are married has been declining. A 2011 study by the Pew Research Center found that among Americans over the age of eighteen, just fifty-one percent were married, down from more than seventy percent in 1960.[5] This drop from almost three-quarters to only

3. See Richard Lyman Bushman, *Mormonism: A Very Short Introduction* (New York: Oxford, 2008), 58–59.

4. Ibid., 59.

5. PBS NEWSHOUR, "Why Are Fewer Americans Getting Married?" *Public Broadcasting Network* (Airdate: December 30, 2011). Available online at http://www.pbs.org/newshour/bb/social_issues/july-dec11/marriage_12-30.html (accessed September 3, 2012).

half is for the most part due to a rise in the age of marriage. In 1960 the age of marriage was at an all-time low—half of all women married while still in their teens.[6]

In addition to the rising age of marriage, divorce rates in the United States have also climbed, reaching their peak during the 1970s through the 1990s. Later marriage, cohabitation, and divorce are all indicators of the instability of the love match, according to marriage historian Stephanie Coontz. The love match and male-breadwinner marriage became the norm during the post-World War II American economic boom. However, for a complex variety of reasons, Coontz argues, in the recent two decades we have witnessed the "disestablishment of marriage."[7]

What are Mormons' reactions to this unprecedented change? Independent research by the Pew Forum has confirmed that, in sharp contrast to the general population of the United States, the dominant Mormon culture subscribes to the male-breadwinner model of marriage (at least in theory, if not in practice) and places incredibly high emphasis on parenthood.[8] So what about the members whose lives do not fit this pattern?

---

6. Ibid. For a history of marriage, see Stephanie Coontz, *Marriage, a History: From Obedience to Intimacy or How Love Conquered Marriage* (New York: Viking Penguin, 2005). For a personal essay that reviews recent sociological research on marriage, see Kate Bolick, "All the Single Ladies," *The Atlantic*, November 2011, http://www.theatlantic.com/magazine/archive/2011/11/all-the-single-ladies/308654/ (accessed September 3, 2012).

7. Coontz, *Marriage, a History*, 278.

8. According to an independent 2012 Pew Forum Study on American Mormons, 81 percent of Mormons said being a good parent was "one of the most important things" in life, compared to 50 percent of the general public. Almost three-quarters of Mormons similarly said that having a successful marriage was one of the most important things; 34 percent of the general public agreed. "Living a very religious life" was "one of the most important things" for more than half of the Mormons (55%) but only one-fifth (20%) of the general public agreed. With regard to ideal family roles, 58 percent of Mormons said that a marriage where the husband provides and the wife stays at home was more satisfying than marriages in which both spouses work outside of the home (only 38% thought so). Opinions on marriage roles were reversed among the general public: 62 percent said it was more satisfying for both spouses to have outside employment, and less than one-third (30%) preferred male-breadwinner marriages. For the full report on the poll, see The Pew Forum On Religion & Public Life, "Mormons in America: Certain

In the early 1990s when Americans were still reeling from economic changes, increasing divorce rates, and experiencing the backlash of secular feminism, LDS Church leader Elder Bruce C. Hafen and his wife, Marie Hafen, coauthored a book on the intersection of Mormon family life and American culture. Marie Hafen specifically wrote several chapters to and for Mormon women out of a desire to help them set realistic expectations and to encourage them to develop their individual skill sets. At this point during the early 1990s, as many as forty percent of the adult women in the Church were single at any given time, whether widowed, divorced, or unmarried—with divorce being the greatest cause.[9]

Based on my analysis of the interviews in the Claremont Mormon Women Oral History Project, even though single Mormon women represent some forty percent of Mormon women—not a small minority—those single women interviewed for this oral history project reflect a tendency to feel marginalized in American Mormon congregations. Being widowed, divorced, or never married requires a significant amount of self-confidence and wisdom in order for these women not to see themselves solely through other people's eyes. These women had several options: they could question the LDS Church culture, question themselves, or simultaneously question both Church culture and themselves.

---

in Their Beliefs, Uncertain of Their Place in Society," January 12, 2012, http://www.pewforum.org/Christian/Mormon/mormons-in-america.aspx (accessed September 3, 2012).

9. Marie Hafen writes, "Career-oriented education is important because women typically experience so many different phases of life—and because they can't always control when and what those phases will be. For example, at any given time, from 35 to 40 percent of the adult women in the Church are single, whether widowed, divorced, or not having married—with divorce being the greatest cause. The never married are the smallest group, since only 3 percent of LDS women never do marry. In addition, over 90 percent, including both married and single women, must work for some part of their adult lives. What these statistics boil down to is that a young woman who believes she will always have a husband who will fully support her, making it unnecessary for her to work, is living in a dream world. Husbands die, or they can be disabled by accidents or illness. Children grow up, missionaries need financial support, and most mothers live healthy, vigorous lives for many years after their children leave home." See Bruce C. Hafen and Marie Hafen, "Celebrating Womanhood," *The Belonging Heart* (Salt Lake City: Deseret Book, 1994), 291.

Women who drew a line between Church members' discourse on singlehood/marriage and their own personal sense of self-worth and connection to God tended to assert that, over all, the Church increased their sense of well being rather than detracting from it. They were able to lay claim to the Church. For them, it was a church for the forty percent as well as the sixty percent.

Chieko Okazaki, first counselor in the General Relief Society Presidency from 1990 to 1997, articulated this confident position. A Japanese-Hawaiian-American woman herself, she also explored the concerns of countless Mormon women around the world. In order to represent *all* women of an increasingly global and diverse church, she set about discarding a life script for women and replacing it with scriptural principles about the equal worth of all souls—black and white, bond and free, male and female, Mormon and gentile, married and single.

In this chapter I share insights from single Mormon women who have been widowed, divorced, and never married. I then demonstrate how Okazaki sought to integrate and elevate these women in the Church as a way of comforting those who mourned and lifting up the poor in spirit.

Widowed

In addition to dealing with grief and purposelessness, widows lost social capital in their congregations. Further, younger widows who had been sealed in the temple faced uncertainty about marrying again. While self-confidence, spirituality, and friendships enabled them to cope more serenely with these challenges, losing a husband to death nevertheless wreaked havoc on these women's emotions.

For instance, loneliness crept in and robbed Pamela of peace months after cancer had robbed her of her husband:

> When he died I was at peace because I felt that he had put in his time. But it's a difficult adjustment, even when you know that it's OK. The adjustment changes. At first I remember the euphoria of the moment. And then, after a month, when I was trying to do a heavy routine of activities every day to keep myself busy I just felt that I was climbing a hill and falling backward. . . . Now, I have greater understanding about being lonely. You have so many experiences that you have only shared with your spouse. You have a common language

> of a word or two or a remembrance of what was funny or what was hard and when you lose your partner all of those shared experiences are gone. Your children share some. Your siblings share some of them, but you don't have anybody who has shared those forty-nine years of life experience.[10]

Jenny was widowed twice. The first time, she was a mother with young children; the busyness of meeting financial demands on her own and the assistance of her parents with the children made the experience different from losing her second husband later in life. While she grieved both times, the second loss left her truly without companionship:

> The first big crisis in my life was the death of my husband. The children and I were overwhelmed by grief. The change that grief brought about was a new depth to my emotional life as well as a vastly increased understanding of others' sorrows. My husband's passing also led to a change in the way the family worked. I could no longer be there around the children; I had to find babysitters. I had to find a way to work full-time, doing all the home and school-work that's involved in teaching high school, and still be a mother and devote time to my children after school and in the evenings. I found this life very demanding and exhausting, and it took all my energy, intelligence, and abilities to manage it. I think it would have been easier if there had been a husband in the home for support, relief, and even conversation. . . . Then, three years ago . . . another crisis came into my life. My [second husband] was diagnosed with [cancer]. . . . He was hospitalized most of that summer, and I spent each long day at his side, watching him fail. He died [in September]. That crisis has again led me to deep grief with a new dimension I hadn't known before—acute loneliness. After [my first husband's] death I grieved, but I had the children to care for and my parents to support me. After [my second husband's] death I was simply alone. It was a searing, painful loneliness that took a long time to adjust to. Since I had never been alone before, I had to cope with this totally new way of living.[11]

For Jenny, marriage divided the weight and responsibilities of family life between two people; and without family in the home at all, she felt acute loneliness.

---

10. Claremont Mormon Women's Oral History Collection, Library of the Claremont Colleges, Claremont, CA, hereafter COHC, #006 (2009), 7.

11. COHC, #081 (2010), 20–21.

In addition to the loneliness, these women often experienced a lack of purpose. For many of the women, it was the first time in their adult lives that their path was no longer set by their husband's career or their children's needs. They had to decide on their own how to create a new life.

> I think being a widow is probably, other than my sister's death, as hard a thing as possible. I had to learn something after [my husband] died. I was so ripped apart. Our life together had been a real roller coaster ride. Wherever [he] had a job or wanted to go to school, I would pack up and go. We just did it. We had wonderful, incredible things happen. Wonderful friends through the process. For a few months there I was just so numb. I didn't much care about anything. . . . I know I have to create a new life without [him].[12]

After a thrilling shared journey with her husband, Cheryl had to gain confidence in making decisions on her own. When faced with a problem, or touched by a happy memory of her husband, she would write a letter to him. Even though these were one-sided conversations, writing letters kept her in touch with her deceased husband; it also made her frustrated:

> When I'm considering a major decision and want his input but I can't get it, I tell him that I hope he likes my choice in the matter because I'm just going ahead with it. That's what I have to do. It's all a part of creating a life.[13]

Cheryl explained that after a period of uncertainty and reluctance to fly on her own, she discovered that she preferred to fill this season of her life giving music recitals and teaching art, rather than accepting what seemed to her a constricted life, simply because her husband had died.

> Soon after [my husband died], all the widows and widowers in the ward called and invited me to join in with their home evening. I went once, and I just thought, I can't do this. These are wonderful people, dear people, but full speed ahead. Every bit of my time and energy is going toward something else.[14]

These women noticed a distinct change in how they were treated by Church members after their husbands died. Suddenly, bishops' wives

12. COHC, #060 (2010), 13–14.
13. Ibid., 14.
14. Ibid., 14.

became welfare recipients and homes of professional fifty-year-old women became off-limits to missionaries.[15] They were pained and annoyed to realize how much their social capital had depended on their husbands and how much being a single female reduced their access to priesthood blessings. Jenny chalked this up to the fact that there are more women in the Church than men, and that men are the rare and rough diamonds needed to lead the Church:

> I know that the Church says it's for everybody, but really the emphasis is on families. If you're single, it's really just not the same. I guess it's kind of an inferior position. There are a lot of women in the Church, and missionaries used to say that you have to convert the men, because then whole families will join. Women are not quite as valuable. I know that's true—women are not as valued. The men are needed to do the leadership positions, and as for women—you can fit them in anywhere, or nowhere.[16]

Sally, who was baptized into the LDS Church while in college, spoke about coming full-circle in the Church with regard to marriage:

> Even in my very early days in the Church, I felt a difference because I was not married and didn't have the priesthood in my home. When I became the wife of a non-member, I was married but without priesthood in the home. Then, along the way, I became the wife of a bishop. From one end to the other. And then, the day he died, I became single, without priesthood in the home again. That was such a shock. Within days after he died, I went from being the wife of a bishop to being on the ministering visit list.[17]

One experience, in particular, convinced her that single women are treated much differently from married women. When her husband was serving as bishop, the missionaries often came by unannounced; they were always welcome. As the bishop's wife, she also enjoyed signing up to feed the missionaries dinner. She had signed up a couple of months in advance; in the meantime, her husband, the bishop, died. A week later, she received a phone call from the new bishop; his urgent problem was that this widow couldn't have the missionaries over to her house as

15. See both COHC, #081 (2010), 25, and #031 (2010), 13.
16. COHC, #081 (2010), 25.
17. COHC, #031 (2010), 12–13.

a single woman—could she find a priesthood holder to join her and the missionaries for dinner at her house the following week?

> It was those kind of things that came as a real shock that I was back to where I started from. So now I've been a single parent for the last seven years, without priesthood in the home again. I hear from other members, men and women, that we don't treat single women differently. BUT WE DO! And I have now been on every side of this issue of marital status and there is a big difference. Men and women deny it, but single women are treated very differently.[18]

Younger widows also found themselves thrust back into the murky ocean of romance. They noticed the fierce competition for a Mormon husband among single women, as the male-to-female ratio becomes increasingly lopsided with age. Sally, who lost her husband while in her forties, was invited to speak at a singles fireside in her stake. Afterward, some of the women approached her with the assumption that she was divorced. When one woman realized that this woman's husband was the late bishop and that she wasn't divorced, the woman said to her, "So, what are you doing here? You already have your temple marriage!" Shocked and amazed, even in retrospect, by the bitterness implied in this statement, the narrator emphasized, "Remember! I was the speaker! I was there because I had been asked to give the talk!"[19] Apparently, with all the Mormon women who deserve a Mormon husband, a young widowed woman who has been sealed to her husband should not get another.

Such is one of the unanticipated consequences of the doctrine of eternal marriage. A woman who enjoyed a wonderfully happy marriage to her best friend is expected to spend the rest of her life alone after his death. Additionally, Jenny had a longer marriage the second time around, but since she was sealed to her first husband, she could not be sealed to her second husband:

> I do feel sad that I'm unable to be sealed to [my second husband]. He was my life companion for almost thirty years. We talked about everything constantly, we enjoyed many interests and activities together, and he was always my best friend. The Temple president told me that a year after my own death someone else (my children, he suggested) can do proxy work and have us sealed to each other. Then

18. Ibid., 13.
19. Ibid., 13–14.

> I'll be sealed to two men, and we can work all that out in the eternities. I have mixed feelings about being sealed to [my first husband] because I was married to [my second husband] for so much longer and more recently.[20]

In spite of all these challenges and perplexities, widowed women found strength in themselves, in God, and in each other. Self-confidence enabled women to not internalize condescending remarks, and a strong sense of self also allowed women to believe that God was a benevolent Being who would answer their prayers—that He *wanted* these women to enjoy the freedom and joy of achieving personal goals. Good friends filled the vacant spaces and moments in time.

Laura, who was a published writer, possessed the spunk to dismiss the unsolicited advice of a well-meaning but condescending neighbor. She had her writing life and her Southern California community, and she was involved in Church roadshows and other productions. In fact, having this "good foundation of activities" in place provided her with stability during the crisis of her husband's death:

> It was a big adjustment for me to live on my own. But . . . I had this good foundation of activities. I wasn't going to move. In fact, my neighbor up the street, a very good friend of [my husband's], came down and said, "Above all, . . . don't move for at least a year. You'll make a big mistake if you do." I thought, "Who wants to move?"[21]

It annoyed her that he assumed she needed his advice. She herself knew what was best.

However, previous abuse could make this kind of self-confidence extremely difficult to obtain. Cheryl had been sexually abused as a child but ended up marrying a wonderful man whose faith in her emboldened her even after his death; his encouragement coupled with therapy helped her to overcome her self-doubt and self-blame. She explained that this abuse when she was young "determined so much of how I see the world and how I look at myself." She has empathy for people who have been abused in any way because it is so debilitating to the human psyche. It took her until her sixties to overcome a "victim's mentality" that had held her back her entire life; the expertise and sensitivity of a good therapist made the difference. She observed that so many women

20. COHC, #081 (2010), 23.
21. COHC, #009 (2009), 11.

in the Church are afraid to not be perfect and afraid to question authority because they take to heart the religious teachings about perfection and obedience:

> I think so many women in the Church are afraid to not be perfect. We hear that term so much. So many women really suffer because they don't measure up, and they are so stressed and anxious about things, to get them all right. We are really, really hard on ourselves. We've got to have enough belief in ourselves to stand up for ourselves, to know within ourselves that we have so much ability and strength that we are the ones who make a huge, huge difference in the Church. If women just went on strike, things would topple.[22]

Widowed women shared some spiritual experiences that reinforced their personal decisions and unique life courses. Jenny felt inspired to inquire about a teaching position at a school that was closer to her home than the first position she had quickly found after her husband's passing. She was hired immediately at the closer school, and it proved serendipitous for her family's well-being.[23]

Cheryl felt her deceased husband cheering her on when she hung back in the doorway of a class of college art students on her first day as an instructor. She felt a gentle shove that propelled her over the threshold of the classroom. She elaborates, "I felt his presence, like he was cheering me on, during the class period. I sensed that he really cared and supported what I was doing. That gave me courage to tackle the difficult moments. . . . Then I had to discover my own gift and accept what I had to offer."[24]

Similarly, Sally, who had suffered infertility and was only able to have one child at the age of thirty-four, remained convinced that the Lord's timing and wisdom governed her life. When her husband died when she was only in her forties, this self-assured and independent woman was able to dismiss assumptions that she was divorced and the accompanying disdain; she had faith in the Lord's purposes and believed that special blessings sustained her daughter as well:

> We were fortunate that despite his poor health that he lived as long as he did. It was a real loss, especially for her, when he died. But

22. COHC, #060 (2010), 11.
23. COHC, #081 (2010), 9–10.
24. COHC, #060 (2010), 14.

> now, as she continues to grow up, I see so much of him in her. I see so much of her dad in her. I have no doubt. I feel evidence all the time of [his] continued involvement in her life. She had a patriarchal blessing . . . and that was the first thing . . . expressed in the blessing, that her father is very aware of what is going on with her and is part of her life.[25]

Finally, friendships with peers filled the empty spaces and eased the pain of missing a spouse. Living in Utah when her husband died, Cheryl began having dinner gatherings full of friends and good conversations. She said that she didn't feel it was fair to put the responsibility for easing her loneliness solely on her grown children. Rather, she wanted to make the most of her present life: "I have had to learn that when I am so lonely for [my husband], that I find ways to cope and not put it on my family, who feel their own loss of their father."[26]

Divorced

Since American Mormons are culturally and economically integrated into the wider society, they are also experiencing consequences of the instability of the love match. In addition to dealing with financial concerns, divorced Mormon women in the oral histories faced self-doubt and religious doubt. Strategies similar to the ones used by widowed women likewise increased the resilience of women who found themselves raising children without a spouse. Significantly, all of these women said that being in charge of a family's emotional and physical welfare was more than a one-person job. Therefore, they absolutely needed financial or childcare help from parents, friends, or Church members.

Most of the women interviewed who divorced during this tumultuous time period had married young and were unprepared to provide for a family. The economic hardships caused some of these women to turn to parents, extended family, and the Church for support. The Church also provided them with emotional and spiritual support. Some women expressed only positive feelings about the Church; others shared difficult experiences of not having found the assistance they needed. Some shared both the benefits of their Church sisterhood and the challenge of being divorced in such a family-oriented community.

25. COHC, #031 (2010), 12.
26. COHC, #060 (2010), 14.

Rachel, who became a single mother with five children after her divorce, emphatically saw no conflict between the course of her life and LDS Church teachings:

> I have never ever ever felt suppressed in *any* way being a member of this Church. . . . I am a very strong assertive woman and I have had to be that way. . . . [As] a single mother and woman . . . [I have] never felt the Church put me down in any way.[27]

Such difficult circumstances were exactly what her faith in God helped her to face and overcome; she never expected that she would be spared challenges because of her religion.

Similarly, Mackenzie, who had joined the LDS Church in her twenties in New York, never had the expectations of the "traditional family" common to Mormons of the Intermountain West. When she was divorced, she did not express feelings that life and God had been unfair to her. Rather, she increased her faith to find ways to work through the heartbreak and worry for her children. For instance, she saw her baptism as a spiritual confirmation of her choice. "If I had turned my back, I would have felt like I was turning my back on Jesus."[28] As a single parent, her prayers for employment were always answered, though she admitted that paying tithing was initially a difficult thing to do. "The Church has offered solutions," she concluded.[29]

At the same time, Mackenzie, who joined the Church in 1979, remembered that at that time, single women were not encouraged to receive the temple endowment. "You were supposed to wait until you got married or went on a mission." The temple and marriage were, in her mind, permanently linked. She delayed going to the temple as a single woman. "Even though I was divorced, that was still my picture [to go with a husband]."[30] Paige lived alone and had lost three husbands to divorce or death. Her grown children lived far away, and the temple was "bittersweet." She admitted, "Right now, it is just too much about all the things I do not have or do not understand. I maintain a . . . recommend though."[31]

---

27. COHC, #088 (2010), 6.
28. COHC, #083 (2010), 8.
29. Ibid., 8.
30. Ibid., 11.
31. COHC, #069 (2010), 15.

For some women, Mormon church life poured salt into their wounds; they expressed alienation if they perceived their individual experiences as being outside the norm. The Relief Society was a bunch of "perfect sisters and their perfect families. . . . Old women, single women, divorced women, widows, and those without family are isolated."[32] In her experience, some non-Mormon churches were "more Christian" and more concerned with "the least of these" than were the Mormon congregations she had attended One of the young women she had taught in church had lost her husband as a newlywed. She persisted in attending meetings for a while, but finally despaired when she realized her new peer group was made up of "gray-haired ladies;" she became tired of having to re-hash her tale of woe and be pitied. Paige found the language toward singles in the Church "patronizing." "No matter how much verbiage is given about the worth of single members, it is just darn tough to fit in if you are not of the mold."[33]

Similarly, church relationships had the potential to cut both ways—to support or to increase the pain. Rachel said that "the Church" never put her down, but individual members sometimes had a tendency to be judgmental. Of the divisive question of women staying home to raise children or working outside the home, she commented that she did both at different times. "We just have to do what we have to do."[34] Because of the uncertainties of life, she urged young women, including her own daughters, to "be prepared" to provide for themselves and for their children. She was pleased that her own daughters had done so. People can be critical, but Rachel's opinion is that we have no right to judge until we've walked in someone else's shoes.[35]

These women coped by seeking out friends. Mackenzie reflected upon how difficult it had been to go to church immediately after her divorce, but her need for support from Church members for herself and her children overrode her feelings of alienation and discouragement.[36] Some twenty years later, she exulted in the "eternal friendships" she had found in the Relief Society. "Nobody's perfect and everybody has their

32. Ibid., 15.
33. Ibid., 17.
34. COHC, #088 (2010), 7.
35. Ibid., 7.
36. COHC, #083 (2010), 6.

trials—family, health, work."[37] The Relief Society provided her with community: she used the word "we" to describe how they had shared burdens with each other. For her, the Church meant "support."[38]

Megan, who was divorced, observed a normativity of marriage in Mormon culture that can unintentionally alienate people whose lives do not conform; at the same time, she acknowledged how gracious and helpful her Relief Society friends were to her after her second husband's death.

> I had one experience, right after my divorce, at a Relief Society function. I was at the buffet table, went to take something and a woman asked if I was a member of this ward, had I been invited by someone. These sound like very innocuous questions, but I was very tender then and the tone of questioning upset me. These experiences have certainly taught me not to be judgmental and to welcome all!—to greet them, love them. During those difficult years when I was single, my Sisters were there for me. Some took me to concerts, some had me to dinner, phoned me. Now since my dear [husband's] death, I have a wonderful church friend. . . . I think that since we share so many similar stories, we have become very close. She phones me frequently and even with her busy schedule, brings me dinner sometimes. It is often the little things that make daily life easier when one faces challenges.[39]

Ultimately, what kept these divorced women loyal to the Church was their conviction that a loving God was watching over them. God had not left them alone. Mackenzie and her children were evicted from their apartment while she was undergoing a divorce. It was "the worst time of [my] life," she reflected. It was prayer that led her to feel comfort from God, and to find solutions to her problems.[40]

Never-Married

Although those who were never-married tended to be financially independent, they have been, at times, the recipients of criticism, pity, or unsolicited advice. Coming from the position that it is the indi-

37. Ibid., 12.
38. Ibid., 12.
39. COHC, #001 (2009), 13.
40. COHC, #083 (2010), 6.

vidual's right to decide the course of her life, these single women called for flexibility in how the Church's general counsel regarding marriage and family life is understood and applied.

The single Mormon women interviewed of the current generation do not share the economic concerns of their mothers' generation. Many of these women feel that being unmarried has a silver lining. Single women embraced their unique opportunities to work toward personal goals financially, professionally, academically, and socially. The youngest generation of women interviewed emphasized that they thought developing maturity was a prerequisite to marriage; they called this concept "independence" and "self-reliance."

Divorced mothers had repeatedly instilled in their daughters a need for an education so that they would not have to face the same kind of financial crises.[41] The women who divorced in the 1970s and '80s were pleased that Church leaders were encouraging young women to go to college and prepare themselves to work outside the home. In contrast, "When I grew up, when you graduated from high school, you would pick a silver and crystal pattern," Mackenzie recalled.[42]

What is difficult for present-day single women is the feeling of rejection. Erin had never married or had children, but she was confident, successful in her career, and self-reliant. She still spoke of occasional feelings of loss and inadequacy.

> I am a sweaty palm dater to put it mildly. I'm okay until someone says "Okay I'll pick you up at 8:00 on Thursday night," and from that point on I try to figure out a way to get out of it. The longest I've ever dated somebody was four months, and it was two months too long. It was two months too long because I became comfortable with the fact that there was somebody else there, and I didn't want to go back to not having somebody else there. I am perfectly fine with being single until there's another option or until it's brought up to me that I'm single. The best example is when my mom called once. We were chatting one day, and she mentioned my best friend from high school who I really don't have any contact with any more who is married and has three children and is a doctor and all these other things. She talked about Suzanne and something about her having another child; I don't remember exactly what the conversation was about. We

41. COHC, #088 (2010), 7.
42. COHC, #083 (2010), 12.

> hung up the phone and my mother called back five minutes later and said, "Oh honey, I'm so sorry. Did that bother you that I brought up Suzanne?" I said, "No." Then I hung up the phone, and I felt really bad about myself.[43]

One challenge singles mentioned was the tendency in Mormon circles to equate marital status with adulthood—regardless of whether or not an individual woman personally felt confident in herself and ready for such a relationship, and regardless of the Lord's timing. Because the Church teaches emphatically that family is a central tenet of the Gospel, some singles said they felt anxious about marrying later than what was expected; others expressed concerns about ending up in an unhealthy marriage:

> As a child and a teenager I didn't have the desire to date or marry. Marriage seemed very, very negative to me as a kid, which may seem ironic growing up in the Church. But in my own family, marriage seemed less appealing. [My siblings' marriages] were negative, troubled relationships. . . . . I just never saw anything that looked appealing; so I cared about going to school instead. . . . I've kind of grown into the idea of marriage and I really think it actually is largely grace that . . . helped me have a positive view of marriage. Part of it has been watching my own friends and like I said my freshman [college] experience was so formative—being with other women who both loved the Gospel and really wanted to have careers and be successful. Watching those friends and really positive marriages and getting to balance those. I think a lot of it is the experience of having been a missionary and just being close to the Gospel and making that the center of my life. So I would say at this point in my life, I have a positive view of marriage and I plan to get married and I plan to have children and that seems very appealing to me. It's been a long road, which is good, I got a lot of education. The timing is great.[44]

Some women had seen their mothers or sisters become dependent in their marriages and then badly treated or betrayed. Financial, emotional, and spiritual independence, therefore, were very important to them as they reflected on their experiences and their hopes for the future. Several said that they believed their eventual marital relation-

43. COHC, #008 (2009), 18.
44. COHC, #074 (2010), 7.

ships would be healthier because of the self-reliance they had developed before marrying.

These single women made peace with their lack of conformity through personal revelation. While some expressed feelings of alienation in a family-oriented Church, many said they feel there is space for diverse perspectives: the Lord wants them involved and understands and supports their personal decisions.

Specifically, they have sought revelation from God about their personal circumstances. An unmarried woman named Emily reflected back on her twenties when her mother's unexpected death had created a crisis in her family. The family's crisis coupled with her illness left her in a no-man's land of single adulthood—she was old enough to be on her own, but she felt limited by her own struggles and by her family's expectations:

> I finished my [bachelor's degree], began a teaching licensure program that fall, and dated a boy, but my school plans and engagement were off by February, so I moved back home to re-group, and to figure out my next move. This was when [my sister] was planning her wedding, and being back home was like being sucked into a vortex which was very hard to escape from again. I no longer had school as an excuse to be in another state. My health was not good. My dad and [my sister] were angry with me for wanting to [leave home again to find work]. Holding fast to the counsel I'd received from a wise bishop the previous year, though, I knew staying [at home] would not be a healthy thing for me. Just before I'd graduated from college, my singles ward bishop had met with me and listened to my family situation and my personal health concerns, and told me, "Whatever you do, don't go home. What happened to your mom would happen to you. It's like a sponge in water. The sponge soaks up all the water. No more [you]." Then my bishop had brought in his clerk to give me a priesthood blessing, and he told me in the blessing that I needed to choose a career and work toward it.[45]

This account of individualized revelation exemplifies a theme of the oral histories. Also, Emily made the point of saying that it is not family in and of itself that leads to happiness, but healthy family relationships along with a sense of individual purpose in life.

Rachel observed that her own daughter was "more prayerful" about choosing a marriage partner than she had been. It was a good thing, too,

45. COHC, #110 (2011), 11.

because her daughter ended up with two children with special needs; their father was devoted to them and able to go with the family to the temple.[46]

Toward Flexibility

The single Mormon women who were interviewed repeatedly mentioned the need for flexibility in applying the Church's teachings on family. Personal revelation reassured them that their unique paths in life were acceptable and even expected by the Lord; they served a wise purpose. As the women felt this was the case, they especially appreciated the non-judgmental support of Church members, and hoped for a shift in Mormon culture toward a less rigid implementation of Church teachings. A 30-year-old single woman named Danielle summarized this view well when she said:

> I think that family values are wonderful and something that I definitely want to take to heart. I do feel like the family can be overly structured for people, overly defined and our discussions about gender and the church are kind of painful for me because I feel like we're quite rigid sometimes saying men are inherently this way and women are inherently this way, therefore men should do these things and women should do these things. That has not been my experience. . . . I think of Elder Oaks, specifically where he's talked about marriage and family, talked about the fact that there are always exceptions to rules. But since he's giving a general talk he will talk about the rules and I think that those kinds of statements are important to me. I think that's the kind of attitude I'd like to see fostered in the Church a little bit more. That we teach the principles of the Gospel and we trust individuals that they are able to implement them in their lives in an appropriate way.[47]

The Teachings of Chieko Okazaki

Chieko Okazaki cracked open the floodgates and let in a wave of women's voices. Women's experiences informed her leadership and her doctrinal understandings. She was a staunch proponent of family—seeing it as the greatest bulwark against anomie and the greatest pathway

46. COHC, #088 (2010), 7.
47. COHC, #074 (2010), 8.

toward the godly life. While she did not want to undermine the sixty percent of married women in the Church, she nevertheless wanted to validate *all* women in the Church, whether married or single, American or international. In fact, she was especially concerned about the needless shame Mormon mothers tended to carry around as if they were "scapegoats" for the ills of society.

At the heart of her understanding of the Gospel was the idea that the Christian life leads to a godly and egalitarian society. Her understanding of the Gospel was based on her understanding of ideal human relationships. Thus she did not strive to shore up traditional marriage and family for the sake of social order and institutional stability; rather, she sought to shore up the individual woman and her faith in the goodness of God for the sake of a *better* culture—the culture of Zion. To this end, she believed it was expedient to throw out damaging cultural scripts and to turn women (and men) directly toward the Lord.

Okazaki diagnosed the main challenge faced by Mormon women, in general, as a lack of personal boundaries—that is, a lack of individual self-worth apart from their identities as mothers and wives. She told a group of Mormon psychologists that many Mormon women do not distinguish between where they end and their children begin. "They feel a sense of confusion about who they are, because many competing voices lay claim to them and they try to accommodate them all." When she became a member of the Relief Society general presidency, she was "appalled at how many women were tormented by guilt about their responsibilities as mothers." For instance, if a child deviated from what was expected, it became a burden that the mother bore. "It has taken a long time for me to understand this," she said, "and although many of you [counselors and psychologists] have had far more clinical experience than I and understand this phenomenon in greater detail, I think you will agree with me that many Mormon women do not know how to recognize and maintain personal boundaries."[48]

Okazaki believed that the solution to this epidemic of self-doubt was to help women develop a strong sense of self—not through having people in authoritative positions bombard them with advice (no matter how sound or well-intentioned), but through encouraging women to seek out personal revelation.

---

48. Chieko Okazaki, "Boundaries: The Line of Yes and No," *AMCAP (Association of Mormon Counselors and Psychotherapists) Journal* 21, no. 1 (1995): 5.

A strong sense of self is not selfish, Okazaki stressed; and in fact, it better enables women to reach out to others in need. As she told the psychologists who counsel Mormon women:

> I have always had a strong and healthy sense of myself. This sense of myself manifests itself in a sense of confidence. . . . I have, I believe, strong boundaries. Because I know who I am and whose I am, it is easy for me to reach across the boundaries to other people—to meet a need, to share a joy, to perform a service, to understand a sorrow.[49]

Okazaki said that she had a strong sense of self because she didn't simply accept cultural "scripts." A life script is a prescribed set of rigid roles and timetables that women and men in any given society are expected to adhere to subconsciously. Okazaki likened the process of conversion to the Gospel with the process of conversion to the principle of personal revelation. Speaking to the LDS psychologists, she said:

> You all understand the simple, yet profoundly mysterious process of conversion—how a man or woman writes a script for his or her life, or accepts one written by others, and then lives it out as though there are no alternatives and no choices left. Every individual who has been converted to the Gospel and has joined the Church is a living, walking testimony to the power of changing a life script. I think that women, more than men, may feel trapped in scripts handed to them by someone else. Even when they accept these scripts willingly, I believe that violence is done if they believe that they *must* accept them because they have no choices.[50]

Concerned that women more often than men tend to feel trapped by life paths imposed on them by others, Okazaki believed that "the power of the Holy Ghost and the power of imagination can combine to suggest alternatives and to give the courage to try on a new role—even for a couple of hours—while the courage builds to make needed changes."[51] For Okazaki, spirituality was part and parcel to the personal strength and sense of wellbeing that God wants for all women and men to experience.

A theme of Okazaki's writings is that a woman's personal strength and a man's respect for his wife are crucial for an egalitarian marriage

49. Ibid., 5.
50. Ibid., 11.
51. Ibid., 11.

and family. Indeed, she believed that one of the main purposes of the restoration of the Gospel was to prepare a godly society, to create a whole new culture based on Christian living. "After all," she pointedly said, "Jesus asked husband and wife to become 'one flesh' (Matthew 19:5). But you can't become 'one flesh' if the husband is the flesh but the wife is just a pretty embroidered dishtowel or a cardboard cut-out of a woman."[52]

For Okazaki, a holy woman was a strong woman. She recounted a Hawaiian folktale about the goddess Hiiaka. Instead of holding up the image of a meek and childlike mother, Okazaki painted a picture of a powerful goddess who restored a dead fisherman to life for the sake of his children. By becoming "stronger individuals" first, women could become "stronger partners" as wives and as mothers, and I would add, as Church members.[53]

> Women need to see themselves as strong, as capable of hard labor for a goal, as deserving of the pleasures of achievement, as worthy of honor. Their sacrifices need to count for something. They need to see how their efforts are acts of salvation, deeds of redemptive love. They need to see that they are important and that they make a difference in the lives of the people they love the most. Often, they are crippled and burdened because they get exactly the opposite message.[54]

The "opposite message" she was referring to was the story of the scapegoat in the Book of Leviticus about the Day of Atonement in ancient Israel:

> And thus, the innocent animal would become guilty and wander away in the wilderness to die of starvation and thirst or to fall prey to wild beasts. I have had a sense that many Mormon mothers are wandering in just such a wilderness, burdened with guilt that they have accepted but of which they are innocent. It is true that much is expected of LDS women in the latter days. Mothers bear a great responsibility. But guilt is a burden they need not pick up. They need not make themselves responsible for the deficiencies of society. They are not responsible for bearing the burdens of both fatherhood and motherhood. It is not for them to bear unmerited guilt for divorce, juvenile delinquency,

52. Chieko Okazaki, "Cleaving: Thoughts on Building Strong Families," *AMCAP Journal* 26, no. 1 (2001): 31–32.

53. Ibid., 35.

54. Okazaki, "Boundaries," 14–16.

> drug abuse, teenage sexuality, theft, and violence. They need to know where they stand in their own eyes and where they stand with the Lord. That precious knowledge is not something they should let someone decide for them.[55]

Okazaki affirmed single women, respecting the fact that there was great diversity in LDS homes. Instead of seeing this diversity as evidence of the decline of family values, Okazaki saw it as an opportunity for women to find more fulfilling and egalitarian relationships. She took a patient and democratic view of such sociological change: each woman would be able to learn from her intuition and from the Lord what roles and responsibilities would make the best use of her time; proscribing the same script or timetable for every woman would be counter-productive.

> All of us women have an image of the ideal family—a marriage in the temple to an active priesthood holder, and children who are obedient and faithful. But President Ezra Taft Benson has pointed out that only fourteen percent of American households in 1980 match the traditional image of a family—working husband, full-time mother with children still in the home. Reliable statistics indicate that only one out of five LDS families in the United States have a husband and wife married in the temple with children in their home. As Elder M. Russell Ballard has already reminded us, there is great diversity in LDS homes. But all of these homes can be righteous homes where individuals love each other, love the Lord, and strengthen each other.[56]

Giving the example of two quilts, Okazaki taught that both were handmade, beautiful, and warm. The difference was that the Hawaiian quilt had a strong, predictable pattern, while the "crazy quilt" was unpredictable and irregular. Her point was that sometimes our lives are "unpredictable, unpatterned, not neat or well-ordered":

> Well, there's not one right way to be a quilt as long as the pieces are stitched together firmly. Both of these quilts will keep us warm and cozy. Both are beautiful and made with love. There's not just one right way to be a Mormon woman, either, as long as we are firmly

55. Ibid.

56. Chieko Okazaki, "Strength in the Savior," *Ensign*, November 1993, http://www.lds.org/ensign/1993/11/strength-in-the-savior?lang=eng (accessed September 3, 2012).

> grounded in faith in the Savior, make and keep covenants, live the commandments, and work together in charity.[57]

Okazaki disagreed that people who were having trouble in their personal relationships should simply be told to adopt "traditional roles of relating to each other and stop making a fuss about it." Instead, she advised counselors to "consider very carefully the strengths and weaknesses of everyone in the family—even pray for inspired insight—and then find ways to help husbands and wives become partners to each other and help parents and children become partners to each other." Rigid gender and age roles could be like "chains"; but Christ came to set people free.[58]

> The Church has nothing to fear from the strength of women. On the contrary, it desperately needs women—and men, too—who are not trapped in dysfunctional roles that involve playing out scripts that don't really work. Partnership is a mutually supportive relationship that recognizes and honors both the differences and similarities between men and women, that draws deeply on the strengths of both, that focuses on working toward mutually decided goals, and that celebrates the contributions of both in the home, in the community, and in the church and kingdom of God. Help both men and women to work for partnership and to move away from the limitations of rigid roles.[59]

Partly because she had grown up in a Hawaiian, Buddhist family, Okazaki valued cultural differences. Moreover, she did not believe that any culture had the monopoly on Christian practices; every culture had inherited false traditions that unnecessarily imposed damaging scripts on individuals.[60]

---

57. Ibid.

58. Okazaki, "Cleaving," 31. Okazaki further argues that the "ritual of the scapegoat is part of a religion that Christ replaced with the true atonement. Christ did not preserve those rituals involving women in his gospel either, but rather acknowledged women as his disciples, honored motherhood, and gave the first evidence of the resurrection to a woman. No matter who may condemn women to the scapegoat's guilt, it is not Christ and it should not be anyone in his church who would bind that burden on a woman. Nor should women pick up that burden and bind it on themselves. Christ died and rose again to free us from burdens." See Okazaki, "Boundaries," 16.

59. Okazaki, "Boundaries," 14–16.

60. Chieko Okazaki, *Lighten Up!* (Salt Lake City: Deseret Book, 1993), 122.

Distinguishing between what she considered part of the "Gospel" versus "culture" allowed her to view the Church as a work in progress. She looked forward to and worked toward a day when the Church would be purified and when there would no longer be rankings according to gender, ethnicity, or economics.

> The Gospel is pointing us toward a time when we can see others—all others—truly as God sees us, as one blood, one flesh, as brothers and sisters. Remember that God is truly the father of us all, that in Christ the divisions and the divisiveness between men and women, between different national groups, between different economic circumstances are done away with; that all are alike unto Him; and that even those who do not know Him are known and loved by Him.[61]

She worried about the tendency among people in the majority to unintentionally build walls that exclude minorities: "This acceptance must be truly universal. If the Gospel gives us tools with which to take down the walls of national or cultural difference, let us not just build another wall to encircle a new Latter-day Saint tribe."[62]

Conclusion

To return to my initial question: "Is it possible to emphasize a theology based on eternal kinship relationships without alienating unmarried church members?" I would argue that this is where theology becomes extremely important, for it defines the place of the individual woman as a part of the whole. If the Church has already arrived, then it is safeguarding and upholding correct religious and cultural traditions ordained of God. However, if the Church itself is a work in progress, then it is still in search of the heavenly society tantalizingly sketched out in scripture as the City of Enoch.

Despite the fact that women have been scripturally scapegoated through the millennia, their voices reveal that they, like Mary Magdalene after Christ's resurrection, are often first to behold the Lord. Many single Mormon women have been convinced that God wants them to be strong and capable, not weak and insecure.

---

61. Chieko Okazaki, "The Gospel and Culture: Definitions and Relationships," *Pioneers in the Pacific*, ed. Grant Underwood (Provo, Utah: Religious Studies Center, Brigham Young University, 2005), 89–90.

62. Ibid., 90.

Primarily because of Joseph Smith's revelation on the "new and everlasting covenant," Mormons commonly understand that only a man and woman *together* receive exaltation:

> Therefore, when they are out of the world they neither marry nor are given in marriage; but are appointed angels in heaven, which angels are ministering servants, to minister for those who are worthy of a far more, and an exceeding, and an eternal weight of glory. For these angels did not abide my law; therefore, they cannot be enlarged, but remain separately and singly, without exaltation, in their saved condition, to all eternity; and from henceforth are not gods, but are angels of God forever and ever. (D&C 132:16–17)

This premise gives rise to questions, though: why would a marriage be necessary for exaltation in the next life? And what is the nature of such a relationship? Does it look like nineteenth-century Mormon polygamy? Twentieth-century male-breadwinner marriage? Or something else entirely? Traditional dynamics of Mormon marriages in the twentieth century have been presumed to answer these questions—marriage in the next life will be like it is here, "only it will be coupled with eternal glory, which glory we do not now enjoy" (D&C 130:2).

Such a prospect is not necessarily appealing to all women. Additionally, forced out of necessity to become strong in mind and independent in thought and action, many single Mormon women hope and believe that heavenly marriages are egalitarian and unified, not hierarchical in nature.

Chieko Okazaki drew from the scriptures and from contemporary Mormon women's religious experiences to expand the possibilities in people's minds about the nature of a Christian family and church. For her, the dominant American family model of male breadwinner marriage was not the pattern followed in heaven. Therefore, the timing and script of a marriage were of less importance than its quality and equality. Being single is simply a phase of life that is longer for some women than others—a phase that can be just as purposeful as motherhood.

It seems evident that in the face of rapid sociological upheaval with regard to family structures in the twentieth century that the Church has taken on the mission of defending the traditional family—two parents and multiple children per household. For Okazaki, having a fewer number of respect-filled marriages in the Church is better than having a greater number of unhealthy marriages. Faith, hope, and charity can be practiced in any household, not only in married ones.

In a way, the story of single Mormon women provides a case study on the topic of institutional change: the women at the grassroots level *do* influence the discourse of sensitive leaders to varying degrees. Okazaki's work encourages me to think that the personal religious convictions of single Mormon women can become better incorporated into the Church's discourse as a whole.

Chapter Four

Motherhood

Allison Keeney and Susan Woster

If you ask a preschool-aged girl what she wants to be when she grows up, she might say, "I want to be a teacher," "I want to be a mommy," or "I want to be a princess and live in a castle." Her choices are likely to reflect the roles she has observed in the women around her or in the characters in bedtime stories. As a young girl matures, her idea of a future career typically centers on her own interests or perceived interests.

In a Pasadena third-grade class, at the last day of school, a small gathering of parents join the students in their end-of-year celebration. The students have worked hard all year and are eager to move on to the fourth grade. In preparing for this last day of school, the third grade teacher had each child draw a picture of his or her future self and career. The result is a lively display of drawings, in which each child's nine-year-old self is participating in his or her future dream job. The crowd sees illustrations of boys and girls as actors, singers, musicians, artists, astronauts, dog walkers, personal shoppers, clothing designers, snowboarders, dessert chefs, and movie directors. Some have multi-careers, such as a violinist-director-architect, or a designer-basketball player-director-actor-screenwriter. There is only one young LDS girl in the class, another multi-tasker, who illustrates herself as a mother. More specifically, she wants to be a mother-park ranger-writer-wife-family history researcher.

If asked whether they want to have children one day, most of the children in the class would say yes, but that is not what they are naturally thinking about at age nine. Why would the LDS child be the only one to include "mother" in her future plans, when other children in the class are also from homes with positive mother figures and loving parents?

The Church of Jesus Christ of Latter-day Saints teaches women—from an early age—that motherhood is a divine calling, and that she will have a sacred, central role in an eternal family. A girl is brought up to believe that she'll one day be responsible for the care and nurturing of a child of God, and for virtually every little LDS girl, the message comes through loud and clear.

At the same time, all members of the Church—men and women alike—are instructed to gain knowledge. Education is important in the Church. Mormon women have always been encouraged to develop their talents, be educated, be knowledgeable about the Gospel, and do good works. One of the standard LDS scriptural cornerstones, the Doctrine and Covenants, includes the following:

> Whatever principle of intelligence we attain unto in this life, it will rise with us in the resurrection. And if a person gains more knowledge and intelligence in this life through his diligence and obedience than another, he will have so much the advantage in the world to come. (D&C 130:18–19)

The excerpts included below are from women who, in most cases, have integrated the two major Mormon tenets of knowledge and motherhood. Though the daily lives, opportunities, and options of LDS women have evolved over the last seventy-five years, the central role of motherhood has not.

Eve and Role Models

In the Garden of Eden, God gave two commandments—to multiply and replenish the Earth, and to refrain from eating the fruit of the tree of knowledge of good and evil. One of the standard works of scripture in the LDS faith, the Pearl of Great Price, offers an additional perspective on the story of Adam and Eve in the Garden of Eden. In this interpretation, the two commandments constitute a conundrum—both cannot be obeyed simultaneously. Because Adam and Eve were not mortal in the Garden, they were not able to multiply and replenish the Earth; conversely, Mormons believe that eating the fruit of the tree would cause Adam and Eve to undergo an actual physical change in which they would "surely die"—in other words, they would become mortal.

While dwelling in the perfect Garden, Eve desired to have her eyes opened to the possibilities beyond her idyllic existence in Eden. Once out of her Garden "nest," she experienced not only sorrow and pain attendant with mortality, but also the fruits of work and the natural desire to multiply and replenish the earth. Latter-day Saints believe that Eve desired to move forward; her decision to eat the fruit was not simply because the serpent tempted her.

Eve, the first human mother on the earth, did not have any role model to follow, and she was not, of course, able to learn in a formal way; however, many Latter-day Saints believe that Eve, as a woman, was endowed with spiritual gifts of nurturing. In addition, according to LDS teachings, until Eve was expelled from the Garden, she and Adam received ongoing direct instruction and communication from God.

Unlike Eve, women in following generations have been able to look to their mothers and grandmothers as role models and learn from the examples of those women. The importance of both motherhood and education are reflected in the statements of Eleanor, born in the 1930s:

> There are certain expectations of what an LDS woman is supposed to be. We are encouraged to be well-educated, to be prepared with some kind of skill to survive and support ourselves. . . . There's still a standard that what goes on in the home is very important. Children need nurturing and they need the guidance that a mother can and should give. . . . But certainly as you look around, you see that most women are working in some way or another.[1]

Eleanor goes on to emphasize the importance of role models as LDS women form their identities and values by observing other women in their faith community.

> I think women get the patterns of what an LDS woman should be from what we see around us, what other people are doing, how they are applying the basic principles of the Church.[2]

For Nancy, who was born in 1950 and grew up in an upper class neighborhood, motherhood was an ideal to be attained. Her parents thrived in their traditional roles, and she desired to live a life similar to her mother's. She was an active member of the LDS Church, so her spiritual goals coincided with her desires:

> My early ambition for my lifetime was to be a mom like my mother; I thought she led a wonderful life. I loved it when I got to stay home from school for a sick day, because she'd be at home with

1. Claremont Mormon Women's Oral History Collection, Library of the Claremont Colleges, Claremont, CA, hereafter COHC, #004 (2009), 19.

2. Ibid., 20.

> the babies and the little children, and she had friends, a very nice house, a social life and plenty of activities—it just seemed like an active, fun way to live. She also had a housecleaner, an ironing lady, and a gardener, which I just assumed was a normal way to run a household. My father worked nearby, so he was easily available. I wanted to be a mother, just like her.[3]

Raised with all the white picket fence advantages of "The American Dream," she admired her mother, had positive family experiences as a child, and was excited to follow in her mother's footsteps and raise a family of her own.

> I never felt any expectation or desire to do anything else, even though we were all definitely pointed toward succeeding in college. I felt that a housewife's life was valuable, necessary, and fulfilling. During my young years, I didn't know any unhappy housewives among my mother's friends.[4]

Education, although important, was a continuation of what she was learning by example from those around her, preparatory to the domestic life that she expected to live.

> I always wanted to be home. . . . Even though I got a B.A. and M.A. in English, and had taught school for quite a few years, I always knew I wanted to stop and raise a family. So I never had any ambitions beyond that.[5]

Despite wanting to be a stay-at-home mom, she nevertheless pursued an education and embarked on a career. This indicates that she didn't absolutely disregard other dreams, goals, and desires for individual achievement.

Her lifelong dream of staying at home with lots of children was thwarted by her husband's untimely death; the education and work experience she acquired became invaluable to her family in not only a spiritual sense, but as a foundation for the family's temporal well being.

> I was glad I had spent time teaching . . . it was not a big, abrupt change for me to work as a teacher. I had a good job that I could go back to.[6]

3. COHC, #081 (2010), 3–4.
4. Ibid., 4.
5. Ibid., 18–19.
6. Ibid., 18.

Don't Think for Me—Trust Me to do the Right Thing

Like most women in the United States, most Latter-day Saint women who came of age in mid twentieth-century America did not typically feel pressured to have children; rather, they viewed motherhood as an assumed consequence of marriage. Once married, a woman often did not have the luxury of evaluating whether or not she was ready to be a parent. In fact, the term "parenting" was not regularly used in the 1950s. Strong exhortations to be parents were less necessary, since there were not many careers easily accessible to women.

Sonia, born in 1935, did not feel that she was being "forced" to be a stay-at-home mother, nor did she fold to 1960s social pressure to *not* be a stay-at-home mother; instead, she chose what she wanted to do. She was highly educated and able to combine freelance writing with motherhood:

> If it's possible to stay home and take care of the children, I like to see mothers do that, at least until the kids start school. Absolutely, yes. Those kids need a mother there. . . . I used to feel that I could never be "fulfilled" staying at home. But then I got into writing and that was fulfillment aplenty. And I could be at home. In fact, I was one of the few mothers in the neighborhood who was at home.[7]

It is interesting to see that many of the LDS women who were interviewed adhered to traditional roles based on society's expectations as well as their strong core beliefs. Nevertheless, they are far from judgmental or narrow-minded about others' choices, including the mothering choices of their children. The primary concern seems to be that their children maintain a belief in the importance of motherhood.

Eva, born in the 1930s, received her bachelor's degree. When her babies were young, she didn't even accept church callings. Regardless, she passes no judgment on others, and doesn't seem to feel envious of those who take a different approach:

> I always stayed home with a new baby and did not return to accept callings until I felt capable. I felt the best way to serve was to take care of the new baby and keep an orderly home and support my husband in his callings. . . .
>
> I don't think that there's a set pattern about women being home or going to work. Everyone's set of circumstances is different. For

7. COHC, #009 (2009), 13.

> my daughter-in-law it works beautifully. She's a pediatrician and why shouldn't she use that skill. So she works two days a week and the family just gets along beautifully. . . . I think as long as . . . it is not affecting your relationship with Heavenly Father or your husband and it's not hurting your children, it's OK.[8]

When is the Grass Greener?

Betty Lynn's story is a bit different. She is from a small town in Utah, where virtually the entire population was Mormon. She was born in 1935 and never questioned the Church nor its teachings. She always knew she would have a family one day. Unlike many of the young girls in her town, she also had clear educational and career goals from an early age:

> When I was a teenager I knew exactly what I wanted to do. I lived in a very small town of about 100 people. . . . I was the eldest of the family and I had a lot of responsibility around the house, taking care of the children and whatever, but I remember the Trailways Bus going through the small town and said to myself, "Someday I'm going to be on that bus. I'm going to travel and go somewhere where it is interesting and where I can learn about the world." That was implanted in my mind in my early teens and I knew exactly what I wanted to do. I wanted to make my environment beautiful and I wanted to live around beautiful things. I can say that my mother . . . encouraged my interest and she too was interested in improving the surroundings. I decided by the time I was in junior high school that I wanted to study to prepare for a career in interior design. . . . Both my parents, but particularly my father, really encouraged us. . . . He wanted his girls to be educated and he worked very hard to support us.[9]

She left her small town and worked her way through college, eventually graduating and working in the design field until she got married.

> My husband . . . did not want me to work after we were married. . . . I finished the jobs I was working on once I was married and I continued to do a few design jobs as they came. However, I was also very pleased with the fact that I was married to someone who could

8. COHC, #002 (2009), 5, 9.
9. COHC, #113 (2010), 3.

make a good income, and as the children were born I could stay home with them.[10]

Betty Lynn found fulfillment in raising her children and through Church work. She feels that her life turned out well. She didn't wonder what she was missing.

> I can truthfully say that I enjoyed the time with my children.... I was also very involved in Church assignments and I think that was more or less my outlet when my children were young. I didn't have any other responsibilities then, and I could truly enjoy my time with them....
>
> I didn't get married until I was 25. I felt that was a great advantage and had I planned it couldn't have been any better. I believe every young woman should get an education and work some time in her career before getting married.... I never had that hunger during the time I was with my children—that I needed to be working or to be doing something more fulfilling than being with my children. I did have great opportunities to serve in the Church and was given big responsibilities. I learned leadership skills I wouldn't have learned any other way than in the growth I received serving in the Church.[11]

Her own daughters completed their educations and proceeded to engage in exciting and lucrative careers:

> Both my daughters have tried to work once they had children. One daughter knew when she held her first baby that she could not go back to work. My other daughter, because she has a unique career, has had nannies for her children in the past. Her children are now two and six and she has decided she would rather be home with them.[12]

Though they both had prestigious careers that they had built up over years, in the end each of the daughters was in a financial position that allowed her to step out of her profession and stay at home with her children.

Sharon, born in 1942, was able to engineer her life in such a way that she could work *and* be at home with her children. With her experiences, she has been able to look realistically at both sides of the fence.

> I would say that I'm in an unusual situation because although I have worked for pay on a modest scale my entire married life, I was also home with my children almost all the time. I very seldom was

10. Ibid., 5.
11. Ibid.
12. Ibid., 10–11.

> away from the children because of any Church responsibility. I'm an unusual case. Many people do not have that luxury. . . .
>
> I had an experience when I was still in graduate school, expecting my first child, which shaped my view to a large degree. I was living in student housing. Everyone around was a young married person. Very few of the women were in school or working. All of their husbands were students but almost none of the women. . . . I, on the other hand, was a full-time graduate student, teaching for my department and also giving some private lessons on the side. I remember a hot day in early spring, expecting my first child at the end of July, seeing the women outside in the playground area, with their little ones, laughing and catching up on news and playing with the children. . . . I could not bear to see them or listen to them because I was not free to spend my time the way they were. . . . I later found out that some of those same women thought that I was free, since I did not have to stay home with little children. Some of them had not had the opportunity to finish college and would have loved to go to graduate school. . . . The other side looks very desirable if you have never actually been there.[13]

Sharon gained insight by being able to more clearly catch a glimpse of the plight of the "traveler" who may feel that she has been routed to one path over the other. Ironically, she has been able to travel both roads, and as such has a realistic view of each.

Mothers and Their Daughters

What of the differences between the generations? Can the bonds of motherhood, hopefully forged when a baby is born, continue to be strengthened once a daughter is an adult?

Julia, born in 1961, who had postponed having children until she was in her mid-thirties was surprised at just how strong the bonds of motherhood were:

> That was the most momentous part of my life, having a baby. Going from just doing whatever we wanted to do, going on a vacation, traveling every month to having this baby that needed us, to being unable to leave for an hour, to having this person who needs you all the time. But . . . as hard as it was, I didn't want to go back.[14]

13. COHC, #005 (2009), 22–23.
14. COHC, #024 (2010), 6.

After her first baby was born, though she was able to care for her baby on her own, her mother adjusted her work schedule so that she could spend at least two days a week helping out. She found that during that time, other bonds were formed.

> [My mother] did that for several months. It was just heaven sent and I have to say that I never loved my mother more. . . . That was something that was intangible. I just needed her here. It was so good. She bonded very well with my . . . daughter. That was a good experience for her. . . . it was so nice to have her be that person who loves your baby almost as much as you do.[15]

Julia's mother died about four years later, so she was especially thankful for the time the three generations had had to bond with one another.

Women born in the 1960s and later have opportunities that their mothers did not. As time has passed, there has not been as much of an uphill battle for women to progress into fields and professions that were traditionally considered to be in a man's realm. One might wonder whether a smart or educated mother, with an educated and accomplished grown daughter, envies the wider array of options that her daughter has. Instead, several of the these examples show the joy these women feel on behalf of their daughters. Perhaps, a mother realizes that her daughter has worked toward her own potential while at the same time inheriting the realized talent or unrealized promise of her mother—potential provided by nurturing, example, life experiences, or even by actual inherited abilities and inclinations. By this legacy, a daughter is able to realize dreams that her mother may have attained had she been provided with the same depth and breadth of opportunity.

Frances, born in the 1940s, raised her family in diverse locales. She rarely worked outside the home and devoted her life to being a mother. She is happy for her daughters and for the opportunities that they have had. She does not see those opportunities as something taking away from their abilities to be wonderful mothers. When asked "How do the attitudes and experiences of your four daughters differ from yours in terms of motherhood, marriage, education, and work?" Frances answered:

15. Ibid., 7.

> Well, for one thing, they are all marrying much later than I did. Of course I always told them to do that. I would always say, "Now, don't rush to get married."
>
> My daughters all married between the ages of 26 and 31, which is late for Mormons. But they pursued a lot of education and my daughters' upbringing was somewhat unusual with all our foreign experiences, somewhat unusual because of the circumstances of my husband and his unusual background. So they always grew up with an awareness—I would say, not typical next door, mainstream USA—always knowing that they were a little bit different but not in a bad way just in a different way.[16]

Her daughters have gone to top universities. Three of her daughters pursued medicine and the other has a high level position at a university on the East Coast. The three who are married have children and have continued balancing parenting with professions. All of her daughters are active in the LDS Church and participate in positions of responsibility within their respective congregations. Despite the impressive credentials of her daughters, she nevertheless emphasizes the importance of children cultivating kindness and charity:

> I wanted my children to be kind. We see so much in our world that isn't. I wanted my children to understand the world around them which implies the Gospel—it implies spiritual things, it implies very much the knowledge of the world, to have curiosity and intellectual curiosity to just always be curious and interested whether it is other people, other cultures, whether it is new discoveries in science, whether it is the arts. . . . We need to be kind and understand that the welfare of others is important and to understand what is out there in that world in order to make good decisions.[17]

In effect, Frances and her husband provided their daughters with experiences that may have served as a sort of intellectual and spiritual life coaching. Her daughters went on to realize their own potential, but it is clear that the mother's dreams for her daughters were less tangible than education and career. Instead, the daughters were encouraged to be curious, kind, and understanding—because these solid, spiritual, personal qualities were embraced by the daughters, they had a strong foundation to build their lives on.

---

16. COHC, #048 (2010), 20–21.
17. Ibid., 26.

When a woman from an earlier generation succeeds in her career, we might assume that—because she worked so hard to gain recognition—her profession would define her sense of self. However, Joan, born in 1935, reports that despite her mother's successful career, her mother's great pride in life was her children. Her mother, born in the early twentieth-century, was a pioneer in educational advances for underprivileged minorities:

> And as I get older, it's easier for me to embrace the primary role of a woman as being a mother, a companion, a wife, and a grandmother. I am kind of amazed to hear myself saying that and I was amazed when my mother said that to me when I was interviewing her for an . . . article some thirty years ago. I wanted her to talk about which of her professional accomplishments she was proud of, but she said, "Oh, by far I am proudest of my wonderful children." I thought she was copping out at the time, but I guess, as you get older, the other things fade away.[18]

Father and Mother Know Best

Though motherhood involves nurturing and child rearing, LDS parenting is not exclusively a woman's territory. Latter-day Saints are taught that the care and nurturing of souls entrusted to them by God is achieved by a partnership between both the mother and the father.

In 1995, LDS Church leaders published a definitive document, "The Family: A Proclamation to the World," underscoring the importance of the family, including the responsibilities of both the husband and wife to be good parents:

> Husband and wife have a solemn responsibility to love and care for each other and for their children. "Children are an heritage of the Lord" (Psalms 127:3). Parents have a sacred duty to rear their children in love and righteousness, to provide for their physical and spiritual needs, and to teach them to love and serve one another, observe the commandments of God, and be law-abiding citizens wherever they live. Husbands and wives—mothers and fathers—will be held accountable before God for the discharge of these obligations.[19]

18. COHC, #007 (2009), 20.
19. "The Family: A Proclamation to the World," *Ensign*, November 1995, 102.

At the same time, the document underscored traditional roles of husband and wife as parents—a father "presides" over the family, while a mother's main responsibility is to nurture her children. Nevertheless, it reinforces the commitment as partners:

> In these sacred responsibilities, fathers and mothers are obligated to help one another as equal partners. Disability, death, or other circumstances may necessitate individual adaptation.[20]

The world has changed, and the LDS Church more overtly provides men with a definition of their responsibilities as fathers. More Mormon men today participate in parenting and appreciate the importance and complexity of raising a loved little person. Marie recounts how involved fathers today are in the raising of children, as compared to the fathers in earlier generations:

> I think it's important for parents to be available, but it's important for fathers to be available, not just mothers.[21]
>
> My father certainly never did household tasks, and he didn't do any childcare either. Nobody expected it of that generation. I see some changes in my generation as a parent. In my children's generation as parents, I see huge changes. The fathers feel as much responsibility for their children as the mothers do. The fathers show greater appreciation to the mothers and recognize that childcare is a very hard job. Some of this comes right from the pulpit. Conference talks, especially. The men are told that they need to protect their wives and cherish them and appreciate what they do, to give them opportunities for personal growth, not to think that they are too good to do certain household things. They are told that roles can be divided in convenient ways, and that the husband is not the lord and master of the house. If they see themselves in that role, they should repent.[22]

For Kelly, the importance of teamwork between mother and father is realized in her daily routine. Through various choices and necessity, her husband is the stay-at-home parent while she works outside the home four days a week:

> Several of my friends who were pregnant at the same time said to me, "How can you trust him to look after your child?" It weighed

---

20. Ibid.
21. COHC, #005 (2009), 22.
22. Ibid., 20.

upon me, and finally I told him that was what they were saying. He said, "What are your friends doing having children with men they don't trust?"[23]

In another scenario, Wendy, a mother of four, recently switched parenting roles with her husband in mid-life. She is impressed with his dedication in filling the role of the stay-at-home parent:

> [My husband] had experienced a serious health scare . . . all stress and lifestyle induced. We needed to change gears and a quieter existence was beckoning. . . . [My husband] stays home, taking care of our brood, and I work [as a school administrator]. [He] still works freelance . . . when he wants to. . . . He works at night mostly, after everyone is asleep. . . . We have a couple of teenagers now. Four different schools, four different schedules—[My husband] is manager of our household, making sure everyone has immunizations, piano lessons, volleyball games, golf team practice, doctor appointments, play dates—even preschool at our home sometimes. I think he enjoys the balance we've created.[24]

Wendy's education enabled her and her husband to find a relatively stress-free solution to the problem of ratcheting down his career-related stress. She continues to strengthen her bonds with her children and is now able to see her husband experiencing that bond as well.

The parents above, as well as the parents whose decisions were criticized by friends, exemplify the LDS Church's council to "help one another as equal partners." The women are *sharing* parenting joys and responsibilities with their partners, not shirking their responsibilities as mothers.

Where Are We Now?

All of the women in this chapter are mothers. Though not all LDS women marry or have children, the majority of those who become mothers understand and embrace their roles, working toward the ideal as the primary nurturer in a loving family. Whatever their circumstances, generations, and abilities, most of these women value their own or their daughters' educations or self-sufficiency while prioritizing the importance of motherhood and responsibilities to their families.

23. COHC, #107 (2011), 7.
24. COHC, #118 (2011), 5.

LDS Church teachings likewise emphasize the profound importance of motherhood. The following statement from 1942 is still quoted and embraced in many LDS circles today:

> Motherhood is near to Divinity. It is the highest, holiest service to be assumed by mankind. It places her who honors its holy calling and service next to the angels.[25]

As society changes, generations accumulate, opportunities widen, and personal necessities vary, the message of the importance of motherhood remains as strong as ever.

25. "Message of the First Presidency," *Deseret News Weekly Church Edition*, October 1942, 5.

Chapter Five

Adversity

Pamela Lindsay Everson

The Church of Jesus Christ of Latter-day Saints promises its members happiness and an abundant life by following its teachings. But can it really deliver?

Twentieth-century Mormon women look at adversity through a unique lens. Peering through what some perceive to be rose-tinted glasses, they use the gospel of Jesus Christ to give purpose to their pain. They see mortality as a brief proving ground and accept the reality of trials as building blocks and stepping stones. The love of God and the atoning sacrifice of Jesus Christ serve to motivate them to bear well their trials and return victoriously to a heavenly home.

The source of their optimism is both doctrinal and cultural. Scriptures teach that "Men are, that they might have joy" (2 Ne. 2:25). Leaders tout the link between good living and a good life, and congregations sing "Happy are We, Happy are We." Even the primary children grow up thinking God wants them for "Sunbeams," to "Shine for Him each day!"

Within this context, Mormon women approach conflict with the hope of finding redeeming grace in their struggles. They are prepared for the fight. Yet, life happens, often with an intensity unimagined and a magnitude unsustainable. Like a tsunami, crisis can disarm its victims. When an LDS woman experiences the loss of a husband and friend through an act of infidelity, her world is shattered; when she feels the disabling effect of illness, she feels useless; and when she turns to God for help and gets no response, she replaces trust with doubt. The good life becomes elusive; expectations fade in the face of reality.

The juxtaposition of happiness and suffering presents a paradox. Some women see it as God's plan. Opposition in all things is a core principle of Mormon theology (2 Ne. 2:11). Accepting opposition enables them to choose happiness and those virtues that are compatible. Others find no solace. Expectations are not met, and situations preclude happiness within the parameters of the Gospel. While exploring LDS women's responses to crises of death and illness, faith and identity, disaffection and abuse, we will consider individual LDS women's perspectives as they seek to reconcile this gospel binary.

Death and Illness

Women suffer when those they love suffer. "I can't say that I've never had anything bad happen in my life, but when something bad happens to my children, it feels ten times worse," declares one woman representatively.[1] Motherhood clearly broadens the scope of a woman's suffering.

Happiness is Spiritual Reward

Dee tells of the physical bonding between mother and child, and the spiritual compensation that accompanies loss:

> The coroner ruled it a crib death. What a sad time we went through afterward. Like all mothers who have lost an infant, I was struck by the emptiness I felt. I had been carrying a cuddly baby in my arms for four months, smelling her special scent as she nestled her head into my neck, hearing her sweet gurgles in my ear. It was all gone. My arms were empty. . . .
>
> We buried our baby girl . . . next to her sister. My ward family was marvelous. So many people from our ward made the two hour drive to the cemetery, even though they had known us only a few months. That spirit of giving has meant a lot to me over the years and I've thought about it often. . . .
>
> Nearly all of my major challenges have involved loved ones—a mother who struggles with emotional stability, a brother who was gay and died young of AIDS, two daughters who died as infants. Other challenges occurred as my children got older. When our only living daughter was in college, she developed signs of mental illness and has since been diagnosed with schizophrenia. While her condition has

1. Claremont Mormon Women's Oral History Collection, Library of the Claremont Colleges, Claremont, CA, hereafter COHC, #056 (2010), 17.

> become more stable over time with medication, she lives a reclusive, limited life and shows little interest in communicating with anyone. Family get-togethers are different now than they used to be—there's always the pain and the sense of loss—though we try to make the best of a disappointing, tragic situation. . . .
>
> Two of my sons chose to leave the Church as young adults. One turned his back on the Church six months after he returned from his mission. . . . Then, within a couple of years, my youngest son decided not to go on a mission and has been inactive ever since. . . .
>
> I know I am a better, wiser, more compassionate, patient, and spiritual person because of these experiences. My faith has been my teacher and my mainstay, and always will be. I've had a good life.[2]

Dee's staggering losses try her on every level—and yet she concludes with the affirmation, "I've had a good life." Like their early predecessors who sang as the sun set on fresh graves strewn along the prairie, twentieth-century Mormon women continue to join in the chorus, "All is Well, All is Well!"

To what specifically can we attribute this Mormon optimism? Dee points to the centrality of the Gospel in her life as the source of her sanguinity. She elaborates:

> It's important to me to have a nurturing spiritual life and a relationship with a personal, compassionate God I can envision and communicate with. The Church gives me that. I want to believe that families can be together forever. The Church gives me that. I want to be part of a people who will do anything for you in your time of need. Again, the Church gives me that. Some may find these yearnings simplistic, even infantile, but I've sorted through the alternatives on occasion, and the Church wins every time.[3]

Dee's affirmation of faith is reward enough to offset her physical losses. Sustained by an attentive Father in Heaven, and confident in the manifestations of His goodness, she finds a winning formula for happiness.

Mormon women report diverse demonstrations of God's love. They come as general impressions, vivid revelations, and audible instruction. They occur randomly and through supplication. They bring about a renewed sense of spiritual focus and intense gratitude and joy.

---

2. COHC, #052 (2010), 11–13.

3. Ibid., 15.

Such spiritual rewards are part of the Mormon paradigm. They are listed most often as the source of happiness among contemporary Mormon women. Some perceive them to be a gift, and some expect and depend upon a heavenly connectedness.

The power of spiritual gifts is manifest in the early tradition of the Saints. When an unnamed pioneer woman was asked to recount the "dark" days of the early Church, she responded with surprising enthusiasm:

> I can never call them dark days, Sister. We were starving, we were dying, suffering was then consuming life itself, but it was that which gave its brightness to the flame; the flame of pure religion was burning then. God was with His people. I would give a thousand days of the present luxury and folly for one hour of that exalted life.[4]

Though extraordinary, this woman's account speaks to the motivation for an "exalted life." The spiritual high associated with pure religion and God's presence among His people compensates for considerable physical hardship.

While modern LDS women seldom encounter comparable extremity they do recount profound and life changing gifts of the spirit. More often than not, it is not the removal of their trial, but a spiritual experience that revitalizes their faith. Patty tells of a single incident that confirmed God was in His heaven and mindful of her plight. It was enough to sustain her in her trial:

> He just wrapped me up in His arms and calmed my soul. And that's all I needed. He was there and He was aware of what I was going through. And I could dust myself off and deal with the problem because God was in His heaven.[5]

A heavenly show of support satisfies this petitioner that she is not alone. She derives strength and confidence through a spiritual connection.

Theresa describes a more literal intercession in her trial:

> Those were very dark days. All the feeling of depression that I felt I was beginning to lose returned a thousand-fold. One Saturday evening I was alone with the children. I was so depressed I wanted to die. I felt there was nothing to live for and it would be so easy to end

---

4. Elizabeth Wood Kane, *Twelve Mormon Homes: Visited in Succession on a Journey through Utah to Arizona* (Salt Lake City: University of Utah Tanner Trust Fund, 1974), 30.

5. COHC, #049 (2010), 12.

> it all. A cloud of darkness seemed to close in upon me. I walked into the bedroom and threw myself on the bed. I had lost all desire to live. I wanted to die. And then I heard a small clear voice. It said, "Paul wrote a letter to the Corinthians. In it he said, 'Do not be worried and troubled. Pray and ask God for what you need, first thanking him for his good gifts. And peace will be in your heart!'" It was a talk [my son] would be giving in Sunday School in a few hours. I had taught [him] these words, and yet I was hearing them for the first time. They sank deep into my very soul.
>
> I slid from the bed to my knees. Tears flowed down my face. I thanked my Heavenly Father for these gifts and as Paul promised the Corinthians, I felt that peace. I got up from my knees, knowing full well that Heavenly Father loves us and is watching over us.[6]

For Theresa spiritual reward came in the delivery of her trial. From the depths of despair and depression, she was lifted from her bed and healed through divine power. For her, it was a gift from God.

Not every woman, however, receives spiritual consolation. Despite a common desire to access God and feel His nearness, many women report an impenetrable wall of silence.

Happiness is a Necessity

In lesser numbers, some women report their trials punctuated by failed attempts to communicate with God. Antithetical to the validating experiences of the former group, these non-events are marked by abandonment and doubt. Questions of God's disposition and whether He exists at all cause them to reconsider their faith.

When Elaine's twenty-four-year-old sister lost her new baby on the operating table and two weeks later her sister's husband was diagnosed with cancer, Elaine desperately sought help. Receiving no spiritual support, despite weeks of intense fasting and prayer, she wondered where God was, and how He could be so cruel:

> It was really a difficult time. I thought for sure [my sister's] husband wouldn't die. Her baby had died. God wouldn't take her husband too. For a while there, it was tough for me to pray for things because I thought, "Why should I ask God for anything? He already knows

6. COHC, #010 (1970), 32.

what He's going to do, and nothing I say will change His mind." It took me a few years actually to get over that.[7]

Elaine's brother-in-law died six weeks after the baby. Gravely disappointed with God for her sister's sake and her own, she concludes that He was impervious to their family's needs. Time however, brought her around.

Several factors contribute to coming around to a spiritual reconciliation. For believers, holding on to their faith is critical to their salvation. While momentarily upset with God, and what He allows, Elaine could not afford to jettison Him for good. Like Job, who wrestling with God, wants both to subdue Him and submit to Him, Mormon women are caught between conflicting emotions. Attempting to privilege their will, they sometimes threaten to usurp His authority and authorship, and in doing so jeopardize their own role as His children.

Coming around also involves a removal from the situation. Like Elaine, the large majority of narrators speak with the distance of time and space. Those in the midst of crises tell a different story, but the hindsight of most is one of renewed faith. Later in Elaine's life, as the mother of a troubled teen, she displayed a distinct change of attitude:

> I gave my emotions away to Heavenly Father. I gave Him my mouth, every word, every response, because it was beyond me how to parent in this case. . . . I think somehow, with Heavenly Father's help, [my husband] and I parented beyond ourselves when it was most difficult to do. I know that Heavenly Father knows what my prayers are.[8]

From accusations of blame to complete trust, Elaine evolved to a position of faith.

In a similar vein, Laura speaks of a dire need to hear from God, and the threat His silence presents. Having joined the LDS Church with a desire to more fully participate in her religion and have access to a more personal God, her hopes were high:

> My daughter had a health crisis. . . . That really challenged me. She has scoliosis and needed back surgery. I had two good friends who had this surgery and I knew how horrible and life changing it was going to be for her physically and emotionally. . . . I did not want my daughter to have to go through that. I had never prayed for a

7. COHC, #022 (2009), 9.

8. Ibid., 18.

> miracle before, but I really wanted one. I wanted God to make this go away. He had to. I had been saving chips and was ready to trade them in.

Time passed with no response to her prayers.

> I woke up at three in the morning and realized the temple opened at five. So I got up and put my clothes on and drove to the temple and was there for the five-thirty session. . . . I was impatient to get through the session because I had things to say to God when I got up to the celestial room. I remember not feeling anything, and being frustrated because God had to know what I was there for. I didn't feel comforted or at peace, I was just agitated and upset. . . . I started to think there wasn't a God. I felt detached from any spiritual experience I'd ever had, any confirmation I'd received. . . . I just wanted God to tell me that he heard me and cared, to just send me some kind of assurance. . . . I was that low.[9]

Laura does receive what she felt to be a clear and unmistakable answer to her prayers. It came in the form of a Relief Society president who "unknowingly" knocked at her door with dinner. Certain that God had finally heard her prayers and sent this woman on His errand, Laura's faith was restored and she was fortified through her trial: "I didn't get the miracle that I wanted, but I feel like something more miraculous occurred. . . . It changed my perspective."[10] She too came around.

Feeling keenly the unmet expectations of her new faith, Laura is paralyzed by notions of failure. Her confidence unraveled, and she became desperate for spiritual resolution. With a dramatic shift of focus, Laura seized upon the miracle of the dinner offering. Identifying divine fingerprints on the timely gift, she was able to find solace and restitution in her ordeal. The tale became a personal one of faith lost and found.

Peace and confidence hang on a spiritual resolution. It is imperative to many of these women to experience some sort of confirmation of faith. While of particular necessity during times of crisis, the ongoing lack of communication can create a trial of its own.

In a church founded on personal revelation, expectations abound. Mormon teachings on prayer and revelation assume a two-way conversation with God. Decisions are made, callings accepted, and counsel

---

9. COHC, #056 (2010), 17–18.
10. Ibid., 19.

and comfort garnered, all in His name. When women feel outside of this dynamic, when they feel singularly unrewarded in their petitions, happiness remains elusive.

Another woman, Lynn, comes around through the back door and finds resolution in full disclosure. She states:

> I never felt like God talked to me. . . . You have this sense that God is talking to everybody but you. I felt guilty about it. I tried and I tried. Finally, one day I had an epiphany, well, not really an epiphany. I just decided, "You know, I'm trying to live an ethical and moral life. I'm through worrying about this. If God wants to talk to me, I'm available, but I'm not going to feel somehow lesser because I don't feel what these other people feel." So that was pivotal in terms of my attitude.[11]

Tired of waiting on an unresponsive interlocutor, Lynn puts the responsibility on God's shoulders to make the connection. For her, honesty was more settling than the pretense. Her candor however, brings mixed reviews. She continues:

> So here we were . . . in this free for all Sunday School class, and I tell this story . . . that God doesn't talk to me, and someone said, "We know. He told us." Hah! It was a fun, interesting group of people.[12]

In another ward however, Lynn was the one to inject a little humor:

> [My husband] came home one time and told me that the stake president said to him, "It must be awfully difficult being married to someone who is spiritually handicapped." I found that a little shocking. I guess if you say that God doesn't talk to you, that's how you're seen. I said, "Does that mean we'll get a special parking sticker at church?"[13]

Happiness is Growth Opportunity

As Mormon women look for comfort in the arm of God, they also strive to make use of temporal and transcendent blessings proffered through suffering. In 1972, Elder Spencer W. Kimball (later to become Church President) wrote:

11. COHC, #030 (2009), 14.
12. Ibid., 14.
13. Ibid., 21.

> No pain that we suffer, no trial that we experience is wasted. It ministers to our education, to the development of such qualities as patience, faith, fortitude and humility. All that we suffer and all that we endure, especially when we endure it patiently, builds up our characters, purifies our hearts, expands our souls, and makes us more tender and charitable, more worthy to be called the children of God. And it is through sorrow and suffering, toil and tribulation that we gain the education that we come here to acquire and which will make us more like our Father and Mother in heaven.[14]

This economy of suffering contributes to a positive disposition. Putting one's tribulations to work concurs with the Mormon values of thrift and productivity. Eternal progression motivates choice and behavior. And through the stretching and conditioning of opposition, LDS women perceive their souls refined.

Gabby demonstrates a remarkable willingness to endure temporal loss for a greater spiritual gain:

> In [the 1990s] our two beautiful boys were born. . . . We had waited a long time for more children, and all of us were over the moon! Both boys were very precocious and made life very fun for all of us. However, one night [my son] had a massive seizure. Within a few weeks we learned he had a class four brain tumor. A year later, after major surgery and months of chemotherapy he passed away at age three and a half. Although I sincerely wish [my son] had not died, his illness and eventual death brought a maturity and religious conviction to my three girls that continues to bless each of their lives. Suddenly the gospel teachings had real meaning for them and they each grabbed on faithfully with both hands. I can honestly say [my son's] death is the best experience we have had as a family. It blesses each of us every day.[15]

By transforming pain into a positive opportunity for growth, this woman utilizes suffering. She turns her loss into a very personal lesson for the family.

Leanne's "schooling" involves a stiff correction from God. Attempting to influence a priesthood blessing, she finds that an unforgettable insight into spiritual matters is compensation for her sorrow:

---

14. Spencer W. Kimball, *Faith Precedes the Miracle* (Salt Lake City: Deseret Books, 2001), 98.

15. COHC, #094 (2010), 4.

> [My husband] gave [my son] a blessing while he was surrounded by all this medical equipment. . . . [He] didn't bless him that he would live. All night long I was so mad at him. I thought, "What are blessings for? We want our son to live, so you bless him so that he'll get over this and be healthy!" But he didn't bless him that way. I didn't say anything to him at the time with all the commotion going on, but I tossed and I turned all night. In my mind I had created this whole scenario, where in the morning I was going to call the bishop and ask the ward to fast for our baby. He needed it, we needed it. But that morning I got a phone call from [my husband] telling me that [our son] didn't make it. . . . Finally when [my husband] and I were together, I asked him why he didn't bless him to live. He told me he wanted to bless him that way, but the words just weren't there. He couldn't do it. I think that's the first time I realized that the priesthood is real and that my husband took it seriously. I don't think I had ever realized that before. I think that was a lesson I had to learn, and apparently I had to learn it in a very painful way. That really chastised me, I'm telling you. Heavenly Father let me know in no uncertain terms that there is power in the priesthood and you don't abuse it.[16]

This woman's consolation comes in the form of a Heavenly rebuff. Receiving a chastening message rather than one of approbation, Leanne nevertheless feels rewarded by the confirmation of God's authority and acknowledgement. Having acquired knowledge in "no uncertain terms" galvanizes her spiritually and sustains her in her temporal travails.

Sami is another who identifies purpose in her suffering. At twenty-two she left the family's Buddhist religion and converted to Mormonism. Estranged for a time from her mother who opposed this radical breech, Sami continued in her faith. She married, had a daughter, and served actively in her ward. When her husband was struck with cancer at age forty-three, she had her beliefs put to the test:

> We didn't know what hit us. Every day his situation deteriorated. The doctors didn't know what we were dealing with. We had very little chance to talk about anything. Somewhere in all of that I knew and he knew that his memorial service—it wasn't a funeral—was going to be [his] Big Missionary Moment. The service was not only to celebrate him and honor him, but I felt the responsibility of doing

16. COHC, #018 (2009), 12.

> what he wanted and that this was our opportunity to share with our non-member family and friends why we believe in the gospel.
>
> I know that Heavenly Father needed [my husband] on the other side of the veil. That's the conclusion that I've come to. That he's busy and is working hard and that he was needed there.[17]
>
> I've had to deal with a lot of things that I never thought I would have to deal with. But I could see that all these things were for my experience and I see the benefit of that, even if they are the very hardest things.[18]
>
> The gospel resonated for me because the joys and sorrows are unified. We can appreciate and experience joy because we can also appreciate and experience sorrow. That's what we signed up for.[19]

Sami's statement of "signing up" is a direct reference to the Mormon "Plan of Salvation." Holding her own experience up against the backdrop of a pre-earth and post-earth existence, she situates herself and her trials within that framework. She believes she has come to "gain the education that we come here to acquire"; and takes comfort in knowing and participating in God's plan. Optimism sprang from the opportunity for Sami and her husband to be busily engaged in advancing the work of the Lord, and in experiencing first hand the order and beauty of His kingdom.

As these three women transformed their sorrow into useful opportunity, they succeeded in offsetting their losses.

Crises of Faith, Identity, Disaffection and Abuse

More often than not, it is matters of faith that stand as the greater obstacles to happiness. While physical adversity lends itself to assurances of a brighter hereafter, spiritual challenges carry the burden of conflict and uncertainty. The threat of spiritual death is grave, and the effects of disenfranchisement are far reaching.

---

17. COHC, #031 (2010), 4–7.

18. Ibid., 9.

19. Ibid., 20.

Betrayal

When women are deceived, let down, or given inappropriate counsel by ecclesiastical leaders, they are not apt to forget it. The sense of being betrayed often brings about a new perspective, or new relationship with the Church, and the outcome may hinge on the ability to distinguish between the offending individual and the Gospel he or she represents.

Hattie recounts the sting of a bishop's deceit and found it almost unbearable to reconcile it with her belief in the Gospel:

> We had a bishop that cheated us out of a lot of money, six figures of money. It was a horrible experience and if it hadn't been for [my two friends] I would have left the Church. But [one friend], who had to be my gift from God at the time . . . said, we would one day look back on the experience and recognize the many things we learned from it . . . but still be unhappy we experienced it. She was right. I learned about evil from this bishop; I learned people will do nasty things to you for their own gain and then lie and get away with it. . . . I would have done things very differently. I would never have trusted him, never cared about him, which was the whole appeal from him to get the money. I would have trusted myself when I looked into his eyes and saw blankness; I was perplexed because I didn't dare conclude what was obvious. But I was better prepared to function in the world because of this experience. It made me a better judge, I'm sure, because I didn't any longer fall into the trap of thinking people who looked like me were going to be good people. . . . It's OK. As [my friend's] good husband says, "It's the Church of Jesus Christ, but also of the Latter-day Saints."[20]

This woman cites this crisis as a turning point for her family. The betrayal of trust, particularly from within the ranks, causes her to amend her Mormon religiosity. Her children become disinterested in the Church after seeing how it was handled; and she no longer attends tithing settlement or speaks of matters of relevance to ecclesiastical leaders. Her experience motivates her to trust her instincts and follow her own pathway to discipleship.

The tendency to establish new parameters of behavior and patterns of thought often characterizes conflict of faith. When Paula is

---

20. COHC, #051 (2010), 35.

put in a position of defending her children or the Church, she comes up with a way to do both:

> We were always taught in Church that if you had Family Home Evening your children would never leave the Church. That was essentially a promise given by a General Authority in a conference talk, so I was very vigilant about Family Home Evening, even when it wasn't going well. At one point Family Home Evening was becoming a disaster at our house, a negative experience instead of a positive one. I realized that we had to regroup and change the experience. We had a twelve and a fourteen-year-old, and two younger children and it just wasn't working. The older boys were sullen and bored. I had to make it fun and change it up, because I was hanging on to that promise that my children wouldn't leave the Church. I succeeded in making Family Home Evening fun and positive, but it didn't really hold because not all of my children remained in the Church. My third child was the first one to leave the Church.[21]

Though Paula did not agree with her children's choices to leave the Church, she was sympathetic and did not disagree with some of their points of contention:

> I think [my daughter] had a right to her feelings about it. . . . I came to realize that, for all of us, our spirituality is our own and that my children have a right to their own spirituality and beliefs. I wasn't the manager of it and should not be. It took time for me to come to that conclusion.[22]

While in years past, Paula felt responsible for her children's life choices, as she got older she realized that her children's journeys and decisions were their own. This freeing of herself from responsibility for others' choices produced a more open canon of thought:

> I feel like there are twelve million LDS Churches, that we all filter the teachings of the Church through our own personality traits and our life experiences. I think that's OK. . . . We all have our own direct relationship with the Church, where we find those things that are important and that bring us closer to God and bring us peace and wisdom.[23]

---

21. COHC, #029 (2009), 10–11.
22. Ibid., 11.
23. Ibid., 12.

As Paula endorsed diversity within the Church, she opened space for herself as a "good enough" mother; and through the various pathways to God, she opened space for her children. Relying on her own interpretation of the Gospel, she found she could be happy.

There are more than a few accounts of women who have experienced grief due to internal strife within the faith. Latter-day Saints anticipate saintliness, and when they experience insensitivity, injustice, or heavy-handed authority, it ignites sparks of dissension.

One sister reports the shock of learning that the very same woman who had seduced her husband (while he was a bishop), was asked to be the keynote speaker at a large meeting. She confirmed that the stake president was aware of this individual's involvement with her husband. She felt he was insensitive.[24] Another woman tells of her bishop driving her son away from the Church by telling him in a militant way that he could no longer pass the sacrament unless he cut his hair.[25] And a third mother tells of a Primary teacher telling her admittedly unruly eleven-year-old daughter that she should not come back to class for a while. She never did go back.[26]

In order to survive dissension within the Church, women at times make generous allowances for human error. They look for ways to make membership easier and get around inconsistencies in behavior and principle. Louise speaks to the challenge of dealing with the human factor in a religious setting. Wondering how she and her husband managed to stay in the Church despite some "very un-Christian" language by respected leaders, she concludes that it is all part of the experience:

> I think I learned from my parents to separate gospel principles from the behavior of individuals, and perhaps from what I learned from many, many overheard conversations as a child when we visited relatives in Salt Lake City. I knew that Church members and Church leaders weren't perfect.
>
> For me the Church has always been about the brotherhood and sisterhood worked out at the local level. I have had lots of wonderful and quite a few terrible experiences in that regard, but truly believe in trying to live in peace and harmony with people who are different

24. COHC, #148 (2012).
25. COHC, #015 (2009), 20.
26. COHC, #065 (2010), 11.

> from me. I cherish the good times and the bad. I like the metaphor of Church membership as a marriage "for better or worse."[27]

As Louise distinguished between man's fallibility and the purity of the Gospel, she preserved the integrity of her Church membership; and by placing herself in partnership with her fellow members, she assumed a shared responsibility for success.

"Cherishing" the bad times with the good also suggests a belief in a beauty associated with coming together as one people under the name of Christ. By invoking the scriptural imperative, "If ye are not one, ye are not mine" (D&C 38:27) Louise espoused the value of working and growing together through opposition.

Alienation

Fitting-in matters to LDS women. The perception that one is outside the flock generates feelings of inadequacy, loneliness, and isolation. Non-conformity can be onerous.

Audrey's world was crumbling. Weighing heavily on her soul were the doubts and culpability associated with a failed pregnancy and a failing marriage. Contemplating life as a single mother in a family and community that she alleges "don't get divorced," she would imagine a place for herself:

> I remember being in the backseat of my parents' car after [my son's] burial. . . . I remember just looking out the window, watching the people walk up and down the dark streets in Salt Lake City, thinking that I was living this entirely separate existence. They were walking through life, I was too, but I felt I had no place in their world; I felt like a round peg in a square hole. . . .
>
> It was painful being around other people. I felt I had no place where I truly belonged and where things worked for me, where things made sense for me. Any attachment I had at that time didn't make a difference to me. I realized that I didn't really belong anywhere. . . .
>
> Then suddenly, I had this complete enlightenment. All of a sudden I was let in on what was really going on. He [Jesus Christ] had relieved all of the pain and this sense of isolation from my mind and from my heart—it just leapt out of my body. It was one of the most profound experiences of my life. . . .

27. COHC, #098 (2010), 4.

> I knew Heavenly Father knew me and understood my situation. I thought, even in my circumstances, in my troubled marriage and my feelings of entrapment and despair, that [my son] chose me to be his mother. I really felt honored.[28]

Audrey's loneliness stands in stark contrast to the joyous communion experienced through divine revelation. Coming from a place of confusion and indifferent attachments, she found herself "let in" to a spiritual understanding and to the love of God.

Prior to Audrey's revelatory conversion, she perceived herself not only outside her community, but also outside the reach of Christ's redemptive power. Despite a belief in the Gospel, she found that the blessings and promises it holds did not pertain to her: "Even though you believe the Church is true and the blessings are true for everybody else, you just don't think they apply to you. It's true, but it's just not true for you."[29] While holding onto her faith in the saving power of Christ's atonement, she missed the personal assurance that He relates to her sorrows.

In the face of such soulful loneliness, Audrey came to appreciate a very personal application of the Atonement:

> Even though my life had been shaped by it, I hadn't learned to apply it to myself. I'd come to understand that if the atonement was real, and if it does all the things that Christ claims that the Atonement does, that the prophets claim that it does . . . and the healing powers of the atonement were true, it was infinite enough and universal enough to cover me.[30]

With the knowledge gained through a heavenly revelation, Audrey was awakened to her position as an esteemed member of an eternal community.

Feeling outside the traditional Mormon female demographic in one way or another proves to be a challenge for many women. While some struggle with issues surrounding spouses and children, the greatest trial for others is the very absence of those relationships.

Within the culture of a church that perpetuates aphorisms such as "Families are Forever" and "No success can compensate for failure in the home," the emphasis on motherhood and family is palpable—and leaves a sizeable gap for the disenfranchised. Despite promise of eternal

28. COHC, #111 (2010), 12.
29. Ibid., 18.
30. Ibid., 18.

fulfillment, those who are bereft of such roles in mortality are susceptible to feelings of marginalization.

As a single and childless woman, Leslie chooses not to let it curtail her joy:

> I'm single and I love children and now I'm past the point when I'm going to be having children age-wise. All I ever wanted to do was get married and have children. My professional life and my job is something that's a means to an end and it's what I do to provide for myself. . . . But it [singlehood] doesn't stop my life either. I think it is important to blossom where you are planted. . . . We're on this earth to be happy despite some of the trials that we face. There are pros and cons to being single, as there are pros and cons to being married. I just have to take advantage of the perks. . . . I've had an opportunity to mother my nieces and my friends' children. I appreciate the opportunity I've had to work in the Primary for six years. I loved that, but I also don't feel sad that I'm on my own. . . .
>
> Why waste time and energy worrying when you can't do anything about it? . . . And it's okay because I think I have a responsibility to find happiness in my life no matter what situation, but it certainly isn't what I expected.[31]

Expectation plays a prominent role in the happiness equation. Putting to rest the deep-seated image of the person that should have been involves a very real sense of grief and mourning.

In Leslie's dialectic of the soul, we see the ping-ponging of emotion between sorrow felt and decided joy. As she attempted to mount a case for the good life of a single woman, her calculated lists of pros and cons, her talk of "responsibility" and "have-to's" belied the raw emotion of loss. Her march toward happiness is one of determination and will.

Anne, like Leslie, is single and childless. She too found herself in a different place than she had expected:

> There's such an assumption—strong assumption—that you'll marry and that when you marry you'll have children. I think those assumptions are so damaging. So incredibly damaging. Because it's just not going to happen for everybody. It's not. Rather than emphasizing what specific relationships we need to have (husband/wife, mother/child) in order to be successful, I think we need to emphasize the kinds of relationships we need to have. By that I mean, the nature of

31. COHC, #036 (2009), 10–11.

> a relationship between yourself and another person as being loving, compassionate, service oriented, considerate and kind.
>
> This assumption that all women marry is a product of the Young Women program. There was no question in my mind. There was not even the acknowledged possibility in my mind that I might not marry when I left Young Women. Here I am seventeen years later, unmarried without children. That's been the most hellish thing in the world for me to deal with. In spite of having twelve years of feminist education, of being a declared feminist, I can't get away from the fact that it's been ingrained in me, this idea that I need to have a marriage and kids in order to be successful, in order to be happy, in order to be making a contribution to my world.... I'm willing to go an unorthodox route and adopt a child or be artificially inseminated as a single woman. The Church is not open to that.[32]

Anne's competing loyalties make it extraordinarily difficult to see her way through this crisis. Declaring herself an emotional hostage of the Young Women rhetoric and the expectations it engendered, she cannot find peace in her current status, nor does she feel free to take alternative steps toward motherhood without jeopardizing her connection with that very same Church. She is fractured in her loyalties and stymied in her pursuit of joy.

A final group challenged by feelings of alienation is that of the so-called *Dialogue* readers. Many of these women feel emotionally or intellectually unsatisfied, and spiritually out of step with those who suggest they "just keep praying about it," or "swallow it whole." They hunger for open, honest discussion, and they thirst for soul mates who speak their language. Discovering the independent LDS publications and communities of *Dialogue*, *Exponent II*, and *Sunstone* marks a turning point in their lives.

Margaret claims that the community saved her membership in the Church:

> White flight changed the face of our area. That was a very hot issue and I got to the point that I was so embarrassed by the Mormon Church's stand on priesthood for Negro men . . . that I was deeply upset. I really was.
>
> Just about the time I felt that I was really going down for the count as far as the Church was concerned, I became a "*Dialogue*

32. COHC, #026 (2010), 13.

Mormon." I started just living for what I was reading from one issue to the next of that fine new journal. . . . I felt that there were people out there who were really thinking like I was. . . . it put me in the orbit of these Mormon intellectuals who had marvelous educations, were faithful members of the Church, and worked really hard at coming up with a synthesis that would do.

I don't know if you have had the experience of just starving for soul mates, even if they are not living next to you, but that's the way I felt with some of these women.[33]

Lynn too, found a home among these people:

I had also plugged myself into the *Sunstone* crowd and helped work on *Sunstone*. So I was becoming very much a part of these communities, these communities within communities. And I still feel very attached to these communities. . . . I found a space where I could talk about the things and ideas I cared about.[34]

Beth, who found this new genre of Mormon literature spiritually invigorating, was surprised that not everyone else felt the same way:

One thing I really enjoyed over the years was *Exponent II*. I loved those! I subscribed to *Exponent II* and to *Dialogue* and to *Sunstone*. I was and am an avid reader. One time a ward Relief Society leader who knew I liked to read asked me to present an evening on Mormon literature. So I pulled in these wonderful pieces that I'd been reading, and all I can remember is that there was a lot of tension in the air and I was never asked again to do that. It surprised me. I had women read excerpts from different writings—none of it anti-church, but it was Mormon literature outside of the mainstream and must have been some kind of threat. Eugene England [*Dialogue* founder] is still one of my Mormon heroes. His *Dialogues with Myself* is like scripture to me.[35]

For some of these women discovering like-minded members who articulated religious issues in a "non-churchy" manner diminished alienation and facilitated a greater satisfaction in the Gospel.

33. COHC, #007 (2009), 8–9.
34. COHC, #030 (2009), 11–12.
35. COHC, #011 (2009), 8–9.

Abuse

A third category of emotionally based crises is that of sexual abuse. It looms surprisingly large in a study consisting of religious women, and sadly involves "religious" men. Coat-tailing on themes of identity, this group deals foremost with shedding false roles and freeing itself from the constraints of victimization. Too immature to comprehend the crime at the time it occurs, and too frightened to get help, these women spent the rest of their lives trying to make sense of who they were and how they would reconcile their experiences with their faith.

One woman, Eleanor, found that maintaining possession of her agency—despite undue influence by another—was critical to her happiness:

> I didn't know it was a crisis at the time, but I was molested as a child. That's been an enormous factor in my life. You feel like it's your fault. It was before the age when I would have heard the chastity talks at church, and then, when you do, you feel like you are a lost cause from the beginning.
>
> It had so many ramifications that it's hard to quantify when you're not mature enough to have any information, and nobody talks about it. It just makes you feel different, and alienated. . . .
>
> My mother did not know about it. I never brought it up to her; I think she died without ever knowing. It was something you're ashamed of. You live with shame. You have sort of a shame based life from that point on.
>
> People would get help today. I didn't until I was an adult. If you don't know what normal is, you don't know you've been damaged. But it does crack your foundation somewhat. It's hard to go on, and to see the person who molested you leave on a mission . . . and become a bishop . . . and teach at BYU . . . and write books. That does crack your foundation.
>
> He did come to me once and apologized. I don't think he was a pedophile. I think he was, as many young men were, charged with hormones and didn't know what to do with them.
>
> I feel like I'm a happy person now and that I've put that behind me. I have my whole future before me. . . . You have to look at the positive things that I have had also in my life. I've had a pretty darn good marriage. We have had wonderful experiences. We have been quite prosperous. . . . My kids are very loving; they stayed active in

> the Church and they love the Savior. I couldn't ask for anything more than that. I'd go through a lot before I would give that up! That has just been a great blessing to me. . . .
>
> I have never lost faith in the Savior. There have been times when I've wondered about the Church as an institution, but I've never, never doubted Jesus Christ and his Mission, and his atonement, and his redemption. Otherwise, I would be completely lost. . . .
>
> I don't have any regrets. I don't want to have any regrets. I don't.[36]

Eleanor's emphatic dismissal of regret and defeat demonstrates a choice to find peace through her own accord. Though she relied on Christ, she also found she must rely on her own determination to seize upon that which she perceives to be good and true.

This pattern of choosing life and goodness over entrapment and despair, repeated in the narratives of so many women, reflects an understanding of the Book of Mormon's teachings on the necessity of opposition. Stated in full, it reads:

> For it must needs be, that there is an opposition in all things. . . . [Otherwise] righteousness could not be brought to pass, neither wickedness, neither holiness nor misery, neither good nor bad. Wherefore, all things must needs be a compound in one; wherefore, if it should be one body it must needs remain as dead, having no life neither death, nor corruption nor incorruption, happiness nor misery, neither sense nor insensibility. (2 Ne. 2:11)

As an animating and vital force, opposition provides women with the opportunity to select and promote goodness. The knowledge that evil will be exploited in the world helps these women to counter such forces and strive to build up the kingdom of God. Those who embrace this precept are more likely to view opposition as something they have the power to combat. For Eleanor and others, choosing happiness goes hand in hand with choosing goodness, righteousness, holiness, and all else that is equated with God.

Still, the pendulum swings back and forth, fluctuating between the promise of joy and the visceral reality of pain. The Church of Jesus Christ of Latter-day Saints offers a formula to happiness—a happiness born of the goodness of God and the overcoming of mortality through Christ. It provides a narrative of growth and self-mastery, a Plan of

---

36. COHC, #063 (2010), 12–13.

Salvation. And yet, its reality often seems far off and unattainable under the stifling weight of adversity.

Perhaps the secret of success lies in Eleanor's thrice repeated denial of regret. Choosing the good life means choosing it again and again and again. Even the early saints had to remind themselves often: "All is Well, All is Well!"

Part Two

Life as a Latter-day Saint

Chapter Six

Womanliness

Sherrie L. M. Gavin

Mormon womanliness and women's roles in Mormonism become increasingly problematic to define in an age of gender studies. Mormon men are clearly defined as priesthood holders, conscribed to a policy of leadership, rank, and title that entirely excludes women.[1] In this policy, males are defined physically (by age) and spiritually (by title) within the Church organization in what can be described as an administrative incline as much as it is an ascent of spiritual title. By comparison, Mormon women above the age of eighteen are all grouped into a single organization, void of specific rank or title. The absence of rank within the singular women's organization does not encourage Mormon women to seek further status within the Church of their own volition. On the contrary, the masculine/patriarchal system in which Mormon ecclesiastical structure operates virtually annuls any gradients that could be used to physically or spiritually define womanliness in the Mormon context.

Given this lack of rank or title for women, it is important to record and analyze the common practices and motivations that women share in connection to the Mormon experience. In doing so, this chapter seeks to discover how Mormon women define themselves within the margins of the institutional Church by means of unspecified titles and ranks. In identifying the personal, yet shared characteristics of Mormon women in the Claremont Oral History Project, we have the ability to better identify what womanliness is to Mormon women.

Attempting to narrowly label all Mormon women within a single definition will inevitably fail. Each woman, Mormon or not, is unique with complex and diverse characteristics skewing the most intelligently

---

1. Maureen Ursenbach Beecher, "Female Experience in American Religion," *Religion and American Culture: A Journal of Interpretation* 5, no. 1 (1995): 1–21.

constructed definition. Further, and as exemplified in the Claremont Oral History Project, the varied levels of full acceptance of Mormon doctrine and policy complicate the question of defining Mormon womanliness. Despite the complexity that variances in orthodoxy produce, I seek in this chapter to highlight some common characteristics and experiences of women within a Mormon context. In order to explore this question of Mormon womanhood, I first turn to official rhetoric from LDS Church authorities in reference to women's characteristics and attributes.

Directives from the Presidency of the Church of Jesus Christ of Latter-day Saints announced in 1942, and again in 1974, that "Motherhood is near to Divinity."[2] These directives echoed Victorian era ideology that women, by divine design, are more spiritually adept than their brothers.[3] One directive further stated that "Motherhood thus becomes a holy calling, a sacred dedication for carrying out the Lord's plans, a consecration of devotion to the uprearing and fostering, the nurturing in body, mind, and spirit [of children]."[4] Moreover, in 2012, the Church magazine *Ensign* published a speech originally given by Elder L. Tom Perry three decades earlier. This speech re-emphasized the preferential tradition of working fathers and stay-at-home mothers as a matter of Mormon historical culture:

> Just as the pioneers made the desert blossom as a rose, so too our lives and families will blossom if we follow their example and embrace their traditions. Yes, pioneer faith is needed as much in the world today as in any period of time. Once again, we need to know that heritage. We need to teach it, we need to be proud of it, and we need to preserve it.[5]

By defining the physical place of womanliness, Perry gives voice to official LDS Church discourse in which Mormon womanliness is crowned in the title of stay-at-home mother.

---

2. "Message of the First Presidency," *Deseret News Weekly Church Edition*, October 1942, 5; Spencer W. Kimball, "Guidelines to Carry Forth the Work of God in Cleanliness," *Ensign*, May 1974, 4.

3. Carol J. Jablonski, "Rhetoric, Paradox, and the Movement for Women's Ordination in the Roman Catholic Church," *Quarterly Journal of Speech* 74 (1988): 164.

4. Heber J. Grant, J. Reuben Clark, Jr., David O. McKay, "Parenthood," Message From the First Presidency, (read by J. Reuben Clark in General Conference), *General Conference Report* (October 1942): 12–13.

5. L. Tom Perry, "The Strength of Our Heritage," *Ensign*, July 2012, 39.

From an ideological Mormon perspective, the act of stay-at-home motherhood is also a spiritual state. In his book, *When Thou Art Converted*, Elder M. Russell Ballard defined womanhood by juxtaposing all women to Mary, the mother of Christ. To him, womanhood is defined by enacting a type of spiritually inspired motherhood. "We need women who can hear and will respond to the voice of the Lord, who at all costs will defend and protect the family," wrote Ballard. "We don't need women who want to be like men, sound like men, dress like men, drive like some men drive, or act like men. We do need women who rejoice in their womanhood and have a spiritual confirmation of their identity, their value and their eternal destiny."[6] By implying that women receive "spiritual confirmation" when acting in defense of "the family," Ballard associated womanliness in actions for and within the family. By clarifying that it is disagreeable for Mormon women to "want" to be like men who can be defined outside of a family unit by clothes, driving skills, or other manly behaviors, Ballard narrowed the scope of Mormon womanliness.

In 2008, Ballad supplemented this philosophy, stating:

> I am impressed by countless mothers who have learned how important it is to focus on the things that can only be done in a particular season of life. If a child lives with parents for 18 or 19 years, that span is only one-fourth of a parent's life. And the most formative time of all, the early years in a child's life, represents less than one-tenth of a parent's normal life. It is crucial to focus on our children for the short time we have them with us and to seek, with the help of the Lord, to teach them all we can before they leave our homes. This eternally important work falls to mothers and fathers as equal partners. I am grateful that today many fathers are more involved in the lives of their children. But I believe that the instincts and the intense nurturing involvement of mothers with their children will always be a major key to their well-being. In the words of the proclamation on the family, "Mothers are primarily responsible for the nurture of their children."[7]

In this, Ballard defines the physical space "the home" as a sanctified environment, making stay-at-home motherhood a preferred, physical and a spiritual state. Though he did not outwardly assert that

6. M. Russell Ballard, *When Thou Art Converted* (Salt Lake City: Deseret Book, 2001), 164, 179.

7. M. Russell Ballard, "Daughters of God," *Ensign*, May 2008, 108.

women are required to stay at home, his emphasis of childhood as being a "short time," with terms such as "crucial" and "focused" rounded by a hint at the modern phenomenon of increased involvement of fathers in comparison to the "intense nurturing involvement" of mothers leaves little question as to his preference for women to be stay-at-home mothers. For Ballard, and presumably the policy makers for the Church, womanliness is clearly defined in the physical and spiritual situation of stay-at-home mothers.

In an attempt to preserve the traditional conception of Mormon womanliness—and perhaps as a means of attempting to include unmarried or infertile women as part of the Mormon experience—a slightly different definition of womanliness began to be developed within the ranks of Mormonism. In this, women were categorized as "nurturers," as well as "mothers." President Gordon B. Hinckley was one of the first to emphasize the "nurturer" definition in 1983, and like Perry, did so by invoking an ideology of Mormon heritage.[8] To these men, Mormon women historically mothered, or nurtured, as a part of the divine Mormon experience.[9] In addition, the softening of earlier authoritative statements against working mothers amended the sacrosanct definition of Mormon womanhood to include a proviso for women who fiscally provided for their families out of necessity, if only as a type of displaced nurturing.[10] Mormon womanhood and womanliness is additionally defined in the historiography of female pioneers who, absent of ecclesiastical rank or title, were said to have nurtured as a divine part of the foundational Mormon experience.

Thus Mormon womanliness is defined in official LDS rhetoric by the act of nurturing. This nurturing within a Mormon context positions women only in familial relationships; included with the title of mother is also a woman who is a "daughter, a sister, an aunt, a cousin, a niece,

8. Gordon B. Hinckley, "Live Up to Your Inheritance," *Ensign*, November 1983, 84.

9. Spencer W. Kimball, "Message of the First Presidency," *Deseret News Weekly Church Edition*, October 1942. 5. Ezra Taft Benson, "The Honored Place of Woman," *Ensign*, November 1981, 104.

10. Quentin L. Cook, "LDS Women Are Incredible!" *Ensign*, May 2011, 18. There are numerous Church resources coming out of the last decade that mention Mormon women in gainful employment without disdain. This is the most recent example wherein working women are considered a part of the Mormon experience, though still partnered in relationship to a family context.

and a granddaughter."[11] Interestingly, in Mormon scripture, the only references to the term "nurture" are directed at fathers (Eph. 6:4, Enos 1:1). Though biblically gendered, the scriptural emphases on spiritual education and spiritual progression as features of nurturing is yet applicable to women given the overt use of the term in reference to women in contemporary Mormon discourse. That is to say, though the biblical definition may be directed at men, the current emphasis is on women as nurturers; therefore, the biblical direction becomes applicable to current Mormon women. Thus, within a contemporary Mormon context, to be womanly is to seek progression and development by the use of physical and spiritual nurturing habits and characteristics; the opposite of Mormon womanhood is not Mormon manhood (or priesthood) but anything that would corrode or impede the act of nurturing.

This chapter explores two aspects of the nurture concept of Mormon womanliness. The first is the physical or action-oriented application of Mormon womanliness; the second is the spiritual application of Mormon womanliness. To be clear, motherhood and mothering was and still is the primary definition of Mormon womanliness in official Church discourse. However, as the Claremont oral histories demonstrate, mothering and motherhood are only a portion of Mormon womanhood, and not the definition of Mormon womanliness. Though the majority of women in this project can be described as mothers, even grandmothers and great grandmothers, the maternal segment of their lives does not define them as Mormon women. Rather, their ability to develop and progress, to wit, their acts of being nurturers to themselves and others becomes the defining characteristic associated with Mormon womanliness.

The Physical (Action-Oriented) Attributes of Mormon Womanhood

For the women of the Claremont Oral History Project, when opportunities were presented for them to act in a way that would lead to self-development or personal progression, they found it to be their duty as a matter of heritage and instinct. Age was not a factor, nor was marital status, education level, calling (rank or title within the Church), or the number of children they had. Acts of service, or what was seen as

11. Barbara Thompson, "I Will Strengthen Thee; I Will Help Thee," *Ensign*, November 2007, 117.

service-oriented instincts within a Mormon context, were definitive of Mormon womanhood.

It is understandable that a primary characteristic of physical Mormon womanliness is the act of service to children, inclusive of, but not limited to the act of being a mother. For most, the mentoring of children seemed as definitive as giving birth. Ginger explained in her experience of living in a remote area:

> See, we didn't have a chapel, it was just us. Well, and one day, there was a knock at my door and there was a man who asked if I could teach primary to his children. I didn't know there was another Latter-day Saint in the town, but he had found me, and we are life-long friends. And I used to go to his house and teach his kids. His wife used to see that; she was inactive. So I would teach the kids and we'd sing. And strangely enough, the girl that I taught that was the daughter of this man—she is still active [in the Church]. My eldest daughter met her when she was on her mission. She has a family and children and she said she'd remembered [me] teaching [her] primary in [her] bedroom. So you never know what you could do—it could be the right thing.[12]

For Ginger, Mormon womanliness meant creating a type of program to teach children gospel principles and children's Church songs simply because she, rather than a formal church structure, was available. Lacking other membership support did not deter her from her act of nurturing other children within a Mormon context. In performing this physical act of service, Ginger felt rewarded. To her, service in this capacity was part of her responsibility as a Mormon woman, and it was not limited to just her own children. Likewise, she was asked to perform the physical act of going to and teaching other children because that was the expectation of the man who had initiated the request. Because this circumstance involved her acting on, teaching, and implementing age-appropriate Mormon dogma for the children in her sphere, Ginger was enacting Mormon womanliness as per her own and others' expectations.

The perception that children were able to learn and respond appropriately after the women engaged them was an important motivator

12. Claremont Mormon Women's Oral History Collection, Library of the Claremont Colleges, Claremont, CA, hereafter COHC, #122 (2009), 7.

for these women. For many, positive actions that were viewed as repercussions of the women's teachings rewarded them with personal and spiritual validation. Likewise, while the act of serving children was seen as womanly, what was deemed as inappropriate discipline of children was seen as distasteful and uncharacteristic of Mormon womanliness.

Brenda explains how her exasperation at motherhood, as a result of the poor modeling from her own mother, led her to seek Church-based alternatives in how to better perform as a mother:

> During the time when my husband was so busy and there were babies to care for and house work to attend, I was fully aware of my lack of skill in raising children. I wanted obedient children but didn't know how to be kind and still have them do what I told them. There were many talks with my Father in Heaven as I tried to learn how to love and teach them. There was one night when my husband was away, I wanted the children to go to bed and I used the intimidation that my own mother had used, shouting and threatening, and knew I was hurting my children. I cried to the Lord that night in my bedroom, lost and broken; He filled me with peace. He did not condone my behavior nor condemn me. . . .
>
> We had mother education lessons in [Relief Society] and I found these lessons to be my life savers. Women whom I admired would share successful experiences and I soaked it up. I learned never to punish a child who told me the truth when he had done something wrong. I would praise him for being honest and we would work out together how he could fix things and help him if needed. I learned to say "yes" if at all possible explaining things they should be aware of. Our children learned responsible decision making and would ask for direction and permission.[13]

In performing actions that she described as "shouting and threatening" that left her feeling "lost and broken," Brenda suggests that she did not perceive those actions to be appropriate or correct within a Mormon context, therefore she sought reprieve in prayer in order to align herself with what she believed was an appropriate Mormon perspective. As a result, by her engagement in Relief Society lessons, she was empowered to develop the active mothering qualities that she deemed to be more nurturing, and therefore, more closely associated with Mormon womanliness. In this cultivation of self, Brenda saw her-

13. COHC, #110 (2011), 9.

self as a better skilled and more successful nurturer to her children, and like Ginger, found additional reward in the actions exhibited by her children in "responsible decision making," which were a perceived result of appropriate nurturing.

In many of the oral histories, appropriate nurturing also invoked a sense of economic responsibility. Hard work, being frugal, and employability were recurrent concepts, though somewhat underdeveloped in the histories—likely because the periods of financial hardship were most often associated with temporary states of being (i.e., in childhood or college years). Still, the ability to live thriftily and teach frugality to children was important and seen as a heritage-driven nurturing characteristic. Gail describes her experience:

> One day when [mother] and I were in our local haberdashery shop where my neighbor worked, the owner offered me a job. Because of my height she thought I was already 14, so even though she got a shock when she found out I was only 12, she still allowed me to work. I have never been out of work since. I started working every Saturday morning, and then moved to every weekday afternoon for one hour a day. I continued this job throughout school and was able to save enough money to pay, in full, for a school trip to Bali in [grade] 10. (As well as starting some short term investments at age 16 on the recommendation and guidance of my father.) Throughout university I worked at a Chiropractic Clinic which paid for another overseas trip and also helped fund my mission. It wasn't easy or pleasant, even embarrassing at times growing up with little money in our family, but I am extremely grateful for my parents' foresight in teaching (and showing me) the principles of hard work and being financially wise, principles I now try to teach my own children.[14]

In Gail's example, she perceived that her drive to be engaged in personal fiscal responsibility was a factor in her ability to serve a mission. In stating that "I have never been out of work since," it is evident that Gail finds employment as an empowering virtue associated with effective nurturing, rather than something that is secondary in choice or something that impedes her progression. She further sees fiscal responsibility as a way of being and an action that enabled her to be successful and competitive with those she believed to have better financial means. As a mother, she is teaching her children this as a matter of

14. COHC, #114 (2011), 3–4.

course; to her and others, a factor in Mormon womanliness is the action and bequest of "hard work and being financially wise."

Just as frugality was a common characteristic of Mormon womanhood, the antithesis of this concept was Mormon women who refused to be engaged in fiscal responsibility. A common theme was the responsibility of women to at least be able to provide for themselves and their families. As Margot explains:

> I am all for birth control. I don't know what the Church's standing is now, but I feel that you should not have children that you can't afford to keep. When we were on our mission, there was one lady at church that had about a 10th or 12th child and living on [government welfare]. She said that she was fulfilling Church teachings because you are supposed to keep having children. To me, that is one thing scoffing at another because the Church also teaches you that you need to be independent. If you can't be independent then I don't think you can be expected to have children that you can't afford to provide for.[15]

Margot believed that the poor financial performance of this woman rejected the ideology of a progressive and developed Mormon woman. The woman in question was Mormon and female, but her dependence on government welfare organizations as a means for survival, coupled with her religious justification in continuing to have children (resulting in her financial dependency), was viewed by Margot as "scoffing" at Church teachings. As a result, for Margot as well as others, lifelong financial dependence as a consequence of child birth choices was uncharacteristic of Mormon womanhood because it outwardly rejected Church preference for financial independence.

Bonnie used equally strong language in expressing her thoughts on the same topic:

> We are encouraged to be strong independent women. We are encouraged to be educated and of value to society. I find you occasionally come up against people who think women are lesser and should be at home only raising children but I find people like this ignorant. . . . I don't know a lot about the Church's standing on fertility and reproduction. I do know that it encourages us to have a family. I am always bothered by those who say we should have as many kids as the Lord allows. . . . I find this ignorant. We are instructed to use

15. COHC, #126 (2011), 6.

> wisdom in all things and I feel my husband and I have done this. We can comfortably care for our five children and while we could cope with more I think it would be at a detriment to the kids, not just financially but in their needs for attention and affection from us.[16]

For Bonnie, Mormon women are to be a "value to society" which is achieved, among other ways, by financial prudence. She associates this with Church teachings; for her, to be financially irresponsible in having additional children would go against a key characteristic of Mormon womanliness. She also notes that her ability to provide appropriate affection would be strained if she had more children. Though affection is most often associated with emotion, it is clear that Bonnie also associates "attention and affection" with the physical characteristic of time—being unable to dedicate time to an additional child was perceived as limiting the progression and development of further children. As a result, Bonnie was satisfied that her ability to successfully nurture was limited to the number of children in her current scope.

Dedicating time to children was a prevalent theme. However, many of the women opted to participate in activities outside of their immediate families and outside of Church callings. Every one of these women were engaged in activities which aided the progression and development of themselves and others, and which the women associated as personal, divine directives. As Faith explained:

> I figured that maybe I am a blessed, barren woman. And I have accepted that. It was hard. But I have accepted that. Because I think in hindsight, now looking back, I think Heavenly Father meant that to happen because I have been able to assist my family in ways I may not have been able to if I had children. I had other responsibility.[17]

Faith saw opportunities in her childless life to aid and assist others—opportunities that could have been impeded if she had children. Her "barren" position left her with increased flexibility, which enabled her to serve others in a capacity that she perceived to encompass as much divine sanction as the role of mother. For her, to progress and assist individuals outside of her immediate family was to nurture in a manner wholly consistent with Mormon womanliness.

16. COHC, #125 (2011), 4–5.
17. COHC, #123 (2011), 5.

In consideration of the ideas presented by these women, it is clear that womanliness within a Mormon context was distinguished as action-oriented progression, development, and independence. Service and education of children was a common theme as were the actions associated with financial prudence. While Mormon men enact Mormon manliness through priesthood advancement and service, Mormon womanliness was defined as the active application of service to others, appropriate care of children, personal independence, and financial prudence.

The Spiritual Attributes of Mormon Womanhood

Spiritual attributes for women are the same as those which are broadly attributed to every Church member who partakes in a post-baptismal confirmation ordinance wherein she is assigned companionship of the "Holy Ghost."[18] There is no womanly title that relays additional spiritual status or ability; every woman in the Church is simply and formally addressed as "Sister." However, for the women in the Claremont Oral History Project, a sense of spiritual direction was shared, but it was not always attributed to Church membership, length of Church membership, or activity level within the institutional Church—that is to say that spiritual direction was a common force, but it was not always associated with an organizational Mormon context. Although the women reported acting in callings and duties within the administrative Church establishment (and sometimes related a sense of spiritual direction in regard to the assignment), the sense of spirituality and individual spiritual direction was more often perceived to progress and develop self, rather than being something that was only relevant or influenced as a part of a Church calling or assignment.

Brenda believed that this experience of a spiritual nature solidified her personal relationship with divinity, far independent of any Church administrative assignment:

> When I left school, I became a nurse. . . . Shortly after I started work, I had been taking my uniforms home to wash on the back of the motor bike I owned and lost them out of the bag that was strapped to the back of the bike. A truck driver had seen them drop and told me the location where the uniforms had fallen when we stopped at

18. Boyd K. Packer, "Prayer and Promptings," *Ensign*, November 2009, 43.

> a traffic light. I went back to pick them up and couldn't find them. I inquired at all the small businesses on the road in the location I was told by the truck driver. I had done all I could do to find them by myself, so now I explained this to the Lord, feeling that I could now reasonably ask for His help. I had no doubt that He would show me where they were and went back over the area expecting to pick them up. I didn't find them and was devastated that my faith had not been responded to. I cried as I went home, broken hearted that He had not responded to me for I knew He was there. I was filled with peace and understood the words "Be still and know that I am God." This had been a Friday and when I returned calmly to work 10 minutes early the next Monday wearing the only uniform I had left, I approached the head nurse in our area to explain that I no longer had most of my uniforms. She was built like a tank and had mastered intimidation with young nurses, but I was not afraid. She eventually told me that the uniforms had amazingly been returned to the hospital and gave them back to me. It was wonderful to get the uniforms back as it would have taken me many months to pay for them on our low wages, but the real blessing was the peace God spoke to my soul.[19]

The sense of spiritual peace for Brenda was grounded in a personal impression that she had of herself as a spiritual individual, rather than only having received spiritual confirmation within a Church administrative title. To be clear, Brenda reported elsewhere that she felt spiritual direction in broad terms when she was in repeated tenures as her ward's Relief Society president. But in an expression of spiritual womanliness within the Mormon experience, Brenda developed and owned what she regarded as the ability to be spiritually empowered and directed outside of Church administrative roles. Her empowerment came as she faced the head nurse unafraid, as well as when she was "filled with peace" as a result of her prayer.

It is also important to note that this perceived spiritual direction came outside of Brenda's role as a mother. In contrast to earlier mentioned LDS perceptions that women have greater, divinely inspired inclinations in regard to motherhood, these women each reported spiritual influences that they believed developed them individually, yet were independent of mothering or Church administrative roles. For them, the spiritual aspect of Mormon womanhood was developed by means

19. COHC, #110 (2011), 5.

of personal and independent spiritual empowerment that was unassociated with maternal title or Church position.

This sense of individual ability to seek spiritual empowerment was important to all of the respondents. Interestingly, they did not perceive this empowerment to be an entitlement due to their church callings, but something that women needed to find for themselves. Mormon ideology concludes that entitlement for spiritual direction is bequeathed to those "on the Lord's errand."[20] However, the respondents generally sought spiritual direction in order to gain personal spiritual empowerment. They actively sought this spiritual empowerment in a variety of different ways and circumstances. When they found it, the power was not necessarily related to their church assignments.

Spiritual development and progression for these women came in varied forms but was unilaterally seen as a requisite part of personal, womanly, Mormon maturity. It was also commonly perceived to be the positive result of prior private conflict and associated with being able to address and resolve personally painful issues.

Quinn addressed this form of womanly spirituality and its associated developmental role in her life in terms of an idea that came to her when she prayed:

> Ten years ago, I went through this thing where I continually prayed to Heavenly Father to show me what was wrong with me. I knew that [my estranged sister] had to see something I couldn't see. I knew that she was right and I was wrong and I prayed for Heavenly Father to show me this flaw, this horrible thing about myself, so that I could fix it and make [her] love me again. The prayers were always left unanswered and so I pleaded harder and harder, convinced that I was so flawed, so horribly wrong that Heavenly Father couldn't even begin to show me what was wrong. I pleaded and begged and promised that if He would show me what I needed to fix, I'd fix it. Finally one day when I was out in the shed working refinishing a piece of furniture I collapsed in tears and prayed again: Please Heavenly Father, show me what is wrong, let me fix it. And then this small thought entered my mind: What if there is nothing wrong?
>
> For me that was the beginning of forgiving. Opening myself up to the idea that there was nothing wrong with me—How do I say this? Acknowledging that perhaps [my sister] was wrong, allowed me

20. Thomas S. Monson, "To the Rescue," *Liahona*, July 2001.

> to acknowledge that [my sister] wasn't perfect, that she was facing her own set of challenges and that this was the way she was trying to address those challenges. It gave me the space to try to forgive her. It was still not an easy process and sometimes I find I have to go back and readdress it. But this lesson I have learned, about forgiveness, is one that I cherish.[21]

Quinn perceived a degree of internal, personal defects and sought spiritual guidance to discover how she could progress and develop beyond her deficiency. In an act of prayer, she comprehended that she was not necessarily wrong and began to forgive her sister. Because she sought divine influence, this insight came to her in prayer, and the negative situation was resolved within her own mind. This was a personal solution to a personal problem, and it was resolved outside of administrative Church roles. Quinn did not seek reconciliation as the result of an assignment, admonition or calling; she sought personal direction for self-improvement.

As Mormon ecclesiastical structure lacks a system that recognizes any degree of female progression, Quinn's example of spiritual ascent is a model of the only means whereby Mormon women can exhibit spiritual increase through individual, personal piety—usually found through the act of prayer—which results in the woman sensing personal growth or spiritual development. This personal development cannot be graded by any current scheme within the administrative LDS Church structure.

Forgiveness was a recurring theme commonly associated with womanly spiritual self-development in the Mormon experience. Divorce and abusive or painful family incidents were the most common motivators for the interviewed women to seek spiritual progression and development. There was a shared sense that forgiveness was a spiritual equalizer, and that however void of rank or title, women were empowered to develop a spiritual sense of self, often as a healing tool or compensation for perceived personal imperfections. Such was the case for Faith, who eloquently connects this ideology within a Mormon doctrinal context, explaining her ideas on the atonement:

> For the Atonement to be effective, it has to apply to me first, especially for others—especially for my own husband. If I want the Atonement to work in him, then I need for it to work in me first. It is

21. COHC, #107, 21.

> forgiveness. Heavenly Father can't really forgive me if I can't forgive myself or forgive the other person, because then greater sin is upon me, if I don't forgive. And I have felt the same about looking at others, and how to not pick on the [imperfections] of others or of myself, because when I do, I am taking away something that is important and good for me to know. . . . The gospel gives me a reason for being. I think that the Atonement is an equalizer. I mean, someone else might be BYU graduated and I came from no real educational background. The gospel makes things simple and across the board and it makes us equal, regardless of our background. Because it is not a matter of Heavenly Father saying, well, you went to BYU, you go over here—or you went to Yale, go over here, and you had a good education, go over here. It's a matter of our personal commitment to the Gospel. Because I might say, that I go to church ten times a week, and somebody else might be five. But in Heavenly Father's eyes, it will be only important that we came to church. That is all that matters to Him, that we came. And that makes us equal. You know, like those who say, I have two children and you don't have any. But in Heavenly Father's eyes, He says "you are My daughters" and that makes us equal.
>
> For me, that gives me purpose. That equality. It gives me a reason for being. For who I am. To live and to love and to hope. I am alive with it! I really am![22]

Faith sees herself as the partner who is divinely assigned to create and drive a sense of spiritual progression within her marriage, within herself, and with those in her personal and professional spheres. She titles herself as a daughter in relationship to divinity, solidifying a spiritual "reason for being." Rather than locating her reason for being in priesthood title, education, religious status, or administrative Church office, she relates that she feels equal being in a state of forgiveness and atonement. In a Mormon context, she has developed spiritually to the point that she believes that title does not matter because it is inconsistent with her perception of Mormon atonement ideology.

Although spiritual attributes within an administrative Mormon context are associated with male-only priesthood titles, most of the women in the Oral History Project, like Faith, disregard men's spiritual titles as superior. The women often related advice from other women, specifically fellow women in the Relief Society organization, as influ-

22. COHC, #123 (2011), 7–8.

ential in their desire to develop spiritually and personally. These women are acting in accordance with inspiration perceived to be from the Holy Ghost. While it is clear that the women deem the advice-giving fellow women as positive and influential spiritual guides, the only title they associate with women is the term, "sister." These narrators shared a sense of spiritual direction, associated it with the progression of self, and often conceived of it outside of LDS administrative callings.

Conclusion

Womanliness in a Mormon context could be disregarded as either too complex or too easy to define. It could be deemed too complex because of the uniqueness of each individual Mormon woman, or too simple if assigning Mormon womanliness to the social and biological state. But in looking at the physical actions and the spiritually based empowerment of the women in the Claremont Oral History Collection, we discover commonalities that can be used to define womanliness in a Mormon context. While women are defined in official LDS discourse as nurturers, Mormon womanliness is better defined as 1) action-oriented tasks such as service to others, appropriate care of children, and the cultivation of personal independence and financial prudence, and 2) spiritual development encompassing an openness to inspiration and the cultivation of a spiritual state focusing on forgiveness and the atonement. This definition may not be applied as a whole to the experience of every Mormon woman; but in an organization that ignores rank or title for women as a matter of policy, it is important to recognize the commonalities that are shared by Mormon women. In defining Mormon womanliness, we come to better understand the experiences of women in the institutional LDS Church. This understanding might pave the way for improvements in the Church organization as a whole, as well as in the Relief Society.

There is no doubt that LDS Church leaders aim to express appreciation for the contribution of women in the Church. However, this gratitude is systematically expressed in terms of the service and sacrifice most often associated with motherhood. Womanhood fails to be addressed in terms defined by Mormon women. Quentin L. Cook attempted to recognize and compliment Mormon women in his "LDS Women are Incredible!" talk in 2011. He conceptualized the beneficence of women as a matter of LDS heritage, framing his talk around the contribution of "pioneer women."[23] In romanticizing the female pioneer experience as a matter of heritage—rather than understanding or addressing what contemporary Mormon women find important—Cook and the administrative Church fail to apply meaningful and personal distinction to its female members, causing many to feel the lack of understanding and appreciation.

Margot expressed her personal spiritual progression in terms of her painful divorce, but she discovered a simple truth that had not always been part of her life:

> My girlfriend was going to a counselor because her husband drank a lot—it was group counseling, and I went along and some of the things the lady said I could relate to my own life and actually, she had us lie down and relax and meditate for a bit. And when I was doing that, my life flashed before my eyes. The terrible situations relating to my marriage, it was as though I was living them again and I couldn't stop crying, and that lady took me aside and talked to me about it. And she said to me, "YOU ARE IMPORTANT TOO." And that was an important change in my life. Because I felt like I had been giving and giving and giving.[24]

Women are undoubtedly important to Mormon heritage, Mormon culture, and the overall Mormon administrative structure. However, the characteristics of Mormon womanliness, shared by the women of the Oral History Project, express deeper distinctions than the typical LDS labels of "mothers" and "nurturers" do. In highlighting some of the common characteristics, we are better able to comprehend a shared, womanly, Mormon experience.

---

23. Cook, "LDS Women," 18. Although Cook attempted to include women who might not be mothers, his conception of womanhood is expressed in his statement that "God placed within women divine qualities of strength, virtue, love, and the willingness to sacrifice to raise future generations of His spirit children." In this, it is clear that even if women are not mothers, "willingness" to be a mother is the preferred spiritually defining characteristic.

24. COHC, #126 (2011), 10–11.

Chapter Seven

Callings

Susan Robison

In the Church of Jesus Christ of Latter-day Saints a calling is a request—a strong invitation to accept a responsibility in the Church organization. The purpose of a calling is to serve God, to strengthen the Church, and to enrich the lives of individuals. The LDS Church has no professional clergy, and members are not paid for their leadership or ecclesiastical service. The time, talents, labor, and resources of all members are needed to share the load of responsibilities and are integral to the operation of the many Church programs—or, as is often stated in the LDS community, to build up the kingdom of God.

The voices and stories of Latter-day Saint women from the Claremont Oral History Project draw attention to the significance callings play in the lives of LDS women. The similarities in their experiences suggest the consistency of LDS Church programs, while the differences in their attitudes, thoughts, and feelings illustrate the individual nature and diversity of their own lives. Their stories and voices challenge the idea that Mormon women are a homogeneous group.

While Mormon women serve in many callings in the Church, they do not serve in all of them. Women cannot hold general or local leadership roles designated as priesthood leadership roles (such as apostle, seventy, stake president, or bishop), nor can they hold most non-priesthood callings that involve leadership over both men and women (such as congregational Sunday School president). Only males have priesthood authority. Some women are frustrated by this limitation of Church authority, but there is no indication that this policy will change.

LDS women, through their callings, offer recommendations, develop and carry out programs, and influence important decisions. The Relief Society president, in particular, can be very influential. She is in close contact with the women; she knows their circumstances and understands their concerns. Because of her unique position, she can be very helpful to the bishop who may rely heavily on her recommendations relating to women and families in the ward.

As presidents of auxiliary organizations—Relief Society, Young Women, Primary—women sit on leadership councils where important issues are discussed and key decisions are made. Still, final decisions and final authority rest with leaders who have priesthood authority. A woman does not initiate her calling, nor can she extend a calling to another individual. A calling cannot come from just anyone. Rather, members of the Church are taught that a calling ultimately comes from God and is extended by an authorized leader acting in God's name. *Authority*, usually implying priesthood authority, is the key word, and is an important principle upon which LDS theology is based.

When a woman is considered for a calling in her congregation, her name is submitted to the proper priesthood authority by the person who presides over that calling (i.e., the Relief Society president for callings in that auxiliary). The priesthood leader is expected to seek divine inspiration in making his decision. He will take into account an individual's worthiness. Is she an active member of the Church? Is her life a good example for others? Will she do this job well? Will it help her in her life? Many factors are taken into consideration, and sometimes there is a concern that prevents a call from being issued. As one oral history narrator explains,

> I think if you have some circumstance that would hinder you from fulfilling your calling, you should explain that to the bishop; if he still wants to call you, fine. I did that once—I got called to be in the Young Women's presidency right after my husband had died. One of the bishop's counselors called me to that position. I was trying to teach school and manage my children during the evening, and life was overwhelming to me. I didn't even say anything to the bishop; I just accepted that call.
>
> I was sustained in Sacrament meeting, and then later that day the bishop called me into his office. He said, "You're doing an awful lot. How are you going to be able to do all this? I wonder if you can." I thought to myself, I thought the calling came from you! But it didn't; it came from his counselor. The bishop just released me then

and there. He thought that it would just be too much for me. He was absolutely right.[1]

Mormons, believing that a calling comes from God, are expected to say yes when they are asked to take on a Church responsibility. Church leaders expect people to accept callings, and family and other Church members also have this expectation:

> When I was called to be the stake Primary president, I wondered how they could possibly ask me to take that on. My husband was in the bishopric. I thought it was unreasonable. I called dad, thinking that he would be sympathetic to me about this calling. He was pretty quiet, then he said, "Well, I guess it depends on whether you want to serve the Lord or not." I thought well, I can do it. So I did it.[2]

People do refuse Church callings. Leaders acknowledge that service is voluntary and people do have the freedom to accept or turn down callings:

> I have never said no to a church calling. I do have to say that I was asked to teach seminary when my youngest was in elementary school. At that point, my husband had taken a job in an office. It was his one, brief couple of years working away from the house. I said that I could do that but it would leave my youngest home all by herself every morning to get ready for school. He looked at me and said, "never mind." So I've never had to refuse a calling. . . . I think callings are inspired, but I also think the person extending the calling needs to understand circumstances. But had I been asked to take a calling after I'd explained my circumstances, I would have taken it. I've never had to say no to a calling.[3]

Another narrator explains her perspective on this issue, illuminating the individual thought and negotiation that goes on in these women's minds:

> Do I believe in taking all callings? On the whole, yes, because they are usually a good and often unexpected opportunity to grow. However, if I sincerely felt I could not or for various serious reasons did not want to accept a calling, I would definitely say so. I think we

---

1. Claremont Mormon Women's Oral History Collection, Library of the Claremont Colleges, Claremont, CA, hereafter COHC, #081 (2011), 28.
2. COHC, #006 (2009), 9.
3. COHC, #090 (2011), 13.

need to speak up and let unit leaders know our situations rather than landing them and ourselves with a potential nervous breakdown.[4]

After a woman accepts a calling, her name and calling is announced in sacrament meeting, and the congregational members are given the opportunity to approve the call by raising their hands in support. They may also raise their hands in opposition to the calling, although such actions are rare events:

> You just have to realize that when you raise your hand to support people, what you're basically saying is, "These are fallible human beings. I'm going to support them in these callings despite the fact that they are fallible human beings. They are going to grow in their callings, and they are going to get better, but they need the members to be patient with them as they make errors." We have to be patient with people and their errors because we're making them at the same time, too. That's how we support each other, through patience in our human fallibility.[5]

When a person has been called, has accepted, and has been approved or "sustained," she is "set apart," which means she is given a blessing by a priesthood leader to be able to fulfill the responsibilities of her new calling. This blessing can offer her comfort and support and can also serve as an affirmation that her calling is inspired.

Most of the women in the Oral History Project believe that their callings were inspired, but a few were not as sure:

> I'll be honest I don't think I ever believed that callings were issued by inspiration. I think they were issued because someone liked someone and thought they could handle something and do what they wanted them to do. I've kind of chosen to not worry about it, and accept that there are some callings that are inspired, but I don't think all of them are. Oh well.[6]

Another woman similarly believes that some callings are inspired while others are not:

> Theoretically, we are to believe that all callings are inspired and that the "call" doesn't come from the bishop, but from God. And I do believe that this is the case most of the time, but certainly not all of the

4. COHC, #080 (2011), 20.
5. COHC, #022 (2009), 27.
6. COHC, #018 (2009), 18.

time. And I can give two specific experiences I had while serving as a Primary president as examples of both uninspired and inspired calls.

One day in the hallway at church, a counselor in the bishopric came up to me to tell me that the bishop had called a certain sister to become our Primary pianist. And it was true that we were in need of one at the time, but I had never heard that this particular sister played the piano so I asked him if she, in fact, played. He said that he didn't know how well she played but then explained what had happened. This sister had told the bishop that she really wanted to hone her piano playing skills and thought that playing for Primary would do so. I said something along the lines of, "Are you crazy? Didn't you find out first if she actually played?" and he responded, "Well, what were we supposed to do? It's not like we could have auditioned her." I said, "Of course we could have! We could have asked her to substitute in Primary for a few weeks to see if this would work." Oh, he hadn't thought of that. She had already accepted the call and she was sustained the following Sunday. Right after Sacrament meeting, she showed up for work, and it was a disaster. She tried her very best, but could not play well enough. She tried and tried, but at the end of Primary, she got up, and ran out in tears. She never came back to Primary and was released soon thereafter. An inspired call? Hard to see how it could have been.

On the other hand, some months later, there was a calling given to a member of the ward that I KNOW came directly from God. There is no doubt. I was sitting in my usual back row spot one Sunday just before church when a certain sister walked by. Let's call her Sister Zelda. As she was walking past me, I heard the words "That's your new Primary secretary." No one was sitting nearby, and I heard those words as clearly as any I have ever heard said to me. My initial reaction was, "Not while I'm Primary president!" I did not care for Sister Zelda. . . . Primary was ending, and my counselor . . . said that the bishop had asked that we consider Sister Zelda as our new secretary. I said, "What?" And she explained that the bishop had been counseling Sister Zelda . . . and she mentioned that she would really like to serve in Primary as the secretary. The bishop said that it was okay with him, but only if I agreed. I still really, really did not want to work with this woman. But I told my counselor about the experience in the chapel before church that very day and added, "I don't need the Holy Ghost to hit me over the head with a shovel to get my attention. If this is the calling she is supposed to have, okay, tell the bishop I said yes." In a fairy tale, we would have

> become the closest of friends and all lived happily ever after. That's not quite how things went. Sister Zelda became our secretary, and she turned out to be a very good secretary. She served as secretary until I was released, and we got along just fine. To this day, I have no idea why she needed to be Primary secretary at that time, but apparently there was some reason for her to hold that calling.[7]

Some of the participants, although willing to serve, were initially hesitant about their qualifications to do the job:

> I was called into the Relief Society presidency as a homemaking counselor, which my husband thought was hysterical. I'm a homemaker, but I'm not a real good house keeper. . . . It had been a struggle to be in a Relief Society presidency. It did not feel like a natural fit. I was short of time, short of experience. I felt very inadequate.[8]

A different narrator remembers her friend's reaction when she received her calling:

> I'll always remember when a friend excused herself to go throw up when the Bishop called her as Relief Society President. Looking back, it was so funny and so understandable.[9]

Other women saw their callings as good fits for their talents, and were confident in their ability to fulfill the responsibility. This was most common among women who were called to be teachers:

> My favorite calling has been Gospel Doctrine teacher. . . . I got to teach the Old Testament, which I just love—especially the Book of Genesis—that has been something that has been really fulfilling and wonderful for me, an opportunity for me where I felt my graduate education could actually serve the church and they weren't two different worlds. That has been really positive.[10]

Many women are asked to fill positions beyond their qualifications. Mormons usually support unqualified people in their positions as they grow into the job and learn skills later valuable to them. Church members emphasize the divine nature of the calling, the person's willingness to serve, and the promise of the Lord's blessings. A woman can learn the

7. COHC, #097 (2010), 12–14.
8. COHC, #057 (2010), 9.
9. COHC, #049 (2010), 24.
10. COHC, #074 (2010), 13.

skills she needs through serving. Thomas S. Monson, the current President of the Church, said: "Whom the Lord calls, the Lord qualifies."[11]

Participants in the Oral History Project spoke of needing and receiving inspiration in fulfilling the responsibilities of their calling:

> One of my favorite callings was as ward Relief Society President for five years. It was a very sacred time and I could feel what I called a "warm hand on my back guiding me" until I was released. I really felt the Lord's help with that calling, which verified to me how important each of us individually is to Him.[12]

Another woman recounts:

> When I moved to the stake I knew only a handful of people. Yet I was called to be Stake Young Women's president. And I just thought, "How can I do this? First of all, I'm not young any more. I have to find the energy for this. Secondly, I don't know anyone." And that's a calling that is really helped by having a network. I probably had to rely on the Lord at that time more than I had in a long time in terms of a calling. . . . It was again a witness to me that the Lord knows who I am, listens to me, and knows what's best for me and provides opportunities.[13]

Church leaders often promise the Lord's help and members take these promises seriously.

In the process of implementing their callings, the participants ran into various challenges. Those who shared their difficult times highlighted issues that face many women as they serve in Church callings. One woman who had served in several Church jobs said that her hardest calling was as the bishop's wife:

> The hardest calling I ever had was the wife of the bishop. I had five children under ten when my husband was called as a bishop; it was a lonely time. He was busy with the ward members and their needs. He gave me enough attention, but it was just hard on Sunday, sitting alone, getting the kids ready alone.[14]

---

11. Thomas S. Monson, "Duty Calls," *Ensign*, May 1996, 43.
12. COHC, #034 (2009), 16.
13. COHC, #037 (2011), 21.
14. COHC, #076 (2010), 18.

Another woman stated there was a strain on her marriage because it was difficult for her inactive husband to understand why she spent so much time on her Church calling:

> I was the Young Women's president, which I really loved, for about two years. I felt out of my element, number one, as I raised boys and there were all these girls—a lot of hormones and giggles. . . . There were a lot of weekly meetings, which put a real strain on my marriage because of my husband's inactivity. He's happy that I'm active in the Church, but during the week, he was having a really hard time at work. When I'm not here, it's hard on him, so it put a strain on things. I think eventually that's why I was released; because word got out. It was really a struggle. I loved working with the girls, but I never felt I really did the job that I might've done had I really been able to put 100% in. I felt like I was torn. Many times, I needed to be supporting my husband's needs rather than doing Church work. Sometimes I just had to say, I can't be there for that. I was the president, so it was hard. But I loved it, I really did.[15]

Two participants raised the issue of a woman's age as problematic in Church callings. One woman described it this way: "As you get older, some people think that since you are old that you are senile and can't do anything."[16] Another woman echoed the same sentiment in a different way:

> I had been regional director and done road shows for regions, for young adults, quartet contests, I've been on every level of teenagers there is. I still love it. I'd still do it again if they didn't think I was too old.[17]

It's not that older members are inadequate, but that they are sometimes seen as being so. Older members of the Church are not incapable of serving in callings, but simply because of their age may not be considered for responsibilities.

Some older women are relieved not to have major Church callings, which require a lot of time and effort. Others feel a sense of loss because they are not as actively involved as they once were, and they are not ready to be relegated to the sidelines. It is a dilemma both for the individuals and for the Church leadership. For the individual, it is

15. COHC, #017 (2009), 11.
16. COHC, #085 (2010), 6.
17. COHC, #023 (2009), 18.

facing a new phase of life and recognizing that younger members are chosen to fill the more demanding positions.

For the Church leadership, it is a quandary to figure out how to use the wisdom, experience, and talent still very much alive in these older members. In his General Conference talk in 2003, Elder Boyd K. Packer addressed the issue of an aging population and suggested to leaders how they might use the talents of the older members. A senior citizen himself, Elder Packer looked for new opportunities for the seniors:

> The aging of the population has far-reaching consequences economically, socially, and spiritually. . . . It will affect the growth of the Church. We [older members] cannot *do* what we once did, but we have become more than ever we were before. Life's lessons, some of them very painful, qualify us to counsel, to correct, and even to warn our youth. . . . Older people have a steadiness, a serenity that comes from experience. Learn to use that resource.[18]

Other difficulties faced by participants in their callings included challenging relationships with priesthood leaders, class members, parents, and other ward members:

> I was a nursery leader with forty-two two-year-olds in the nursery in Texas. It was mayhem. I'd put signs on the door: If your child has a cough, cold, runny nose, diarrhea, vomiting, rash, don't bring him/her into the Nursery. I found that if a child had green coming from their nasal passages, I couldn't wipe it. If I did, the parents would say that the child wasn't sick. So I would have to take the child with the evidence plastered all over his/her face into Gospel Doctrine [Sunday School class]. I'd lead them up to the parents so that the problem was quite evident to everyone.[19]

Another woman's anecdote highlights the strained relationships some ward members can have with one another:

> One job I found quite challenging was teaching 12 year olds in Sunday School. . . . I was giving a lesson about the Priesthood. . . . The discussion led to prayer. One boy who was quite outspoken in class said, "Yeah, when your daughter had her mission farewell, your other

---

18. Boyd K. Packer, "The Golden Years," *Ensign*, May, 2003. Available online at http://lds.org/ensign/2003/05/the-goldenyears?lang=eng (italics in original).
19. COHC #022, (2011), 26.

> daughter prayed to Mother in Heaven." I asked if he was in the meeting. He said, "No." So I said, "First of all, she didn't pray to Mother in Heaven although she did mention and acknowledge her in the prayer. Where did you get that?" He said that his mother said that our family makes up our own religion, and we do whatever we want. I said, "So far we haven't done anything new. We read the same scriptures you read, and we have family home evening and early morning scripture study." His comment disturbed me, and I had to do something about it. I went to the bishop and told him that I would appreciate it if parents would talk to me about any issues their children might not have understood or misinterpreted. Don't let it come through the kids like that. It's not fair to them, it's not fair to me, and it's certainly not honest for the parents to do. . . . More disturbing than the boy's accusation was the fact that no parent called me to inquire about the class.[20]

Some women endeavored to meet their challenges and solve the problems—as they saw them—with new innovations, and they implemented new ideas beyond the scope of the outlined Church programs. These creative attempts were met with mixed success. One woman, undaunted, tried on three different occasions to improve the Relief Society and Young Women's programs through the calling in which she was serving at the time. Her attempts demonstrate her commitment to her calling, her talents, her good intentions, and her final acceptance of priesthood leaders' decisions. Two of her stories follow:

> Soon after moving to Boston . . . I was asked to be the Stake YWMIA president. . . . In those days, our stake covered Eastern Massachusetts, through Cape Cod, and all of Rhode Island. . . . After following the Church organizational structure, I chatted with my counterpart in the YMMIA . . . and we decided things would be tighter if we had a slightly different administrative structure. We suggested that [he] head up the joint Mutual program and sit on the high council as our representative and voice, and that he have three counselors, one for Young Women's classes and activities, one for Young Men's classes and activities, and one Activity Counselor who oversaw all the joint activities. We went to [the stake president] with our idea, which also reduced by two the number of administrators we'd need at both the stake and the ward levels. He peppered us with questions and in the end gave us his blessing and we did it. . . . I was new to the

20. COHC, #060 (2010), 17.

politics of the Church so I had written to Salt Lake to tell them to send all materials to my counterpart in the YMMIA and not to me. . . . Salt Lake took a dim view of this idea, much to my surprise. And when we got visitors from Salt Lake for our Stake Conferences, they would tell us we had to go back to the Church organization. But [our stake president] stuck by us because we were getting results. I remember one visitor from Salt Lake who stayed with me; . . . she listened to our reasons for changing the organizational structure, freeing up precious people when our ranks were already thin in the mission field, and she said she thought the Church should consider what we were doing. [The stake president] said when President [Harold B.] Lee called him to be a General Authority [This stake president was called to be one of the twelve apostles over the Church] he said they had been following what was happening with the Mutual program in our area and that he hoped they could bring some of the ideas to the general Church. We felt at least a little vindicated when we heard that.[21]

I never liked Relief Society, but was asked to be the Relief Society president in 1978. With my counselor, who also didn't like Relief Society, we tried to identify what we did and didn't like about it, and also why things like adult education classes appealed to us. After some discussion and batting ideas around, we decided to put together a program that would take the content of Relief Society, add a few more things that the sisters were interested in, and package it like adult education classes, which we did. We put together a brochure, offered "classes" that ran for various numbers of weeks (instead of doing one lesson a month from each category of lessons), made grids and annotated lesson lists, and advertised "free child care" (i.e., the same old nursery, and we in the Presidency took our ideas and brochures to every woman in the ward. Those who were interested signed up for the classes they wished to take by filling out the attached form on the brochure. About 92% of the women in the ward signed up for classes, and our attendance jumped over 20%. We got the best people to teach the classes, including men in the mix! At the end of the year, I did a survey of the sisters, who—not surprisingly—were quite pleased with the experience. I thought the General Relief Society would be interested in our little experiment, which seemed to me to have been successful all around, but they were not. It came down to us through the Stake President that we had to stop. So we

21. COHC, #051 (2010), 25.

> did. . . . What I learned from this year was that if you listen to what the people want to do, want to learn, and try to meet their needs as they see them, they will flock to the Church. In later years when I was again the Relief Society president, I learned the corollary, that if you make them listen to the same Women's Lessons Part B year after year, they stop coming; that year we had an average attendance of about 12–14 sisters.[22]

Like the woman in the previous anecdotes, there are individuals who have ideas and innovations that may be more efficient, more fun, and maybe even better than a particular Church program or lesson. Also, there are some leaders who encourage innovation while others do not. In any case, when one accepts a calling in the Church, it is understood that one accepts the obligation to carry out the responsibilities within the established guidelines and parameters of the Church.

The term of service in a calling is indefinite and comes to an end most often when the priesthood leader feels that it is time to make a change. Some people find it difficult to be released. They have grown to love what they do, and they have grown to love the people they work with:

> I loved being stake Relief Society president because I had such incredible counselors. . . . We did some amazing things. Those were some of my happiest years. I was sad to be released.[23]

In response to the question of how one can maintain a positive attitude when being released from a calling, Brother In Sang Han from Seoul, Korea, stated that he felt a release from a responsibility in the Church was actually another type of calling—a calling of release.[24] A release necessitates a change, and through change comes growth both for the individual and for the organization. The individual may be given an opportunity to serve in a new Church calling, or may simply be allowed to have more time to spend with her family and the chance to focus on other areas of her life. The Church benefits from a new person accepting a calling and bringing with her new ideas, new determination, and new energy.

---

22. Ibid, 27–29.
23. COHC, #002 (2009), 7.
24. In Sang Han, "Question and Answer," *Liahona*, February 1988. Available online at http://www.lds.org/liahona/1988/02/question-and-answer?lang=eng.

The term of service in a calling may also come to an end when the individual serving in the calling asks to be released. A request for a release may be due to a change in personal circumstances such as moving from the area, health issues, marital or financial difficulties, or individual concerns about the calling:

> After two and a half years as [Primary] president, I asked for a release. I had been having some issues with one of my counselors to the point that I felt it better to be released than to talk negatively about her, something I didn't want to do especially as a president.[25]

The following narrator asked to be released when she had a difficult time connecting to the young women she was working with:

> I was hopeless in Young Women's—finding the girls sulky and unforthcoming. They must have found my accent ridiculous and my lack of understanding of American culture a crime. I asked to be released.[26]

Since new calls are issued all the time and releases necessarily follow in course, the announcement of a release in Sacrament Meeting is a routine matter and does not reveal a failure or conflict but the ongoing process of change.

The participants in the Oral History Project wholeheartedly acknowledged the benefits they received from serving in Church callings and were grateful for those blessings. The women spoke of their personal growth; they spoke of their greater understanding of the gospel, the growth of their testimonies of Church teachings, and their increased involvement and investment in the Church. They even spoke of health benefits:

> I have enjoyed them all [my callings]—some more than others. I have learned and grown from every single one. Whatever I learned in one calling would always help me in another. What I learned from my callings also helped me to be better in other areas of my life—including being a parent, spouse, employee, and member of the community. Callings don't only serve others—you benefit too![27]

25. COHC #114 (2011), 13.
26. COHC 080 (2010), 20.
27. COHC #101 (2011), 11.

> I am now the Primary pianist, which I just love. . . . I get to play the piano once a week. It keeps the arthritis in my fingers at bay. My doctor says it's good for me![28]

Many women expressed their love for the people they worked with and spoke about the life-long friendships they developed with other women:

> I think one of my callings that people don't know much about is when I was the area advisor for the Church sorority, which no longer exists—Lambda Delta Sigma. I was that for eleven years. . . . The women that I worked with as area advisors were from Arizona, California, Utah, Idaho, Oregon—we still get together every year. We have a reunion. There's about twenty or twenty-five, depending on who's not on a mission somewhere! We had such great bonding and experiences that we still enjoy getting together.[29]

Most women felt their calling had a positive influence on their families, and they saw their service as setting a good example for other family members:

> I definitely think my children have a love for primary music because of that calling. I think my willingness to serve had an influence on my kids serving missions.[30]
>
> As far as the impact of callings on families is concerned—You get into it and you just make things happen. We included the family. Everyone was along for the ride. I would like to think for all of the good and the bad that my kids hopefully learned you do not make excuses. You just get out there and you do it. And hopefully, you do not complain too much. . . . I hope that they learned that when you make a commitment you get it done one way or another.[31]

The same woman who said her hardest calling was being the bishop's wife also recognized the blessings she and her family received at that time:

> I will say one thing about being a [wife of a] bishop. He came home one night and said, "You know, I've never really told you this, but I really appreciate you as a woman. You're really a good wife and don't have the problems that other women have." . . . He did gain an

28. COHC #081 (2010), 28.
29. COHC #095 (2010), 14.
30. COHC #090 (2010), 14.
31. COHC #058 (2010), 22.

> appreciation for me at that time. I felt blessed while he was Bishop because I never missed a Sunday in five years. My children were never sick and with five little ones that is a miracle.[32]

Some participants used the skills they developed in their callings to improve their employment and contribute in their work places. Others used what they had learned in their callings to volunteer for positions in their broader communities. They saw their community service as a valuable part of their lives and as an important area of growth for the Church in the future:

> My camp calling was very formative for me. In that calling, I developed many of the skills I eventually used to both get my job and do my job in health education. It taught me practical ways to manage a huge project, how to be organized, how to keep track of the moving parts, and how to recruit people and keep track of what they needed to do to have a successful outcome.[33]

> When I was called as director of Public Affairs, I was the first woman to be called to that position. . . . I have always felt the necessity of being active in my community. . . . We need to make our voices heard. Sometimes we are so busy serving in the Church that we ignore our communities. I can honestly say that I have tried to serve as much in the community as I do in the Church, and I have seen things change.[34]

It is apparent from many of the interviews how much women give to their callings. They embrace the work and give unselfishly of their time, talents, energy, and resources:

> At one point I had eight different jobs in the branch. . . . I think . . . I did everything that there was to do at one time or another. . . . It was a full time job just doing Church jobs. To illustrate, at one point my visiting teaching companion [with whom she made monthly visits to other Church members] lived twenty miles away from me and had no car. We had five or six sisters to visit, but before we could do that, I had to drive out and pick her up then drive back into town. After our visits I drove her back home and then came back to town.

32. COHC #076 (2010), 18.
33. COHC #029 (2009), 10.
34. COHC #046 (2010), 16.

> This was not a hardship to me because she was such a wonderful and devoted woman, a great example to me.[35]

Why do they do it? Why do Mormon women dedicate so much of their lives to their Church callings? A simple answer is they do it because they are willing to help, and they do it to get a job done. However, their own accounts of callings indicate they have higher purposes. They want to serve God, to strengthen the Church, and to bless the lives of individuals. They believe they are doing what God wants them to do:

> I most definitely believe in taking all callings offered to me. Again, I think that everything you do in relationship to the Church provides you a training, a foundation to build testimony on, and helps you realize just who you are, where you belong, and most importantly brings you back to your Heavenly Father.[36]

Mormon women serve in their callings, not without struggle, but with a determination to work through the difficulties and to go forward in spite of the challenges. They may have questions, and even doubts, but they make the decision to engage in the work. The women in the Oral History Project demonstrated their dedication and commitment to their callings.

35. COHC #004 (2009), 13.
36. COHC #101 (2010), 11.

Chapter Eight

Revelation

Lisa Thomas Clayton

Shauna, a life-long member of the LDS Church who lives in Australia, believes in prayer and personal revelation. As a narrator in the Claremont Oral History Collection, she explains the importance of her revelatory relationship with God:

> I came to know prayer through the Church, and through prayer I came to know God. . . . I cannot deny that prayers are heard. The most powerful motivation for me in regard to the Gospel is that I am encouraged to develop a direct relationship with God, that I can pray directly to Him and that I am entitled to a personal reply that does not need to be filtered through someone in some authority position. My relationship with God is personal; and I would not have sought or known that without the Gospel.[1]

LDS teachings encouraged Shauna to develop a relationship with deity, and she reports direct and personal answers to her prayers.

Julie, an author born and raised as a member of the Church in Utah, describes how prayer has empowered her to make choices in her life:

> The only way I have gotten through the challenges of life is to be prayerful and to listen to God. I have received divine help as I made important decisions such as: the choice of a marriage partner, how many children to welcome into my home and how to share the talents God has given me.[2]

These women and others seek and receive divine revelation and then act for themselves—or exercise agency—as a result. They share

---

1. Claremont Mormon Women's Oral History Collection, Library of the Claremont Colleges, Claremont, CA, hereafter COHC, #127 (2011), 9.

2. COHC, #070 (2010), 4.

their experience with an aspect of their religion that has often been misunderstood by those not of their faith. Secular culture and feminist theory have often dismissed conservative religious women as people who do not act independently; however, I have found evidence in the oral histories that the religious women do act agentively and that a revelatory relationship with God is key to their ability to exercise agency. This has, over the years, also been my experience.

"Do you really believe that God speaks to you?" and "How can you exercise agency in such a thoroughly patriarchal church?" These were among the many questions I heard during the time that I, a devout Mormon, worked as an intern at the University of Utah's new Women's Resource Center. I was introduced to feminism as a student at the "U" in the 1970s through the center's workshops and classes. I learned a great deal and enjoyed the association with other women. On occasion, however, my religiosity became the issue, trumping the planned topic of discussion. Many of the other women had found empowerment and acceptance in a thoroughly secular feminism. They questioned why I sought to learn a male God's will and how I could hope to be a free agent within a patriarchal church. They also questioned why I stayed in any organized religion.

That was almost forty years ago and now I'm back on a university campus earning a graduate degree in religion. My devotion to the doctrines of my faith has matured in the intervening years, and I have a profound appreciation for the paths it has encouraged me to travel. As I've spent over three decades endeavoring to receive and heed personal revelation, I've learned how to better talk about my religious devotions with those of varying viewpoints. I find that those who don't share such commitments are more willing to appreciate their validity for me.[3] I find myself fielding—and asking—more nuanced questions than those of long ago at the "U."

Second-wave feminism has come and gone, with multiple feminisms emerging globally that more accurately reflect the wide variety of

3. "Differences do not negate one another, unless some feminists make the mistake of thinking that their feminist context is normative. Rather this diversity is precisely the wonderful richness of feminism, its capacity and necessity of being articulated in many contexts and cultural locations." Rosemary Radford Reuther, "What is Feminism and Why Should We Do it?" *Feminism and Religion*, http://feminismandreligion.com/rosemary-radford-ruether-on-feminism/ (accessed 3 July 2012).

woman's experience. With this multiplication of views, there is a growing body of scholarly work challenging earlier feminist assumptions.[4] My essay will address some of this work, focusing on LDS doctrine and how the narrators in the Claremont Oral History Project converse with God, live their lives, and exercise their agency.

Julie Beck, a recent general president of the LDS Church's Relief Society, often spoke of personal revelation and agency. In the April 2010 General Conference she taught, "The ability to qualify for, receive, and act on personal revelation is the single most important skill that can be acquired in this life."[5] Does Beck's simple, action-inducing prescription describe reality? Does God really talk directly to women? Do LDS women act independently when He does speak to them? And does this revelatory relationship with deity enable agency in their lives? This essay will examine personal revelation, specifically answers to prayer described by LDS women, so that we can consider the role that personal revelation and agency play in traditional religious women's experience. This essay will challenge the frequent assumption that LDS women do not exercise agency but merely submit to patriarchal power. I hope to concretize and document their experiences, expanding common ground for future conversation.

Conversations with God

Members of The Church of Jesus Christ of Latter-day Saints live in a world imbued with God's presence. They believe that He is active in their lives and in their institution.[6] They believe that God communicates directly through living prophets and apostles. They also believe

4. "Historical treatments of women's piety have tended to present a flattened version of modern religious nonfeminists, as if choosing to believe in "absolutes" of morality, theology, and gender roles in today's world renders them unworthy of the careful analysis ordinarily accorded women from the past who professed similar religious certainty." R. Marie Griffith, *God's Daughters: Evangelical Women and the Power of Submission* (Berkeley: University of California Press, 1997), 1.

5. Julie B. Beck, "And Upon the Handmaids in Those Days Will I Pour Out My Spirit," *Ensign*, May 2010, 11.

6. This is consistent with a recent Pew Institute survey, which indicated that 91% of the Latter-day Saints responding believe in a personal God. Available online at http://www.pewforum.org/Christian/Mormon/A-Portrait-of-Mormons-in-the-US--Religious-Beliefs-and-Practices.aspx#god (accessed 20 May 2012).

that God communicates with each member directly through what they call personal revelation.[7] Elder David A. Bednar, an apostle for the Church, teaches that "Revelation is communication from God to His children on the earth and one of the great blessings associated with the gift and constant companionship of the Holy Ghost."[8] The women echo this belief in the oral histories. Lillian discusses her first experiences with revelation in her life:

> I gained a testimony of the Gospel as a young girl. I experimented with prayer and found out that there is a God and He does answer prayers. I remember the first time I could recognize promptings from the Holy Ghost. I marveled that God took an interest in me![9]

Lillian believes in her capacity to hear God's word as direction in her life. This skill is a key element in conversion to the LDS Church at any age. While Lillian experienced revelation as a young child within the context of her Mormon upbringing, Laura experienced personal revelation as she was deciding whether to join the LDS Church:

> I really struggled while taking the discussions because I wasn't sure I wanted to leave my faith. . . . The elders at that point encouraged me to fast and pray and I was intimidated by that because I had never really prayed to God before. I had prayed at God and said rote prayers, but I had never talked to God. . . . I did finally have the experience of kneeling down in my room and hoping that nothing would really come of it. I didn't want angels, I didn't want flaming swords or thundering voices. It was my first experience of getting an answer to prayer. It's kind of indescribable, but it was also very simplistic. There was nothing ground-shaking or earth-moving, there was just a real piercing to my soul. It wasn't a burning in the bosom—I've never had that—but it was such a sure answer to me, that to this day it's prob-

7. Terryl Givens, *By The Hand of Mormon* (Oxford: Oxford University Press, 2002), 209–39. See chapter eight for a discussion of revelation in Mormon doctrine and The Book of Mormon.

8. David A. Bednar, "The Spirit of Revelation," *Ensign*, May 2011, 87. For an explanation of General Conference and its function in the Church see: Jan Shipps, *Mormonism: The Story of a New Religious Tradition* (Chicago: University of Illinois Press, 1987), 131–32.

9. COHC, #034 (2009), 5.

ably the surest answer I've ever received in my life. That was my first awakening to what it meant to have an answer to prayer.[10]

Because personal revelation is employed in the process of conversion, the belief structure of Church members rests directly on this principle; it is the means by which they come to believe.[11] Julie shared this experience:

> As a young child I learned to rely on direct inspiration from God. When I had questions, I sought personal revelation. I read how-to books and listened to other older wiser people, but when I really wanted to know what was right for me, I got on my knees and asked for direction and wisdom.[12]

Julie reveals a surprisingly anti-authoritarian attitude in the context of an authority-oriented church structure. This is tempered by the sense that the "direction and wisdom" she receives should correspond to scripture and current Church teachings.

These women believe that they qualify for revelation through righteous living. They believe that God expects them to act upon that revelation, and that this process is essential to salvation. He will hold them accountable for their choices. Bednar outlines this idea:

> The spirit of revelation is available to every person who receives by proper priesthood authority the saving ordinances of baptism by immersion for the remission of sins and the laying on of hands for the gift of the Holy Ghost—and who is acting in faith to fulfill the priesthood injunction to "receive the Holy Ghost." This blessing is not restricted to the presiding authorities of the Church. The blessing belongs to and should be operative in the life of every man, woman, and child who reaches the age of accountability and enters into sacred covenants. Sincere desire and worthiness invite the spirit of revelation into our lives.[13]

---

10. COHC, #056 (2010), 9. Scriptural descriptions of the Holy Ghost: "a still small voice," 1 Kgs. 19:12, 1 Ne. 17:45; "a voice of perfect mildness," Hel. 5:30.

11. Barbara Thompson, "Personal Revelation and Testimony," *Ensign*, November 2011, 9. See also Richard G. Scott, "How to Obtain Revelation and Inspiration for Your Personal Life," *Ensign*, May 2012, 49.

12. COHC, #070 (2010), 4.

13. Bednar, "The Spirit of Revelation," 87.

These women believe that baptism and the gift of the Holy Ghost, coupled with righteous living, allow them direct access to deity. Though the ordinances of baptism and giving the gift of the Holy Ghost are performed by a male priesthood holder, there is no priest or other authority acting as mediator in women's private conversations with God. These women commune directly with God and take action in response.[14] Marianne experienced personal revelation in this way:

> I finally got to a point where I needed to know, and the only way I could know was to pray about it. That was really scary to me, because I knew I would have to get an answer to a prayer. I don't think I had really ever said a prayer and gotten an answer. . . . After I got down on my knees and prayed, the confirmation was just too strong not to get baptized. . . . I knew just enough about the Church that I just knew that it was where I needed to be, and it is where I wanted to raise my family.[15]

Prayers that ask for information or for a confirmation of belief are common within the Mormon framework. Terryl Givens, in his discussion of LDS scripture, describes this kind of prayer: "That is an asking, rather than an asking for, and that anticipates a personal response, a discernable moment of dialogue or communicated content."[16]

As in many faiths, Mormonism teaches that God is a caring deity who responds to believing supplicants through scriptural passages, visions, dreams, impressions, and miracles. People who have experienced these things report divine solace, communion, and aid. In this chapter, I focus on the supplication and answer model of prayer. I do not question the reality of these women's claims to divine revelation. There is no need to judge whether these communications are in fact from a loving

---

14. Direct access to God without mediation of a priest (once the initial ordinances are performed) is a central concept in Mormon doctrine. Individual prayer plays an important role in many religious traditions, its importance growing with modern evangelical movements.

Griffith, *God's Daughters*, 1: "Prayer is a powerful medium of expression, alliance, and desire. . . . Family members may pray for the healing of sick loved ones, children may pray for relief from punishment of misdeeds; religious congregants may pray together for the dead as well as for the living. Whether they make their petitions in public or private, those who pray seek comfort, assurance, and courage in the face of adversity." Distinctive aspects of the Mormon concept of prayer are seen in the narrators' use of the medium.

15. COHC, #083 (2010), 4.

16. Givens, *By The Hand of Mormon*, 217.

and interested divine being. It is enough that these women believe the answers came from God and, thus, carry the weight of heavenly communication for them. My focus is how these women interact with the perceived answers to their prayers and the trends that are discernable. These oral histories do not reflect a statistically significant sampling, but they do provide a private glimpse into the lives of Mormon women.

Evidence in the oral histories shows that belief in a personal relationship with God, revelation from Him, and the ability to evaluate that revelation enables LDS women to exercise agency. Amy Hoyt, in her article, "Reconceptualizing Agency" discusses this process of "self-interpreted authorization," as she sees LDS women relying on their own abilities to interpret spiritual experiences and personal revelatory moments within the boundedness of their tradition.[17] This "self-interpreted authorization" of personal revelation is evident in the oral histories as the women judge its meaning and determine what their responses will be. These women's choices reflect their theological and cultural boundaries, and within this context they report receiving answers to prayer, interpreting those answers, and, as in Beck's formula, taking action.

Agency

Most of our narrators participate willingly in their patriarchal religion, supporting and recreating the androcentric structure of the Church. Is this evidence of submissive obedience to patriarchy or can it possibly signify independent agency? Agency generally refers to the capacity of individuals to act independently and to make their own free choices or exert power. The LDS concept of agency is nuanced by concepts of God's will, obedience, and salvation, referring both to the capacity of people to act for themselves and their accountability for those actions. Mormons believe they are free to act for themselves—the gift of agency having been given in the Garden of Eden and secured through Christ's Atonement (Moses 7: 32, D&C 58:28). Submission to God's will is the ideal exercise of that gift, but men and women are free to choose their own paths (2 Ne. 2:26).

17. Hoyt, "Reconceptualizing Agency," *Element*, 5:2, Fall 2009, 81.

Many feminist leaders and scholars have assumed the primacy of the autonomous individual, naming freedom as the highest value.[18] It is assumed that this freedom is demonstrated by exercising agency in resisting the structures in place and working to change them, or alternately, by leaving the tradition and critiquing from outside the structure. The LDS woman's relationship to freedom is nuanced by her belief in both agency and personal revelation. Hoyt discusses the need to look again at the acts of traditional, norm-sustaining religious women, which are not typically viewed by feminist scholars as constituting agentive behavior because of the strong association between resistance and agency.[19]

If agency is defined as resistance to norms, it is difficult to perceive agency exercised in supporting religious structures. However, if we remove the agency-as-resistance lens, we see in these oral histories personal agency being exercised in response to personal revelation.

Catherine Brekus, in her article "Mormon Women and the Problem of Historical Agency," explains the expanded use of the term "agency" and observes that most scholars invest far more in the word than the definition of the capacity to act. As feminist historians sought to recover a "usable past" during the 1970s and 1980s, they looked to find "evidence of individual or collective resistance to white male hegemony."[20] Their writings valorized resistant behaviors over those supporting existent forms. Brekus writes:

> "Agency" today has become virtually synonymous with emancipation, liberation, and resistance. When historians write about agency, they often imagine an individual in conflict with his or her society

18. See Miriam Schneir, *Feminism: The Essential Historical Writings* (New York: Vintage Books, 1972). According to Griffith, "Amidst the explosion of feminist scholarship during the past twenty-five years, the accuracy of certain key assumptions has remained largely unquestioned by historians of twentieth-century American women. The standard paradigm for women's history extols the liberation presumably wrought by second-wave feminism, in stark contrast to what is assumed to be women's near-universal oppression in American life prior to that time. Religion, particularly in its more traditional forms, is viewed as a tool for preserving patriarchy, suppressing women's energies and talents, and imbuing them with 'false consciousness' in which hope for a better life is deferred toward expectations of heaven." Griffith, *God's Daughters*, 202.

19. Hoyt, 70.

20. Catherine Brekus, "Mormon Women and the Problem of Historical Agency," *Journal of Mormon History* 37, no. 2 (Spring 2011): 71.

> who self-consciously seeks greater freedom. . . . Because historians have implicitly defined agency against structure, they have found it hard to imagine women who accepted religious structures as agents.[21]

Feminist theorists have looked for resistance to religious structures as the key marker of agency, prizing freedom and autonomy over other values. Saba Mahmood, an anthropologist of religion, notes this bias, arguing that scholars assume that "human agency primarily consists of acts that challenge social norms and not those who uphold them." She also argues that "Liberal assumptions about what constitutes human nature and agency have become integral to our feminist intellectual traditions." These assumptions lead to a fundamental misunderstanding of the traditional religious woman.[22]

Brekus suggests that to better understand such religious women we should reconsider the implicit association of agency with freedom and emancipation and expand the definition of agency to include "reproduction of social structures as well as the transformation of them." She further argues that agency exists on a continuum, a reality we see in the collected oral histories.[23] These are women exercising choice within a social and theological structure—either of their choosing or inheritance. Not all of the narrators support the patriarchal structures without reservation; some of the women exercise their agency in choosing to work for change even while participating in the Church, or to absent themselves from the Church altogether. My goal is to examine the instances of revelation that lead to a variety of agentive behaviors.

Women's Lives

The experiences of two different women will be examined in an effort to reconsider the association of agency with resistance and the role personal revelation plays.

21. Ibid., 71–72.

22. Saba Mahmood, *Politics of Piety: The Islamic Revival and the Feminist Subject* (Princeton, N.J.: Princeton University Press, 2005), 5.

23. Brekus, "Mormon Women," 78–82.

An Australian Convert Changes Her Life

Brenda, an Australian convert to the LDS Church, saw her father as "very kind and patient, [he] always looked to see the other side of a story and was slow to judge people." She had a difficult relationship with her mother who lacked positive parenting skills and used negativity and threats to control her children. Brenda "trusted her father's atheist judgment" until she was taught by LDS missionaries as a teenager. When they encouraged her to pray for the first time she was conflicted. She didn't believe there was a God. She overcame this hesitancy and reports the answer to her prayer:

> There may not be a God but these people believed in Him and so I wouldn't look silly, I had to be sincere in case God was really there. And when I said "Dear Lord" and continued with my simple question of was He there, I was engulfed in the most pure joy and knowledge that my Father in Heaven was there and loves me. I cried and cried unashamedly in true happiness.
>
> I had recently been ice skating for the first time and the boots were too small. There was no padding inside the boots and the cold came up through the blades into my feet. After two hours of skating, my feet were really uncomfortable. . . . I put on my old warm comfortable shoes afterwards and felt such pleasure, warmth and comfort. That was something of how I felt in relation to finding truth. I had been pondering and yearning to know what purpose life had and now I knew God was in heaven, that He loved me and there was a plan for me to get back to Him.[24]

Believing she had identified God's plan for her, Brenda joined the Church despite the early influence of her father's atheism, claiming independence from him and her mother. She applied the pattern of asking God (pondering and yearning to know), receiving an answer (He is there and has a plan for her), and acting upon the divine instruction (choosing to be baptized). We see this pattern throughout her life. She reports numerous answers to prayer in daily events. Despite insecurities from her upbringing, she reports a "peace to her soul" as a result of this communication with God. As a teenager she had often dated young men in and out of the Church yet she felt "distressed, alone, and con-

---

24. COHC, #110 (2010), 3.

cerned" that she wouldn't find someone suitable to marry. She prayed to God and received an answer:

> The Holy Ghost spoke to my mind and told me that there was a man for me that was beyond my comprehension to understand how wonderful he was. I ceased to be concerned about dating.[25]

Brenda observed that God's replies come concerning small issues as well as big questions. She went to nursing school and upon completing that course desired to go on a mission for the Church.[26] She hoped that with her training she would be called on a health mission. She had often helped the sister missionaries in her area and knew that a proselytizing mission was "hard work and discouraging and I thought it would be much more fun teaching people about health issues." Brenda prayed for direction in her choices:

> As I prayed to know what to do I understood that my Father in Heaven didn't want me to choose the easy option. He wanted more of me. In my prayer I finally said that if He wanted me to do a proselytizing mission, I would do it. I received the communication in my mind, "I am pleased with your desire." When I spoke to my bishop, he said I would probably be called on a health mission. I smiled at him and said, "No, I'll be going on a proselytizing mission," and that's what happened.[27]

In seeking God's direction in her life, Brenda "prayed to know what to do." She was willing, as an exercise in agency, to relinquish power in her decisions. She asserted her willingness to go where God would send her, which implied her revealed knowledge of His will. She relinquished the power to God and heard an answer from Him regarding the call. Power plays a role in definitions of agency, as the loss of power is equated with the loss of the ability to act independently. Brenda and others, as devoted and religiously committed women, choose to subject their will to God and the organization through which God operates. Christ modeled this willingness to subject one's will to the divine, and is held up to all as an example for emulation. Ancient and modern

---

25. Ibid., 5.

26. For an explanation of the LDS mission experience see Claudia Bushman, *Contemporary Mormonism: Latter-day Saints in Modern America* (Westport: Rowman & Littlefield Publishers, 2006), 58–74.

27. COHC, #110 (2010), 5

LDS scripture encourage this behavior (Matt. 26:42, Luke 11:2, D&C 109:44, Jacob 7:14).

Brenda chose to go on a mission, but also chose align her will to God's, ceding power to Him. This incident illustrates how the power to act as an agent can, paradoxically, lead to less freedom, not through the loss of agency but as a result of it.[28] This is a difficult result to value if one sees personal freedom and power as optimal goals. The traditional religious woman prioritizes obedience to and unity with God's will over all other ends.[29]

The idea of seeking to relinquish power to God in doing His will has historical precedence in the Church in the practice of polygamy. The women who were approached to participate in polygamy had a history of receiving answers to prayer. They had established a pattern of seeking the Lord's affirmation of their choices through personal revelation and they were intent on submitting their wills to God. They had already sacrificed a great deal as a result of their beliefs. We read how repugnance and shock at the very suggestion of entering into a polygamous marriage turns into acceptance of "the principle" after receiving an answer to prayer. Lucy Walker first rejected the teaching of polygamy but after consideration felt she received a manifestation of its truthfulness:

> When the Prophet Joseph Smith first mentioned the principle of plural marriage to me, I became very indignant and told him emphatically that I did not wish him ever to mention it to me again,

---

28. Enzio Busche, "Truth Is the Issue," *Ensign*, November 1993, 26. "In the depth of such a prayer, we may finally be led to . . . the place where we suddenly see the heavens open as we feel the full impact of the love of our Heavenly Father, which fills us with indescribable joy. With this fulfillment of love in our hearts, we will never be happy anymore just by being ourselves or living our own lives. We will not be satisfied until we have surrendered our lives into the arms of the loving Christ, and until He has become the doer of all our deeds and He has become the speaker of all our words."

29. Griffiths's view of the evangelical experience of prayer: "Christian submission is a flexible doctrine intricately attached to contro—of self and other—and freedom, rather than a rigid blueprint of silent and demoralizing subjugation. Likewise, the practice of prayer is perceived as gloriously liberating, creating possibilities for loving intimacy, healing of body and soul, renewed courage in the face of sorrow, emotional maturity, and perpetual transformation . . . devotional practices of surrender are affirmed as the key to women's fullest spiritual and emotional fulfillment." Griffith, *God's Daughters*, 202.

> as my feelings and education revolted against anything of such a nature. . . . After I had poured out my heart's content before God, I at once became calm and composed; a feeling of happiness took possession of me, and at the same time I received a powerful and irresistible testimony of the truth of plural marriage, which testimony has abided with me ever since.[30]

An apparently immoral proposition, clearly at odds with religious teachings of the time, became a principle worth sacrificing for. Why? Evidence suggests that these women who had established relationships with God, had already sacrificed much to join the Church, and had made decisions within a context of previously received personal revelation ultimately had the power of personal agency. These women exercised agency within the context of their desire to follow God's will in their lives.

Brenda also reports that God's reply to her prayer about her mission was in actual words. "I am pleased with your desire" is perceived by the recipient in an actual sentence structure. In asking for guidance, she articulated a specific need and heard God respond to her plea with specific words. Terryl Givens defines this type of answer to prayer as "dialogic revelation." The Book of Mormon is central to LDS belief and practice, and the idea that the individual has access to divine direction is central to its plotlines and teachings. Givens points out that

> Far beyond a forceful spiritual intimation, one finds in the Book of Mormon that prayer frequently and dramatically evokes an answer that is impossible to mistake as anything other than an individualized, dialogic response to a highly particularized question. The conception of revelation as a personalized, dialogic exchange pervades the Book of Mormon—as well as the life of the Prophet Joseph—like an insistent leitmotif.[31]

Latter-day Saints believe that Joseph Smith, a young and unschooled teenager, approached God with a question and received a visitation from deity in response (JS–H 1:11–20). Young Nephi, a central character early in the Book of Mormon, asks for confirmation of his father/prophet's visions recorded in the book. As the story unfolds he

30. Lucy Walker, as quoted in the "Historical Record: A Monthly Periodical," Andrew Jensen, Salt Lake City, Utah 1882–1890, Vol. 6:229–30. See also Kathryn M. Daynes, *More Wives Than One: Transformation of the Mormon Marriage System* (Chicago: University of Illinois Press 2008), 27.

31. Givens, *By The Hand of Mormon*, 217–18.

later becomes a prophet himself, the leader of his family and ultimately a nation. But at the moment he asks for God's answer he is the fourth son in a patriarchal society. He was not a prophet, a ruler, nor the apparent heir, but rather an individual teenager praying for help in believing in his father's visions. The account of the angelic visitation to Nephi and the attendant vision described in the first chapters of the Book of Mormon establish for the reader the expectation that God will communicate with the individual member, not just the prophet/leader.[32]

Members are encouraged to read the Book of Mormon each day, reinforcing the concept that God will communicate directly with the individual regardless of station.[33] Brenda was taught this principle and we see her living according to it. The obvious paucity of female models for women in the scriptures is ameliorated somewhat by the fact that Nephi was not a powerful patriarchal or royal leader but a teenager. Perhaps this makes him a more approachable model for women.

This dialogic relationship is seen often in the oral histories as women ask for specific answers to prayer and receive them in word form. Women report strong impressions and specific wording in response to their petitions. These conversations with deity reflect Givens' idea of a "personalized dialogic exchange." Here is another example of Brenda's dialogue with God:

> I had looked forward to going to the temple prior to my mission as it seemed everyone said what a wonderful experience it was. No one can fully prepare for the temple and perhaps I was not ready for the commitment that was required. I remember feeling hurt that God should ask me to participate in the ordinances of the temple, ordinances which I didn't feel comfortable about and couldn't fully grasp the eternal purpose of. Didn't He know how much I loved Him? Why did He ask me to do this? I spoke to the temple president but felt no real understanding. I prayed most fervently and in answer to my prayer, the Lord gave me a glimpse of the Celestial Kingdom, closed again before I could see it. The communication that came into my mind was, "I am going to give you everything, and this is all I ask." Suffice to say, I have never doubted that the temple is part of God's plan and as I have progressed spiritually and fully accepted that I can give all things back

32. See also 1 Ne. 2:16, Jacob 7:5, Enos 8.

33. Henry B. Eyring, "The Book of Mormon as a Personal Guide," *Ensign*, September 2010, 4.

> to Him, losing my selfishness, I too can feel the joy of the temple. I still do not understand some of the experience, and I don't have to.[34]

Brenda, with her vision expanded, chooses her path, using her dialogic relationship with God as a guide. She chooses to trust God regarding temple worship, and doesn't require complete control or comprehension.

Brenda's choice to join the LDS Church changed the trajectory of her life, introducing a realm of agency and revelation she had never considered before. Her children have exercised agency as well; some have chosen to be involved in Church membership and one chose not to participate. Even though she has been married for many years, when Brenda speaks of her revelatory relationship with God it is as an individual. She describes a direct and personal relationship with deity that leads to agentive behaviors.

From Utah Girl to Agentive Mother

In contrast to Brenda's early life, Amber was raised in a small Utah town by parents involved in the Church and surrounded by extended family. She has lived as an adult outside Utah where she and her husband participated fully in the Church as they raised their children. She describes her early spiritual life:

> I grew up in a very traditional Mormon home. I had parents who were very active in the LDS Church. I was taught to pray and to read scriptures as a young girl, and I remember being very excited that I was about to be baptized. My parents had prepared me well, my father in particular had prepared me very well for baptism, and I remember it being an extremely important event in my life that had a lot of meaning to me. I also remember as a young girl getting an occasional answer to prayers, something that in my adult life I continue to experience on occasion. It's not a frequent thing. From time to time, and I can only think of a handful of times in my life, there have been distinct answers to prayers. That started when I was a very young girl.[35]

Her experience reflects the training young women receive in the Church in the hope that a relationship with God will be established early. Though Amber claims only a few answers to prayers, she has en-

34. COHC, #110 (2010), 6.
35. COHC, #071 (2010), 6.

deavored to live as God directs. Following a common Mormon cultural pattern, Amber fell in love when she was a sophomore at Brigham Young University (BYU). She prayed about whether she should marry this man whom she felt was very different from herself:

> I soon found out I could not stay away from [my boyfriend.] I had a missionary that I was writing to, the classic BYU scenario. But my feelings . . . would just not go away. We decided to marry and as a lot of Mormon couples do, we married within just a few short months. I mentioned earlier that from time to time in my life that I have received distinct answers to prayers, not often, but I prayed fervently to know whether I was to marry this man who was so unlike me, so foreign to the type of men I had dated. The distinct answer that I got was not yes, but that it will be hard. I thought at the time, no problem! I can handle hard and I ran with it and, at times, it has been difficult. But it has also been a marriage of great respect and love, but it has not been an easy marriage; I don't know if any marriage is easy.[36]

Amber took a "distinct" though not a completely positive answer to prayer and "ran with it." She felt warned that her marriage would be difficult but, exercising her agency, trusted that she could succeed. Amber and her husband have faced challenges and she reports that it has taken great effort to achieve their successful marriage.

In working out her marriage and her relationship to the Church, Amber sought God's help in understanding patriarchy. She built upon her previous testimony of the Book of Mormon and asked for guidance from God, receiving a dialogic reply:

> I received a testimony of the truthfulness of the Book of Mormon as a young married woman. It has gotten me through a lot of trials. I received that absolute testimony of the Book of Mormon that some people never receive. . . . I had to read the Book of Mormon several times before receiving this testimony. I report this as a preface to my thoughts on feminism.
>
> I had my feminist awakening in the late '70s early '80s when I started to question living in a world so full of patriarchy. I seemed to be surrounded by patriarchy. I had grown up in a family where my father was a dominant but loving figure. When I was working, I went through a series of bosses who were overbearingly domineering. I questioned where women fit into this scheme. I turned to the Lord

36. Ibid., 9.

> in prayer not knowing if I would get an answer. This was one of those rare experiences when I received a very distinct answer to my prayer. It satisfied my questions about where women fit into the Church. I had questioned why women seemed to not be viewed as being as important as men and the answer that I got was very simple. The answer was that patriarchy is *for order, for now*. That satisfied me. I've never had to grapple with issues of feminism since then. I also eventually learned to assert myself around men and to not allow myself to be dominated.[37]

Amber's long held concerns were laid to rest as she received a specifically worded answer to prayer. She trusted the message as God's reply and determined to act assertively.

Amber and Fred have sorrowed over their children, who all eventually decided to leave church activity. Though they endeavored to teach their children as they themselves were taught—including taking them to seminary and having Family Home Evening—each child chose to leave the Church in his or her teens.[38] Amber records her reaction:

> At this time, I was several years into realizing that I could not protect my kids from making bad choices. I was beginning to realize that being a close family that tried diligently to keep God's commandments would not guarantee a certain outcome. As each successive child left the Church, my cynicism increased. It became a defense mechanism to help me cope; I could not remain tucked in a fetal position, crying, my entire life.[39]

Amber's children exercised their own agency, resisting her efforts and Church authority. Her own devotion could not guarantee her children's behavior. She shared an excerpt from her journal:

> As Drake struggled through high school with gradually declining grades, I wore out two perfectly good knees in constant prayer on his behalf; I knew going on a mission would be critical for his future but soon realized he would not go. . . .
>
> I am experiencing pain for our son . . . and my own pain which threatens to overwhelm 24 hours each day. . . . I have sensed that Drake was heading in the wrong direction for a few years. I have spent countless days and nights in prayer on his behalf. I have prayed for strength

37. Ibid., 27–28.

38. For a description of seminary and Family Home Evening, see Bushman, *Contemporary Mormonism*, 30, 44–45.

39. COHC, #071 (2010), 14.

> and direction in parenting him; I have felt alone, terrified even, knowing the devastation I would face if yet another . . . of our children left the Church. I have prayed for guidance in encouraging him to serve a mission. He has rejected most of my advice. My worst fears have come true as he has stated that he plans to never attend church again.[40]

Amber doesn't ask God to trump the agency of her children, but seeks to know how to encourage and guide them. For a time she pulled back from participation in the Church, stopped attending the temple, and often chose to be out of town on Sundays. Here is a diary entry from that time:

> I vacillate between feeling like a failure as a mother and reflecting on the wonder and amazement I find in each of our children. I am avoiding friends and family, even strangers, as I burst into tears at the most random times; in restaurants, while riding my bike, and on my morning hikes. A part of me seems to die each time one of my children makes a choice contrary to Gospel principles.[41]

Amber eventually makes peace with her children's choices and has become ever more involved in church activity, teaching in various church organizations and serving in the Relief Society. Her respect for her children, as well as her "wonder and amazement" in them, continues to grow.

As Amber practices her ability to choose, she also recognizes her children's agency. When her eldest son, who is gay, announced plans to marry his companion, the family attended the wedding in support. The family came together in endorsing this marriage. Amber supports her son, but she recognizes the President of the Church as a prophet and knows that he has spoken against same-sex marriage.[42] She lives with these competing loyalties as she navigates church and family life.

These women's stories challenge the agency-as-resistance equation. The culture of revelation in the Church fosters the ability to act agentively, and these women use it to navigate their complicated lives. They enhance our understanding of the traditional religious woman, her motivations, and her use of agency.

---

40. Ibid., 18.

41. Ibid., 19.

42. Gordon B. Hinckley, "Why We Do Some of the Things We Do," *Ensign*, November 1999, 54.

Trusting Self, Trusting Others

As these women build a personal history of revelation they learn to trust themselves and their decisions. This process takes place in the context of a patriarchal authority structure and within a ward, or congregational social unit. Answers to prayer create space for these women to function within these structures. Hoyt discusses the space that is created when personal revelation is invoked, commenting that it is highly unusual to question others' personal revelations.[43] Our narrators nurture a relationship with deity, and when others question revelation that comes from such communion, some defend that space. For example, Laura learned confidence in the answers she receives to prayer during her conversion. She references personal revelation when she disagrees with her Bishop's advice:

> I think God expects us to act on it when He whispers in our ear. It may not always be what we think we're going to hear, but I've never really been disappointed in following eternal truths. . . . I had an instance where a bishop told me that I was out of line because I didn't accept something that came from him. I told him I felt like I received an answer to prayer on the issue, and he said because he was the bishop, he trumped me on that. I didn't believe that, and I told him that I wasn't going to tell him who to call, but when it came to me, my personal revelation trumped his. . . . I wondered if I had done something really bad by confronting him, but I felt strong enough in myself that I persevered. . . . At one point he was again questioning my ability to know something, and I told him that if what he was saying was true, I didn't belong in this Church. I joined the Church based on personal revelation, based on a prayer.[44]

Laura resisted the bishop's efforts to supersede her inspiration. She recognized his authority in the ward, even as she was released from her calling following their disagreement. But she was also confident in delineating her final authority in her personal choices. In this instance she both resisted and sustained the bishop. Laura's history of revelation and agentive behaviors began when she converted to Mormonism and helped her negotiate its patriarchal structure.

---

43. Hoyt, 81.
44. COHC, #056 (2010), 16.

The potential impact of prayer in such circumstances is discussed by R. Marie Griffith in *God's Daughters: Evangelical Women and the Power of Submission*:

> This search for fresh ways to think about power and resistance may also offer a method for considering the practical effects of activities such as prayer: one that would avoid the either/or perspective, by which practices are viewed as either opposing or conserving certain meanings and values, but rather understand them as doing both, upholding power arrangements even while exposing them to unexpected challenges. One way of articulating such a method might be to think in terms of "making room," that is, expanding one's sense of place, creating more out of less or less out of more, taking part in the opening of new worlds.[45]

Laura sustained the bishop's authority and the ward's power structure, even as she created space for her own inspiration.

Debra, a graduate student who was raised in the Church, began trusting personal revelation while on her mission and "made room" for her agentive actions. She learned to do so, even when it went counter to the opinion of an authority figure:

> I had a negative experience on my mission where I felt like I was receiving revelation about a decision I needed to make, and a mission president basically told me that since it wasn't lining up with what he thought I needed to do that I might be receiving my revelation from the wrong place. That was a really challenging experience and to be honest several years later, something I regret. But it was an important learning experience for me to realize that I needed to trust myself and my own revelation.[46]

As Debra navigated a patriarchal church and its authority structure, she learned to understand better the role personal revelation can play. She learned to trust herself and the revelation she receives. These women use the principle of personal revelation to negotiate relationships and to navigate their lives, and also to expand their obedience to

---

45. Griffith, *God's Daughters*, 212. See also Amy Hoyt, "Agency, Subjectivity and Essentialism within Traditional Religious Cultures: An Ethnographic Study of an American Latter-day Saint Community" (Doctoral Dissertation, Claremont Graduate University, 2007), 133.

46. COHC, #074 (2010), 9.

other principles of the Church's teachings. These agentive choices echo throughout the narratives.

The potential for conflict is inherent in a church that encourages both personal revelation and obedience to authority. As Debra says,

> That's just the tension in the Gospel, that we believe in principles that are universally true and believe in being a cohesive group and at the same time we believe in personal revelation. This is just a tension that we have to hold together. But I really appreciate when that's made a little bit more overt and talked about a little bit more in general conference.[47]

There is clearly potential for conflict in a community that believes in both the guidance of living prophets and in individual divine input. The tension between personal revelation (and the agency it engenders) and obedience to authority is inherent in church participation as both values are celebrated by the culture and LDS Church teachings. Our narrators reflect their thoughtful consideration of these principles.

These women live in wards, among sisters who also receive and act upon revelation. Do our narrators recognize their fellow sisters' access to God? Do they respect the choices they make? Are they comfortable with multiple devotions and the complicated equations that result? There is evidence in the histories that they do.

As these women trust in their relationships with God and build personal histories of inspiration and action, they see the potential for such a pattern in other women's lives. Debra feels she knows what God wants for her and supports other women in making the best choices for themselves:

> I always felt a really strong sense of my relationship with God. . . . The bottom line of my experience with being a Mormon woman is that I feel like I have a really strong sense of what God wants me individually to do. So that's really helped me to not feel overly confined by gender roles and Mormonism and also to not feel somehow judgmental about the choices that other women make. To me what matters so much is that women do what they feel is right for them. . . . So to me the bottom line is that women know who they are as individuals and as members of the Church and they make the decisions that they are comfortable with and that are right for them and what will be the most fulfilling for them.[48]

47. Ibid., 14.
48. Ibid., 8.

Debra operates in the space created by personal revelation. She trusts her own decisions and her sisters' choices as well.

Whether to work outside of the home is one of the more publicly observable choices women make, and therefore is one more easily judged by others. At the beginning of this essay, we heard from Julie, a lifetime member of the Church and an author. She declares that prayer creates space for various decisions to be considered:

> Every woman has an individual set of circumstances and should decide for herself what is in the best interest of her family concerning work outside the home. . . . I think every woman has the right to make a prayerful and thoughtful decision. After prayer, counseling with her spouse, listening to the counsel of Church leaders and considering her mental and physical health, each woman has the right to make a choice that is right for her.[49]

Julie feels comfortable supporting decisions made by fellow Church members. She outlines the process she recommends in making those decisions. As her history of personal revelation deepens and her record of agentive behavior expands, she recognizes that fellow travelers also have the capacity to know God's will for themselves.[50] This engenders respect for their motivations, as Church doctrine and culture support both individual revelation and obedience. Though not universal, Julie's attitude is frequently found in the histories.

Conclusion

The Claremont oral histories reveal women who value communication with God and find power in their revelatory relationships. We see women applying Julie Beck's formula to "Qualify for, receive, and act on personal revelation." These women learn the pattern early and as they repeat this process, they build a history that increases self-confidence in their capacity to act. They exercise agency within the context of their religious beliefs.

---

49. COHC, #070 (2010), 5–6.

50. Chieko Okazaki said in general conference: "Let us never judge another. We do not know her circumstances. We do not know what soul-searching went into her decisions. . . . Let us trust the Lord, trust ourselves, and trust each other that we are trying to do the best we can." In "Rowing Your Own Boat," *Ensign*, November 1994, 93.

Conversion to the LDS Church is often in response to revelation, and we see a continued pattern of engaging in dialogue with deity as converts navigate their life choices. These women incorporate answers to prayer in their effort to relinquish power in their lives to God. They express confidence that their fellow female members engage in this same process and trust their choices as well. Belief in personal revelation from God empowers these women to navigate their lives with confidence and negotiate their relationships with authority, enhancing their capacity to act in independent ways. They most often reproduce the social structures they function within, as they support the patriarchal LDS Church rather than challenge these structures.

Removing the lens that sees agency as resistance only, we find that the culture of revelation in the LDS Church empowers women to make choices and creates space for them to act agentively. We better understand LDS women when we recognize that personal revelation is key to their ability to behave as agents in a patriarchal church. The oral histories allow us to listen in on women's conversations with God, providing a rich resource in interpreting their agency and their lives. Perhaps these examples can inform and improve the questions we ask each other. Perhaps they can enrich the questions we ask ourselves.

Chapter Nine

Missions

Elisa Eastwood Pulido

For women who belong to the Church of Jesus Christ of Latter-day Saints, missionary work stands at the epicenter of spiritual experience. In the set of questions used by interviewers for the Claremont Oral History Project, only one dealt specifically with missionary work, yet the words, "mission," "missionary work," and "missionary experience" run as recurrent themes throughout these accounts. Women speak about raising missionaries and being missionaries, and how the injunction "every member a missionary" influences their relations with their friends, their neighbors, their colleagues, and non-Mormon family members. In 1977, LDS Church President Spencer W. Kimball stated,

> Every man, woman, and child—every young person and every little boy and girl . . . is responsible to bear witness of the gospel truths that we have been given. . . . It is our responsibility to pass the truths of the gospel on . . . by example as well as by precept.[1]

This chapter analyzes comments made about missionary work by women who participated in the Claremont Oral History Project, comparing these comments to teachings about missionary work from LDS Church leaders. The chapter examines these comments in light of anthropological theories and feminist thought, and it concludes that Mormon women consider missionary work a personal responsibility, which gives meaning to their lives and the lives of their family members. As will be shown, Mormon women fulfill their missionary obligations by participating in missionary work and by raising children, particularly sons, who willingly serve the LDS Church as full-time missionaries.

---

1. Spencer W. Kimball, "It Becometh Every Man," *Ensign*, October 1977, 3.

The Evangelizing Responsibilities of Mormon Women

In their evangelizing efforts, Mormon women share in an ancient tradition. Acts 18:26 tells us that Priscilla and her husband Aquila taught the gospel to Apollos. Paul, in his epistles to the Romans and Philemon, lists several women as his fellow workers or *sunergos*, including Priscilla (Romans 16:3), Euodia, and Sytyche (Phil. 4:2–3). He also commends Phoebe to the Romans. Phoebe, a servant of the church at Cenchrae, had been Paul's benefactor, and was, perhaps, carrying Paul's letter to them (Romans 16:1–2).[2]

Contemporary LDS women represented in these pages fulfill their responsibility to evangelize by participating in the Church's formal proselytizing efforts as full-time missionaries, through fellowshipping family, friends, and co-workers, through community outreach, by serving short-term local missions, by rearing future missionaries, and by living exemplary lives.

Mormon girls are taught early that even the youngest members can be missionaries by the example they set:

> I'm much too young to go abroad
> To teach and preach the word of God,
> But I can show I know it's true,
> Quite simply by the things I do.[3]

Several women prefer to be good examples rather than actually preaching Mormonism. Maintaining good neighborly relations has always been important to Maude: "I'm not one of those who call on my neighbors purposely to tell them about the Church. I'd rather try to be an example or show charity."[4] When the five-year-old son of Maude's neighbor was run over and killed in front of his house, Maude asked other LDS women to bring food over for the bereaved family:

> One [of the Mormon women] asked whether the people were members of the Church, and I asked if it mattered. I am sure that my

2. Raymond E. Brown, *An Introduction to the New Testament* (New Haven, Conn.: Yale University Press, 2010), 574.

3. L. Clair Likes, "The Things I Do," in *Children's Songbook of The Church of Jesus Christ of Latter-day Saints* (Salt Lake City: The Church of Jesus Christ of Latter-day Saints, 1989), 170–71.

4. Claremont Mormon Women's Oral History Collection, Library of the Claremont Colleges, Claremont, CA, hereafter COHC, #001 (2011), 18.

> neighbors were so distraught that they just welcomed the food and didn't even know that it came from members of our Church. They know that I'm a Mormon.[5]

Connie never mentions the Church to people of other faiths. "I am of the feeling that we want to be missionaries by being good friends and not by trying to convert people. I try to be competent, cheerful, and dependable."[6] Mormon leaders encourage this soft approach along with bolder methods. Mormon Apostle, Jeffrey R. Holland, says that, "Asking every member to be a missionary is not nearly as crucial as asking every member to be a member!"[7]

Still, many of these women feel a duty to let others know what they believe. They look for opportunities to discuss Mormonism by offering to pray for friends in need, by handing out printed Church materials, and by using the significant events in their lives as moments for teaching others about LDS doctrine. The funeral of one woman's husband was his big missionary moment. During the service she shared what she says was most important to her husband—his testimony of Mormonism.[8]

Laurie invites questions about her beliefs by being open about her church activity. When people asked her what she did over the weekend, "I would tell [my colleagues] I was going to church."[9] On one occasion she put the name of a colleague with cancer on the Mormon temple prayer roll. "He was really appreciative. . . . It also gave me the opportunity to share the gospel with him."[10]

Only rarely do the women report that a friend or neighbor joined the Church. Sometimes these proselytizing efforts go well, sometimes not; but, regardless of the outcome, most of these women feel that participating in missionary work is a personal obligation.

---

5. Ibid., 19.
6. COHC, #012 (2011), 35.
7. Jeffrey R. Holland, March 31, 2001, in *Report of the Annual Conference of the Church of Jesus Christ of Latter-day Saints* (Salt Lake City: Church of Jesus Christ of Latter-day Saints, annual), 16, hereafter *Conference Report.*
8. COHC, #031 (2011).
9. COHC, #036 (2011), 12.
10. Ibid.

Evangelizing the Broader Community

For Mormon women, the duty to evangelize extends beyond the circle of family, friends, and colleagues. A few women have used their positions of influence to further Church work in their communities. Though not official representatives of the Church, they feel their interaction with the public results in greater tolerance of and interest in Mormonism. Sarah gives organ recitals on Temple Square in Salt Lake City. After recitals, she interacts with the audience:

> Recently I talked to a family group in town for the Unitarian convention. One of them asked about the new scriptures that we have, the "gold plates" . . . I gave them my most positive, most faith-affirming description of the coming forth of the Book of Mormon.[11]

Holly moved to the Marshall Islands in 1973, after her husband accepted a governmental position. While there, she worked at building the Relief Society, the LDS women's auxiliary:

> There were five [women] who had been baptized. . . . I asked them what they would like to do in Relief Society. They told me they would like to learn to cook. . . . So every Monday night until Thanksgiving I had about 20 members and their friends [come] to my home to cook American food. . . . We finished by cooking two large turkeys with all the trimmings. . . . We had about 55 women in Relief Society each Sunday. . . . Entire families joined, and no one went inactive that entire year. . . . If you listen to what the people want to learn, and try to meet their needs as they see them, they will flock to the Church.[12]

Some of these women have gone with their husbands on short-term, specialized missions, such as humanitarian, performance, and Church Education System missions. Angela, serving as a Public Affairs missionary after 9/11, reported the tremendous friendships she made with Muslims:

> The head of half a million Muslims . . . [came] to our home because he wanted to know how our church is organized. . . . We've been to . . . Ramadan several times. . . . He invited us to his interfaith group this last week where he had six different religions talk about their views

11. COHC, #005 (2011), 27.
12. COHC, #051 (2011), 28–29.

> of motherhood.... I read the statement on motherhood from the First Presidency.... [T]hen I told them about the [LDS] Proclamation on the Family and there were some who wanted copies.[13]

Creativity and dedication in secular and church assignments have led to connections not normally made by the Church. Despite these successful efforts, neither of the two women quoted above believed that they had "gone on missions" for the Church, because they had not been full-time evangelizing missionaries.

Full-time Missionary Services

In cultures all over the world, rites of passage mark transitions to new stages of existence, such as marriage or coming of age. Initiates are generally deprived of their names, secular clothing, and property—maintaining a "sacred poverty."[14] Frequently, rites of passage prepare initiates for future sacred duties.[15] Mythologist Joseph Campbell sees similarities between rites of passage and the mythological adventures of heroes. At the beginning of their adventures, heroes typically retreat from the known world to a realm where they find a resolution to personal conflicts and fears. In the second phase of his journey, the hero proves merit, resists evil, and "learns the secrets of the gods." In the final phase, the hero returns, "transfigured, [to] teach the lesson ... learned [and] ... to make a difference in the everyday world."[16] As it was for Gilgamesh, a hero's goal will often be to find the key to eternal life.

Following this anthropological model for rites of passage, young Mormon missionaries leave home with few possessions, drop their first names in favor of "Elder" or "Sister," dress in a uniform manner, undergo initiation rites in Mormon temples, and work hard to bring their sacred words to strangers. They return home to function as spiritual elders in their Mormon tribe. The symbolism of the hero's path appears clearly in the following two narratives, told by women about their fathers. Heidi's

13. COHC, #002 (2011), 6.

14. Victor Turner, *The Forest of Symbols: Aspects of Ndembu Ritual* (Ithaca: Cornell University Press, 1967), 93–111.

15. Eva M. Thury and Margaret K. Devinney, *Introduction to Mythology: Contemporary Approaches to Classical and World Myths* (New York: Oxford University Press, 2005), 381.

16. Ibid., 137.

father brought the literal bread of life to LDS members in Germany, and Glenda's brought the word of life to the Maori in New Zealand. They returned home to share their enthusiasm with their families:

> My father had served a mission in New Zealand for five years.... He helped Matthew Cowley translate the Book of Mormon to the Maori language. A true believer and a reader of the scriptures, he spoke to me of Jesus and the importance of prayer and we read [together] from the ... Bible.[17]

Glenda's father worked with Matthew Cowley, a famed Mormon missionary in New Zealand, who later became a Church apostle. Cowley helped to give Mormon scripture to the Maori in their own language—and in Glenda's eyes, that made him a heroic figure.

Heidi tells her father's story:

> My father ... went on a mission ... [to] Germany ... about 1920 and he tells of the terrible inflation. ... [The members] were just starving and so he asked the branch president what they could do ... [The branch president] said, well, if we just had a little bread and lard. So [my father] and his missionary companion put in $5 each and with that $10 they were able to buy a whole bakery. ... They brought all this bread and lard to the branch [of the church].[18]

Though Heidi's account focuses on feeding starving German Mormons with actual bread, rather than spiritual manna, the story follows the New Testament pattern where Jesus fed multitudes with very few resources. Like Jesus, this woman's father is a compassionate being who cares for his beleaguered flock. Both missionary fathers mentioned above were salvific heroes in the eyes of their daughters. As enlightened figures and missionaries, they brought spiritual knowledge, wisdom, and practical relief to the people they taught.

Mormons view full-time missionary service as a consecration of time and labor with potent benefits for the missionary, his family, and his

17. COHC, #065 (2011), 2. Matthew Cowley did not translate the Book of Mormon into Maori, but edited the translation. He did, however, translate the Doctrine and Covenants and the Pearl of Great Price, also scriptures in the Mormon canon, into the native New Zealand language. Heidi's father most likely helped Cowley edit the Book of Mormon in Maori. See Lawrence R. Flake, *Prophets and Apostles of the Last Dispensation* (Provo, Utah: Religious Studies Center, Brigham Young University, 2001), 481–83.

18. COHC, #002 (2011), 2.

future family. At the Church's October 2008 General Conference, Silvia Allred, first counselor in the General Relief Society Presidency, stated,

> Missionary work is the lifeblood of the Church. There is no greater work, no more important work. It blesses the lives of all those who participate in it. It will continue blessing future generations.[19]

These sentiments are echoed in the oral histories. For example, Nancy recalls:

> My own father did not want to go, but the mission changed his life. It also changed the lives of everyone in his immediate family and his descendants. Young people should be encouraged to go.[20]

A mission completed by any family member becomes a notable event in the collective family history; litanies of relatives who were missionaries figure in the oral history narratives as a kind of spiritual genealogy. Some of the women begin their histories by indicating which of their ancestors and descendants went on missions, both male and female, blood relations and in-laws (indicating one can marry into a missionary heritage). Jan listed missionary service along with other weighty achievements, such as marriage and education:

> We've been so richly blessed in our children. They all served missions. They all married in the temple. They all graduated with advanced degrees. They have all grown to be faithful, capable, productive and wise adults and excellent parents and have given us twenty-seven outstanding grandchildren and to date, twenty-one great grandchildren! Their service in the Church and the community has been and continues to be exemplary. I could not have wished for a better life than this.[21]

In addition to the spiritual blessings received by families of missionaries, these women believe a missionary's family is also *materially* blessed, such as when needed funds are miraculously found. When Paulette's son received his mission call to the Czech Republic, "a generous donor from his work bought all his clothes . . . my brother helped pay monthly mission costs and all the appliances ran smoothly for two years."[22]

19. Silvia Allred, *Conference Report*, October 4, 2008, 9.
20. COHC, #005 (2011), 27.
21. COHC, #003 (2011), 21.
22. COHC, #069 (2011), 9.

One final indicator of the value placed on full-time missionary service, is the significance the title *returned missionary* plays in the selection of husbands. Parents of eligible women, and the women themselves, perceive completed missionary service as a preeminent indicator of eligibility for prospective husbands. Sometimes that's the only characteristic that matters.

Mormon Women as Full-time Missionaries

Because LDS women are not ordained to priesthood offices, their pre-mission preparation differs from that of young males. The fifth Article of Faith reads:

> We believe that a man must be called of God, by prophecy, and by the laying on of hands by those who are in authority, to preach the Gospel and administer in the ordinances thereof.

Young men serving missions are invariably ordained to the office of elder before departing on their missions. Young women, though not ordained to any priesthood and unable to administer ordinances such as baptism and confirmation, are called by prophecy and are blessed to go on proselytizing missions around the globe, just as young men are.[23] Mission calls to male and female missionaries come from the First Presidency of the Mormon Church.

Mormon women have long been involved in missionary work. Lucy Mack Smith, Joseph Smith's mother, preached Mormonism's message as she and other members of the Church relocated from New York to Kirtland, Ohio.[24] The first "single, official, proselytizing lady missionaries in the Church," Inez Knight and Lucy Jane (Jennie) Brimhall, were blessed by Church leaders before going on missions on April 1, 1898, in Provo, Utah.[25] Jessie Embry writes that

> Until 1898, women were not encouraged to go on missions. Following the Victorian ideal, Mormon Church leaders expected

23. Jessie L. Embry, "Oral History and Mormon Women Missionaries: The Stories Sound the Same," *Frontiers: A Journal of Women Studies* 19, no. 3 (1998), 173.

24. Lucy Mack Smith, *History of Joseph Smith by His Mother, Lucy Mack Smith*, ed. R. Vernon Ingleton (Arlington: Stratford Books, 2005), 293, 297–98.

25. Diane L. Mangum, "The First Sister Missionaries," *Ensign*, July 1980, 61.

them to marry, have children, and care for their families. Teaching the gospel was seen as a male responsibility.[26]

Though women were not officially encouraged to go on missions, over two hundred women participated in non-proselytizing missionary activity prior to 1898.[27] Some women traveled to the Hawaiian Islands with their missionary husbands. Others were called as missionaries before traveling abroad or going to study at universities.[28]

The LDS Church has revised minimum age requirements for missionary service several times, though the minimum age requirement for men has always been lower than that for women. In 1915, the Church put out a call for female missionaries who were "not too young."[29] In 1960, the minimum age requirement for male missionaries was lowered to nineteen. In 1964, the minimum age requirement for female missionaries was lowered from twenty-three to twenty-one years of age. These minimum age standards remained constant for several decades.[30] In October 2012, the First Presidency of the Church issued a policy change which lowered the minimum age requirement for men to eighteen years of age and the minimum age requirement for women to nineteen. The object of this change was to increase the number of Mormon missionaries evangelizing worldwide.[31]

Missions for Mormon women have also varied in kind and length over the past one hundred years. In 1915, the Church actively sought female stenographers to go one missions.[32] One participant in the oral

26. Embry, "Oral History and Mormon Women Missionaries," 171–88.

27. Calvin S. Kunz, "A History of Female Missionary Activity in the Church of Jesus Christ of Latter-day Saints, 1830–1898" (MA thesis, Brigham Young University, 1976), 40–54.

28. Mangum, "The First Sister Missionaries," 61–62.

29. "First Presidency to Serge F. Ballif, January 20, 1915," in James R. Clark, *Messages of the First Presidency* 4 (1901–1915), 335.

30. "First Presidency to Presidents of Stakes and Bishops, June 28, 1960," First Presidency Circular Letters, LDS Church History Library. "First Presidency to Mission Presidents, Presidents of Stakes, and Bishops, February 12, 1964," First Presidency Circular Letters, LDS Church History Library.

31. "Church Lowers Missionary Service Age," LDS Newsroom, October 6, 2012, http://www.mormonnewsroom.org/article/church-lowers-age-requirement-for-missionary-service (accessed December 14, 2012).

32. "First Presidency to Serge F. Ballif, January 20, 1915."

history project went on a "stenography" mission in 1946.[33] During WWII, the only women allowed on missions were stenographers, summer school teachers, or wives accompanying husbands too old to be drafted.[34] In 1971, missions for women were reduced to eighteen months.[35] In 1990, welfare missions were organized. In recent decades, Mormon women have gone on many varieties of proselytizing missions, service missions, and humanitarian missions.[36]

LDS Female Missionary Service, a Tradition of Optionality

Anthropologist Victor Turner's word "liminoid" describes optionality in terms of liminal or threshold experiences. He uses "liminoid" to describe rites of passage and other rituals mandated in primal societies, but voluntary in complex, industrial societies: marriage, seasonal pageants, and attendance at worship services are now liminoid or optional.[37] The term *liminoid* can also be defined as "quasi-liminal."[38] As the LDS Church continues to expect missionary service from young men, a mission remains a *liminal* experience for young males. Attitudes among Church leaders about females serving as full-time missionaries have fluctuated over the years. In 1981, Spencer W. Kimball said:

> Many young women have a desire to serve a full-time mission, and they are also welcome in the Lord's service. This responsibility is not on them as it is on the elders, but they will receive rich blessings for their unselfish sacrifice.[39]

A 1997 statement regarding female missionary service made by President Gordon B. Hinckley seems cooler: "Young women should

33. Embry, "Oral History and Mormon Women Missionaries," 173; COHC #092 (2011).

34. Embry, "Oral History and Mormon Women Missionaries," 173.

35. Ibid, 174.

36. Neil K. Newell and Lloyd D. Newell, "The Power of Compassion," *Ensign*, December 2002, 22.

37. Victor Turner, *On the Edge of the Bush: Anthropology as Experience* (Tucson: University of Arizona Press, 1985), 160–61, 235–36.

38. Mathieu Defiem, "Ritual, Anti-Structure and Religion: A Discussion of Victor Turner's Processual Symbolic Analysis," *Journal for the Scientific Study of Religion*, Vol 30, no. 1 (1991): 1–25.

39. Spencer W. Kimball, *President Kimball Speaks Out* (Salt Lake City: Deseret Book Co., 1981), 30.

counsel with their bishops as well as their parents. If the idea persists, the bishop will know what to do."[40] In the same address, Hinckley stated that the Church needed "some" young women on missions, but that missionary work

> Is essentially a priesthood responsibility. As such our young men must carry the major burden. . . .
>
> To the sisters I say that you will be as highly respected, you will be considered as being as much in the line of duty, your efforts will be as acceptable to the Lord and to the Church whether you go on a mission or do not go on a mission.[41]

Four years later, the First Presidency advised bishops that they "should not recommend [single women twenty-one and older] for missionary service if it will interfere with imminent marriage prospects."[42] President Thomas S. Monson recently issued more encouraging counsel to young adult women wishing to be missionaries:

> While you do not have the same priesthood responsibility as do the young men to serve as full-time missionaries, you also make a valuable contribution as missionaries, and we welcome your service.[43]

The "liminoid," or optional, nature of full-time missionary service as a rite of passage for young Mormon women is well-documented in the variety of attitudes found in the Claremont Oral History Project. At least one woman reported never having felt an inclination to go on a mission.[44] Another woman said she was shocked when her daughter decided to be a missionary. By contrast, at least one woman, Katy, felt that all women needed to go:

> I'm tired of hearing from the pulpit how important it is that all our young men serve missions. I think that girls need to do this too! Mine has, and she is stronger for it. Why do we feel that just boys need that experience? I think it's wonderful for [whoever] wants to do it.[45]

---

40. Gordon B. Hinckley, *Conference Report*, October 4, 1997, 73.

41. Ibid.

42. Richard G. Scott, *Conference Report*, April 2, 2006, 91. Scott cites an unpublished communication from the First Presidency of the Church.

43. Thomas S. Monson, *Conference Report*, October 2, 2010, 3.

44. COHC, #036 (2011), 12.

45. COHC, #007 (2011), 21.

In 1998, Jessie L. Embry wrote that the evolution of Church policy has resulted in fewer Mormon women going on missions than Mormon men, and that "when the First Presidency has asked for more missionaries, they have usually requested men."[46] It appears this trend has recently changed. In the first two weeks after the First Presidency's October 2012 announcement lowering the minimum age requirement for female missionaries to nineteen, missionary applications increased from 700 per week to 4,000 per week, with just over half of the applications coming from women.[47] Church officials appear to be pleased with the increase in the number of females applying to go on missions. Apostle Jeffrey R. Holland stated that though it is not an obligation for women to go on missions, "those who do serve are stunningly successful" and that their service is "enthusiastically" welcomed. Holland also stated that he would be "absolutely delighted if this change in policy allows many, many more young women to serve."[48]

Undoubtedly the lowering of the minimum age for female missionary service will be reflected in the lives of future oral history participants and will provide opportunities for further research into the intersection of Mormon women and missions.

Varieties of Female Missionary Experience

Though women's mission experiences vary, all of these missionaries reported challenges and frustrations and agreed that their missions were difficult. Sometimes they juxtapose conflicting emotions in consecutive sentences: "I loved my mission. It was really hard."[49]

Women who served missions reported disappointment over low retention rates, challenging assignments, misunderstandings with young priesthood mission leaders, primitive living conditions, and health challenges. Low conversion rates and especially recidivism presented grave disappointment.

---

46. Jessie L. Embry, "Oral History and Mormon Women Missionaries," 173–74.

47. Lyman Kirkland, "Church Statement Regarding Increase in Missionary Service Interest," The Newsroom Blog, October 23, 2012, http://www.mormonnewsroom.org/article/church-statement--announcement-leads-to-significant-increase-in-missionary-applications (accessed December 14, 2012).

48. Kirkland, "Church Lowers Missionary Service Age."

49. COHC, #063 (2011), 6.

Some women reported difficulty working with male leaders. Although the missionary handbook of instructions directs young missionaries not to catechize investigators of the opposite sex, Elaine got little support from young elders in her attempts to keep this rule:

> I was afraid [our investigator] was having romantic notions about . . . the sister missionaries. We had begged the elders to teach him. They wouldn't do it because they said that he lived too far away. They had given [us] a tracting area, which was way out of town amongst the farms. . . . That investigator did end up coming to the United States and marrying my [missionary] companion.[50]

In contrast, Geraldine was made the district leader over a small group of female missionaries assigned to a given locality. She reported that the "sister missionaries" were often in competition with the male missionaries, but that they were able to alleviate competitive tension by including young male missionaries in their successes:

> We would teach the lessons, and then we would have the elders come in and give the last lesson. So they were always part of it. We worked together very well. We had lots of baptisms.[51]

Some women experienced significant health problems on their missions. Lauren relates that, "The hardest experience on my mission was when I got malaria. . . . I think out of the group that was there, six of us had malaria before we were through."[52] Later, working with her husband, a mission president in South America, her health was "absolutely terrible. I completely lost my hearing. I got a lung disease down there too. [My husband] had a heart attack, and that ended it."[53] Lauren might have had a negative view toward missionary work, but she is actually very positive. When asked about her experiences as a missionary, she answered:

> Oh, wonderful, don't you agree? There is no other thing quite as wonderful. I'm so glad [one daughter] studied one summer in Spain and became the first sister missionary in Spain; [another daughter] served in Switzerland; [my son] served in Japan; and [another daughter] is now serving in the Church Family History Library.[54]

---

50. COHC, #022 (2011), 11.
51. COHC, #073 (2011), 3–4.
52. COHC, #092 (2011), 5.
53. Ibid., 12.
54. Ibid., 12.

Participants who were missionaries speak of satisfaction in overcoming obstacles in the mission field. They view missions as a chance to emulate the itinerant service of Jesus—a challenge Christian women have accepted for over two millennia. For Mormon women, sharing the spiritual gifts that missionaries are perceived to possess is their moment of greatest authority in the Church. While these women do not claim to have functioned as priesthood holders in the Church, they do claim to have been enlightened.

Missionary Children

A primary song often sung by Mormon children three to twelve years of age teaches them this Mormon imperative—they must obey God's will and become the Lord's missionaries. It also lays the responsibility for raising and teaching these young missionaries at the feet of their parents—specifically at the feet of their mothers:

> We have been born, as Nephi of old,
> To goodly parents who love the Lord.
> We have been taught, and we understand,
> That we must do as the Lord commands.
> We are as the army of Helaman,
> We have been taught in our youth.
> And we will be the Lord's missionaries
> To bring the world his truth.[55]

These children's verses refer to a body of valiant, young warriors mentioned in the Book of Mormon, who "had been taught by their mothers, that if they did not doubt, God would deliver them."[56]

Mormon women do hold themselves personally responsible for raising sons who will choose to go on and complete missions. Interestingly, no female narrator has yet attributed a son's lack of missionary service to a weak or unsupportive father. The responsibility to raise missionaries is communicated to women through scripture, song, and the speeches of Church leaders, who emphasize the power and influence of Mormon mothers. In May of 2003, at a Brigham Young

55. Janice Kapp Perry, "We'll Bring the World His Truth," in *Children's Songbook* (Salt Lake City: The Church of Jesus Christ of Latter-day Saints, 1989), 172–73.

56. Alma 56:47.

University Women's Conference, Mormon apostle M. Russell Ballard outlined the steps it takes to raise faithful missionaries, telling the women in attendance: "You have an irreplaceable and an unparalleled influence with our children and youth because you have such a natural propensity for the things of the Spirit."[57] In an October 2007 General Conference address, Julie Beck, then General President of the Relief Society in an address entitled "Mothers Who Know" said that despite trying economic circumstances

> Mothers who know . . . bring daughters [to church] in clean and ironed dresses with hair brushed to perfection; their sons wear white shirts and ties and have missionary haircuts. . . .
>
> Mothers who know . . . plan for missions, temple marriages, and education. They plan for prayer, scripture study, and family home evening. . . .
>
> Think of the power of our future missionary force if mothers considered their homes as a pre–missionary training center. Then the doctrines of the gospel taught in the MTC would be a review and not a revelation. That is influence; that is power.[58]

As can be seen, mothers in the LDS Church are thought to have a powerful influence in their children's spiritual lives, due to a belief in the natural inclination of women for spiritual matters. Whether or not a boy embarks on missionary service for the Church is therefore seen to rest, to a large degree, on the efforts of his mother to train and prepare him to be a future missionary.

The emotions of Mormon mothers who successfully bring a worthy child to the threshold of the missionary experience can only be described as ecstatic, for while two years of missionary service is the goal for all nineteen to twenty-six-year-old males, not all go. Joanna asked her stake president

> why I was such a baby when I sent my sons on missions. I said that I'm either going through the changes of life or I'm really feeling the Spirit. He said that I was feeling the Spirit . . . I do believe that was what it was. (It might have been the other one too!) It was so joyful

57. M. Russell Ballard, "Raising the Greatest Generation of Missionaries," Paper presented at Brigham Young University's annual Women's Conference, Provo, Utah 2003, 2. Available at http://ce.byu.edu/cw/womensconference/archive/2003/ElderMRussellBallard.pdf (accessed August 29, 2012).

58. Julie B. Beck, *Conference Report*, October 7, 2007, 80–81.

> to send sons off on missions and to know that they were worthy to go and that they wanted to go and were prepared to go. I knew that I had done my job.[59]

While successful parenting is thought to bring young men into missionary service, mothers include the personal growth their sons made while missionaries as one of the incentives for sending them:

> I've really grown to appreciate what a mission does to create life for the missionary, not to create converts. There are more effective ways for that. I appreciate what it has done for our daughter and the difference it made for [my husband].[60]

Women listed increased maturity, the ability to accept responsibility, experience in foreign lands, and the ability to speak foreign languages among the benefits of missionary service.

Recipes for Success

Many sacrifices are made in Mormon families to ensure children will be able to complete missions. Mothers go to work. Families scrimp and save. Missionary funds are started for toddlers. Strictures are also imposed on lifestyle to ensure that missionaries reach the front. Many families feel they developed a pattern for living, which made missionaries out of their children. Marla lays out the disciplined structure that produced missionaries in her home:

> We immersed ourselves in the Gospel. We never watched regular TV prior to church. After church we would watch selected Disney movies. Watching the kids grow up was really a testimony to that recipe. . . . It just felt right, I felt inspired. It was something I did because I wanted my kids to stay innocent and sheltered. I really worked hard on that and censored what they took in both with their temporal and spiritual food.[61]

Inez praises the formula that made missionaries out of all of her grandchildren:

---

59. COHC, #014 (2011), 11–12.
60. COHC, #062 (2011), 21.
61. COHC, #021 (2011), 13.

> They've all been on missions; they all are lovely, wonderful kids. They follow all the pattern . . . family home evening, scriptures morning and night, family prayer every night and morning.[62]

Serena remembers that in her family, "it was not 'if' you go on your mission, it's 'when' you go on your mission. . . . It was always expected."[63]

Other parents want the decision to go on a mission to belong to their sons. Elizabeth and her husband wanted to have a more hands-off approach, assuring that their son would go on a mission because he wanted to, and not because he felt coerced:

> [My husband] and I always made it clear to [my son] that we wanted him to serve a mission, but in the last few years, we feel that it was really his decision to go and he was responsible for doing his own personal preparation. We never had to try to make that decision for him. He got there for the right reasons.[64]

A Source of Anxiety: Children Outside the Missionary Pattern

Raising children according to a prescribed pattern does not guarantee success. The children of some active Mormon parents choose not to go on missions, even as children from some inactive, or part-member families, choose to go on missions. While only one mother regretted that a daughter chose not to go on a mission, both mothers and grandmothers report a great deal of anxiety over sons and grandsons who refuse to go on missions, are sent home from a mission, or who choose to leave the Church after completing a mission. They wonder where they failed in rearing these children. Sometimes they blame the Church. For example, Charity complains that in the last decade, worthiness standards for young missionaries have been raised. In her opinion, the change "left a lot of kids out who will just go farther away if they are considered not worthy to go on a mission."[65]

In addition to mothers, other congregational members are responsible for preparing young men for missions. The bishop and his counselors, who lead local congregations, have a direct responsibility

62. COHC, #032 (2011), 10.
63. COHC, #037 (2011), 22.
64. COHC, #019 (2011), 10.
65. COHC, #060 (2011), 17.

to mentor youth, particularly young men.[66] One mother feels that ward leaders let her son down:

> The bishop was out of town and the second counselor came in and grabbed [my son] by the back of the shirt, pulled him away from the sacrament table and out into the hall and told him that he was not worthy to bless the sacrament and he could never do it again until he cut his hair. . . . He never blessed the sacrament again. He went back to high school and decided that if he wasn't worthy, he might just as well try some of these other things. . . . Now, I think that's terrible priesthood leadership. At that time, you didn't go in and volunteer for a mission, the bishop called you. The bishop wasn't available that whole year, and so [my son] was never called to go on a mission. So I feel that the Church let my son down in that case. I'm sure it was extreme, but they did nothing to correct it.[67]

Only one participant reports having a rebellious son who was helped by concerned members and who subsequently went on a mission.[68] Most often, mothers blame themselves for a child's failure to go on a mission. Camilla recalls:

> Our oldest two sons served missions for the Church. Our youngest son chose a different path . . . I look back and wonder what . . . made him decide he no longer wanted to attend church. . . . I made a big mistake. I forced him to go to a youth conference one weekend. . . . I was wrong—wrong . . . to force him to go. I seriously regret my actions and wish I could go back and do it differently for him. So maybe I was the one who turned him away from the Church, I don't know.[69]

This mother is still haunted by the forced activity of one weekend. She believes that her son's decision to become inactive in the Church hinged on that single event.

Mormon prophet, David O. McKay taught that, "No other success can compensate for failure in the home."[70] The failure to send one's son on a mission is viewed by several of these participants as that kind

---

66. The Church of Jesus of Christ of Latter-day Saints, *Handbook 2: Administering the Church* (Salt Lake City: Church of Jesus Christ of Latter-day Saints, 2010), 55.

67. COHC, #015 (2011), 20.

68. COHC, #018 (2011), 35.

69. COHC, #053 (2011), 22.

70. David O. McKay, *Conference Report*, April 1935, 116.

of failure. Many carry a heavy emotional burden when their hopes for their son are dashed by the refusal of that son to go on a mission. Dee describes how she managed to come to terms with that disappointment:

> Two of my sons chose to leave the Church as young adults. One turned his back on the Church six months after he returned from his mission, where he had served as Assistant to the President and baptized over fifty people. Then, within a couple of years, my youngest son decided not to go on a mission and has been inactive ever since. . . . Mormon mothers feel they've failed when their children reject what they've been taught. It's a heavy burden I struggled with for a long time. I've come to peace with it, however. I did the best I could raising them and my role now is to maintain a relationship with them that makes them feel loved and valued. I feel better having come to that position. . . . I find it's not productive to dwell on the negatives.[71]

Dee focuses on what she can do in the present to improve her relationships with her children. She does not rethink past decisions.

After years of reflection, Jean also managed to separate her feelings about the quality of her parenting from her children's mission decisions:

> I just always assumed that my son would serve a mission. . . . As [our son] grew up and went through high school, I began to realize that this might not happen. . . . He always came to church with us, but the minute he left home for college he stopped going. At one point I did pointedly ask him if he was going to go on a mission and the answer was "No." That was hard to take from a personal perspective. In some ways I felt that I had failed as a mother. As the years went on I just assumed that none of our children would serve missions.[72]

Jean states that she eventually realized that her son's decision "had no bearing on whether [she] was a good mother or not, and a mission might not be for everyone."[73]

Elaine, who was in danger of miscarrying, promised God that if she could bring her pregnancy to full term, she would raise her son to serve God, a promise that, of course, included a full-time mission in her child's future:

---

71. COHC, #052 (2011), 12–13.
72. COHC, #058 (2011), 20.
73. Ibid., 20.

> I was extremely dedicated to my parenting. We had family home evening and family council, and prayers morning and night. We never missed a church meeting. . . . I lost count of the times . . . [we] read the Book of Mormon completely through with our children. My sons graduated from seminary. They were both Eagle Scouts. . . . The eldest . . . kept a picture of the Savior in his locker at school. I passed his room every night on my way to bed. He was always on his knees with his Book of Mormon in front of him. We sent my son away to college, and the unthinkable happened—he left the Church. I agonized for quite some time. I had promised the Lord a profitable servant, and I failed. . . . In my despair I offered God my life if He would just bring my son back. The answer was immediate: That has already been done, thank you.
>
> It has taken ten years, but I have come to realize that in my arrogance, I thought I could raise a perfect child, and when that didn't work, I thought I could atone for him! I had no right to promise God a profitable servant at all. I could only promise to raise my son the best I knew how. In God's plan, children retain their agency.[74]

This mother is now able to laugh at the "godlike" expectations she had, not only for her own parenting, but for her son's behavior as well. Nevertheless, the maternal anxiety and self-blame that accompany a son's refusal to go on a mission haunt many Mormon women years after the event. A few manage to "forgive" themselves, crediting the children's own right to choose whether or not to become missionaries.

Conclusion

Women in the Church see missions and missionary work at the epicenter of Mormon religious experience. They evangelize themselves as well as raise missionaries. Those who have gone on full-time missions see their missions as spiritual offerings, and report tremendous satisfaction with the experience. Despite risks and complications involved in their service, they regard their missions as time well spent. Female missionaries participate in the transformational powers of the liminal missionary experience, and, for a while, share in the authority of the evangelizers.

Mormon women see the rearing of missionary children, especially sons, as one of their primary responsibilities. The continuation of the Church, in the absence of other formal ministerial training, necessi-

74. COHC, #022 (2011), 31.

tates participation in full-time missionary service for males, who will become future leaders. Mothers participate in the training of clergy by preparing and sending sons on missions, and the failure to do so is acutely felt. Because of familial investment in the outcomes of missionary service, it is possible Mormon mothers may never be able to separate themselves from either the pride or the pain of their children's decisions with regard to missionary service.

Perhaps feminist theologian Rosemary Radford Ruether has some good advice for Mormon mothers on the topic of parenting children who will hopefully participate in God's work one day:

> We need a different model of divine parenting, based not on domination and dependency, but on wise nurture that guides those who are dependent, as weak or wounded persons into graduate adulthood where they are able to enter into reciprocal and responsible relationships with each other. . . . God does not create in a way that crushes our freedom. God grounds our finite freedom and presents to us free choices of good possibilities. God strengthens us against our own failures to live up to this potential. . . . Both humans and God are reciprocal partners in building a redeemed earth. God cannot redeem the world apart from our free and loving response to God, which is, simultaneously, a choice to love and support one another.[75]

The model of divine parenting suggested here by Ruether is one that mirrors Mormon teachings about God's design for humans and doctrines about human "agency" or freedom of choice. Many Mormon women want to partner with God in building a redeemed world by participating in missionary service. They also hope their children will choose to partner with God in building a redeemed earth—by serving as missionaries around the globe. However, as Reuther states, our redemption as human beings rests as much on our free response to God as it does on God's efforts to help us live up to our human potential. While few Mormon mothers reported freedom crushing behaviors, the choices their children make need to be viewed as free responses those children make to God, apart from their mothers' efforts to help them achieve a spiritual potential.

---

75. Rosemary Radford Ruether, "Feminist Critique and the Re-visioning of God-Language," in *Mormonism in Dialogue with Contemporary Christian Theologies*, ed. Donald W. Musser and David Paulsen (Macon, Ga.: Mercer University Press, 2007), 274.

Part Three

Relationships with the Institutional Church

Chapter Ten

Agency

Amy Hoyt

Introduction

Feminist theory is one of the most important academic trends in the twentieth century and has been incredibly influential. Within religious studies, it is virtually impossible to study women without using feminist theory.[1] Feminist theory has usually portrayed traditional religious women in America (often referred to as "conservative" religious women) as either oppressed or working from within their religion to subvert it. This inclination is due to the fact that contemporary Western feminism is culturally bound to American and European political notions.

The tendency for feminist scholars of religion to measure traditional religious women against liberative norms comes out of the inheritance of liberal feminism within the United States and Europe. Beginning in Europe during the eighteenth century (with Mary Wollstonecraft's publication of *A Vindication of the Rights of Women*) and continuing in the nineteenth and twentieth centuries in America (with the abolition and suffrage movements), what has been called the first-wave of American feminism was a liberative form of feminism—based upon European and American understandings of legal rights, equality, and freedom.[2]

---

1. Marilyn Strathern, *The Gender of the Gift* (Berkeley: University of California Press, 1988). Strathern noted that anthropology has had similar challenges and that a myth has come to exist within the field that there was no prior study of women except by feminist theory. She challenges this and demonstrates that anthropologists were studying women without a feminist analytic prior to the second wave of the American women's movement, which was eventually incorporated into the academy in the form of women's studies programs.

2. Rosemary Tong, *Feminist Thought: A Comprehensive Introduction* (Boulder: Westview Press, 1989); Sheila Ruth, ed., *Issues in Feminism* (Mountain View,

The goals and values of liberal feminism were naturally taken from the goals and values of European and American political categories and were based upon a liberal, human subject—one that was an autonomous, free individual, who was capable of making independent decisions.[3]

During the second wave of American feminism, liberal political goals once again figured prominently within the women's movement as feminists worked in the Civil Rights movement and for the passage of the long-proposed Equal Rights Amendment.[4] Liberal feminism has enjoyed particular influence over most types of feminisms because most other feminisms have replicated its commitment to the liberal human subject. Even those feminisms that trace their roots to post-structuralism have adopted liberal tendencies.[5]

The liberal influence within feminist theory has led to an emphasis on the feminist theoretical category of agency because it has been typically understood to demonstrate freedom. Within feminist theory, agency has been debated for years. While the debate has taken many forms, feminist scholars have rarely questioned an underlying premise: that agency is demonstrated through the resistance of norms. Since resistance has been equated with agency, women's acts that sustain traditional religions are not viewed as constituting agency. In other words, women in traditional religions can only exhibit agency when they are rebelling against their traditions.[6] This has resulted in a host of research that looks at various ways that women resist, rebel, and subvert their traditions and has left those religious behaviors that sustain, support, and propel patriarchal religions largely unexamined.

In order to work through some of the problematics of the feminist theoretical category of agency, particularly when applied to the lives

---

Calif.: Mayfield Publishing, 1995), 445–51.

3. Wendy Brown, *Politics out of History* (New Jersey: Princeton University Press, 2001).

4. The ERA was first proposed in 1923. For an alternate history based upon the work of women see Kim Blankenship and Anne Bezdek, "Rediscovering American Women: A Chronology Highlighting Women's History in the United States," in *Issues in Feminism*, ed. Sheila Ruth (Mountain View, Calif.: Mayfield, 1995), 455–69.

5. Saba Mahmood, *Politics of Piety* (New Jersey: Princeton University Press, 2005).

6. See Mahmood, *Politics of Piety*; also Pamela E. Klassen, *Blessed Events: Religion and Home Birth in America* (New Jersey: Princeton University Press, 2001); Mary Keller, *The Hammer and the Flute: Women, Power and Spirit Possession* (Baltimore: The Johns Hopkins University Press, 2002).

of traditional religious women, I conducted an ethnographic study of American women in the Church of Jesus Christ of Latter-day Saints.[7] One of the purposes of ethnography is to test the adequacy of theory for explaining human actions. Examining the feminist theoretical idea of agency is necessary because theories of agency that are based solely on resistance are inadequate to explain the practices and behaviors of the women who participated in the study. Latter-day Saint women offer an interesting framework in which to examine agency because they adhere to an unapologetically patriarchal religion and the category of agency is an indigenous concept (although there are some key differences between the LDS view of agency and the way in which the term is generally used in feminist writings). This does not mean that the feminist theoretical category of agency must "match" the LDS definition of agency in order to be useful, but it must at least be able to adequately describe the actions, including religious practices, of Latter-day Saints.

I am interested in looking at the lives of contemporary American LDS women as a way of pointing out specific ways that the feminist category of agency can be expanded. The gaps in theory become evident when placed alongside the "real lives" of those being theorized about; in this case, traditional religious women. My findings indicate that the feminist category of agency needs to be reconceptualized, since the majority of women involved in traditional religions are not involved in their faith to resist and subvert it.

After briefly discussing two theorists who have approached agency with a wider lens, I will draw upon both their work and my own ethnographic findings of LDS women to propose a new way of understanding the feminist category of agency.

Agency

Prior to feminists' interest in agency, social theorists had been debating theories of human action, or agency, for decades.[8] Many feminist theorists have largely ignored this wider literature on agency to support a definition of agency as resistance.

---

7. My ethnography was conducted during 2005 and 2006.

8. Ira S. Cohen, "Theories of Action and Praxis," in *The Blackwell Companion to Social Theory*, ed. Bryan S. Turner (Oxford: Blackwell, 2000), 73–74.

Social theorist Anthony Giddens has dealt explicitly with theories of agency, and has largely been able to avoid a narrow definition of agency. Giddens defines agency as actions or thoughts that people engage in as they relate to events in the world.[9] Giddens does not claim that all actions are necessarily conscious or intentional, but that actors produce and reproduce society by "skilled performances."[10] For Giddens, agency is limited by social conditions, but these structures are not necessarily limiting, they can also be enabling.[11] Giddens offers an interesting way of conceptualizing agency—it is used to negotiate a human actor's relationship with society, and is constantly shifting. Although Giddens does believe that all interaction contains three essential elements—communication, power, and moral relations—issues of power and politics do not over determine his concept of agency.[12] For Giddens, agency can be used to resist *or maintain* social norms.

Saba Mahmood, a feminist theorist, explicitly deals with the feminist theoretical category of agency. Mahmood aims to shift the analysis of agency within religious practices from a singular focus on resistance toward culturally and religiously specific frameworks that consider *both* resisting and supporting religious norms as valid examples of agency. Mahmood argues that liberal and progressive politics have become naturalized within the study of gender and that because feminist theory is committed to both analysis and politics (in other words, it asks the questions and attempts to resolve the problems) freedom has become normative to feminism.[13] Furthermore, liberalism has married notions of freedom with the idea that self-fulfillment comes from individual autonomy. Within this framework, as long as a person can demonstrate that she is acting *autonomously*, "even illiberal actions can arguably be tolerated" as she is thought to be living out her "true" desires.[14]

---

9. Anthony Giddens, *New Rules of Sociological Method* (Stanford: Stanford University Press, 1993), 81. Giddens says that agency is "the stream of actual or contemplated causal interventions of corporeal beings in the ongoing process of events-in-the-world."

10. Ibid., 168.

11. Ibid., 169.

12. Ibid., 133.

13. Other scholars have made the argument that feminism includes both analysis and politics, but Mahmood is unique in linking the twin commitment to the tendency to define agency strictly in terms of resistance. For other scholars who have written on the dual role of feminist theory, see Diane Fuss, Judith Butler, Marilyn Strathern, and Wendy Brown.

14. Saba Mahmood, "Agency, Performativity, and the Feminist Subject," in *Bodily*

The challenge with this construct, according to Mahmood, is that it is difficult to locate autonomy or freedom *when one is compliant with norms*. As a result, resistance or subversion has become valorized as a demonstration of one's capacity to act freely and enact one's true desires. Thus, "even in instances when an explicit feminist agency is difficult to locate, there is a tendency among scholars to look for expressions and moments of resistance that may suggest a challenge to male domination."[15] In short, feminist theorists run the risk of projecting a desire for freedom and autonomy upon women who do not necessarily share these goals. Feminist theories of agency have replicated this pattern by emphasizing women's resistance to norms.

In order to adequately address the women Mahmood studied, she contends that "it is crucial to detach the notion of agency from the goals of progressive politics."[16] Furthermore, "If we recognize that the desire for freedom from, or subversion of, norms is not an innate desire that motivates all beings at all times, but is also profoundly mediated by cultural and historical conditions, then the question arises: how do we analyze operations of power that construct different kinds of bodies, knowledges, and subjectivities whose trajectories do not follow the entelechy of liberatory politics?"[17]

Mahmood does not claim to offer *the* theory of agency; instead she encourages the construction of culturally specific theories that examine behaviors that uphold *and* diverge from religious norms as constituting agency. Thus, agency is expanded and consideration may be given to "projects, discourses, and desires that are not captured by these terms."[18] Mahmood reminds feminist theorists that "we cannot treat as natural and imitable only those desires that ensure the emergence of feminist politics."[19]

Mahmood's pull away from agency that is understood as only acts of resistance is critical in order to increase the possibilities for identifying agency. However, I contend that unless agency is conceived of as a *fluid continuum* or spectrum, which includes more than modes that

---

Citations: Religion and Judith Butler, ed. Ellen T. Armour and Susan M. St. Ville (New York: Columbia University Press, 2006), 184. Italics added for emphasis.

15. Mahmood, *Politics of Piety*, 8.
16. Ibid., 14.
17. Ibid., 14.
18. Ibid., 15.
19. Mahmood, "Agency," 187.

either resist or maintain norms, it will be stuck within another dualistic theoretical construction.

Reconceptualizing Agency

Giddens and Mahmood each offer insight into the retooling of the theoretical category of agency. The benefit of Giddens' theory of agency is that it is not overly dependent upon power relations. Implicit in his theory of agency is the ability for one to either be in compliance with social norms, or to go against them. Because he is uncomfortable with dualism in social theory, it is likely that he would be uncomfortable with a dualistic definition of agency.

For Mahmood, agency is either the support *or* the resistance of norms by an individual who has some level of volunteerism but is limited by religion and cultural expectations and boundaries.[20] This definition is revolutionary within feminist theory because it allows women's actions and practices to be validated as agency, even when they support patriarchy and religious tradition that appears oppressive of women. However, despite Mahmood's excellent work in redefining agency, for her, agency is still locked within a duality; agency is *either* used to uphold norms *or* agency is used to detract from religious and social constructs.

I aim to build upon the careful work of Giddens and Mahmood by highlighting the *simultaneous* nature of agency. I contend that agency often includes a fluid engagement within a spectrum of behaviors, including resistance *and* maintenance of norms, which fall between the poles of autonomy and limited freedom. Theories of agency must take into consideration the influence that the self—both conscious and subconscious—has on one's actions, as well as the limits that are imposed upon the self (usually by the self) within the communities in which these subjects are embedded. In other words, for our purposes, a woman is constantly mediating how she will act (consciously and subconsciously) and weighing her actions between individual motives and her communal loyalties (which can be the same). However, loyalties between the self and community will constantly be renegotiated so that diversity will be inevitable in actions, even moment to moment.

20. Pamela Klassen, "Agency, Embodiment, and Scrupulous Women," *Journal of Religion* 84, no. 4 (Oct. 2004): 592–603. Klassen quotes a manuscript version of Mahmood's *Politics of Piety* and cites page 281.

Naturally, these mediated responses result in behaviors that range from resisting norms to upholding norms and *often these occur simultaneously*. Concepts of agency must be attentive to the marriage and constant renegotiations between self and community and the flexibility of behaviors that occur as a result of this fluid union. Thus, all modes of agency can be construed as constituting some form of simultaneous engagement between self and community, within a continuum between autonomy and determinism.

The reconceptualization of agency as a *simultaneous* negotiation between the self and her community is a rejection of theories of agency that are based upon individual bodies that navigate systems of power within a deterministic paradigm. It is also a rejection of the idea that humans act completely autonomously, independent of all kin, social and biological interests. Instead, agency is mediated by loyalties between the self and the community that shift depending upon the context. As such, I propose that acknowledging the simultaneous nature of agency offers a helpful way of analyzing behaviors without positioning agency within a dichotomy of resistance/support. This retooled concept of agency is useful for analyzing the actions and religious practices of traditional women who are bound by the need for individual salvation but committed to the strengthening of kinship and religio-cultural communities.

Latter-day Saint Agency

Before looking at the women I worked with in the LDS community, I want to briefly touch on the LDS concept of agency. Agency is part of the theological language that Latter-day Saints use to explain the role that humans have in influencing their ultimate destiny. The women I worked with commonly referred to this principle as *free agency*, although in recent years LDS Church leaders have been referring to it as "moral agency."[21] One LDS leader explains that "If, through our unrighteous choices, we have lost our footing on that path, we must remember the agency we were given, agency we may choose to exercise

21. Although the women I interviewed referred to it as *free agency,* in recent years there has been a shift away from this language as several LDS Church leaders have referred to it as *moral agency.* For instance, see L. Lionel Kendrick, "Our Moral Agency," *Ensign*, March 1996, 28; David A. Bednar, "And Nothing Shall Offend Them," *Liahona*, November 2006, 89–92.

again. . . . How do you reclaim that agency? *You choose to act in faith and obedience.*"[22] In other words, for Latter-day Saints, agency is the ability to choose between disobedience and obedience to God. Agency is also part of the everyday vernacular that believers use to explain events. It is not unusual to hear a congregant in a monthly testimony meeting speaking about how her children used their "free agency" and have gone astray, or, although less often, how they used their agency to serve the Lord. During my ethnography I observed that although the LDS theological definition of agency includes behaviors that are both in concert with and in opposition to God's will, when the term "agency" was used, it was most often used to describe the actions of someone who had made a choice that was contrary to the will of God.

Within the LDS Church, agency is a central element within a belief system that proposes that humans are engaged in a life-long test to prove their devotion to God and Jesus. Within this tradition, members can use their agency to "choose the right," or they can use their agency to be disobedient to God's laws and the covenants they have made with Him. Latter-day Saints define agency in terms of their ability to make a "free choice" between options, usually between good and bad choices.

The Latter-day Saint concept of agency has an autonomous aspect to it, unlike the determinism within some feminist notions of agency, such as post-structuralism. One contemporary LDS leader explains that "as sons and daughters of our Heavenly Father, we have been blessed with the gift of moral agency, the capacity for *independent action and choice.*"[23] This description exemplifies how agency is thought to be choices made by "free" and "independent" individuals who are not hampered by social constructionism and systems of power that act to subjugate them.

While LDS concepts of agency have some similarities to feminist renderings of agency, my point is not to make hard comparisons between the two, although I think this would make an interesting project. Rather, I am interested in how LDS women show the simultaneous nature of agency.

---

22. Robert D. Hales, "To Act for Ourselves: The Gift and Blessings of Agency," *Ensign*, May 2006, 4–8.

23. Bednar, "And Nothing Shall Offend Them," italics added for emphasis.

Ethnographic Particularities

My ethnography focused on a community of Latter-day Saints who were located within four congregations or wards, each adjacent to one another in a suburban environment in northern California.

I conducted in-depth interviews with thirty-one women and fifteen men, ranging in age from twenty-seven to seventy-nine. Because of the complementary gender norms that are embedded within the LDS cosmology, I worked with both men and women to gain a wider picture of the community, although my primary focus was upon the women. I used the insights and conversations with the men as a way of delineating differences, similarities, and nuances that I might not have been privy to had I exclusively interviewed women.

The wards I observed were approximately 85% Caucasian, mostly middle-aged and middle-class. There were some variations in age, racial and ethnic background, and class, but the average congregant was a white, middle-class family member in the throes of raising children. The racial and ethnic diversity of the particular LDS community that I worked with, albeit slight, consisted of families who are Chinese, African, African American, Tongan, South American, Mexican, Malaysian, and Vietnamese. The women and men I worked with had varying family situations, and most of them had children. Many of the women I worked with hold college degrees, particularly because they are encouraged by the Church leadership to become educated.[24] On average, the women I worked with had completed 3.4 years of college, with the most educated woman holding two master's degrees; almost every woman attended some college. Of the women I studied, slightly more than fifty percent held bachelors or higher degrees.

Practicing Agency

The practices, or actions, of the women I worked with both resisted and supported religious norms. I have demonstrated that for LDS women and certain theorists, agency is not necessarily linked to a strict logic of resistance. I have introduced the retooled concept of agency as a way of recognizing the multiple impulses that inform agency, as played out between the self and community along a spectrum between

24. Gordon B. Hinckley, "Inspirational Thoughts," *Ensign*, June 1999, 2.

subjugation and autonomy. I will now explore the varying outcomes of agency that the women I interviewed employ, demonstrating that agency is used to transgress religious norms, to sustain religious norms, or to *simultaneously* transgress and sustain religious norms.

Within this religious community were several groups of friends who spent considerable time together outside of institutional Church activities. One group of ten to twelve women in their late twenties to mid-thirties was stylish, socially savvy, fun, and adventurous. These women also were fairly exclusive, remaining within their social circle. In early January, this group of women gathered to shoot boudoir photos to give to their husbands on Valentine's Day. One woman, a photographer, took the pictures and each woman sat for twelve poses to make a calendar for her spouse. Some of the women were a little bolder in their pictorial poses than others.

Somehow, the women's photo session came to the attention of the highest ranking local leader, the stake president.[25] He was not enthusiastic about the activity, although by all reports he was kind and gentle during his inquiry. He asked the woman who had organized the photo shoot to meet with him and talk about it. Another of the women who lived in a bordering area was asked to meet with her stake president. Obviously, this would be incredibly intimidating and upsetting—for a younger woman to be questioned by a local high-ranking, male Church leader about her sexual behaviors. According to some of the women I spoke with, the stake president was worried that some of the women's teenage children would see the photos. Overall, from various conversations I have had with different people, it seemed that his main concern was really about the degree to which pornographic influences had seeped into the local LDS culture.[26] Many of the women were shocked when they realized that their activity was cause for concern and that the local Church leadership objected. What is interesting is that, although two women were questioned, the group decided to proceed with their

25. The stake president is an ecclesiastical leader within the LDS Church who oversees several bishops in an area.

26. This is also evident in several addresses that current LDS leaders, including the LDS Church President, Gordon B. Hinckley, has given to the men in the Church. Gordon B. Hinckley, "A Tragic Evil Among Us," *Ensign*, November 2004, 59–62; Dallin H. Oaks, "Pornography," *Ensign*, May 2005, 89.

original plans. Most of the women compiled their individual boudoir calendars and gave them to their husbands.[27]

I was fascinated by these women. These were women who attended church each week, were stay-at-home moms, and would not consider themselves feminists. They drove mini-vans and large SUV's and dutifully performed their Church callings. Many of the women I spoke with indicated that their choice to go ahead with the calendar, despite the disapproval of the leadership, was based on what they were comfortable with. They regretted that the stake president didn't approve but felt ultimately that they (and their husbands) were comfortable with the project. After the gifts were given, many of the women commented that the calendars had livened up their sex lives and that they were glad they had made them.[28]

However, in smaller conversations, away from the bravado of the group, some of the women worried that they might not be seen as devout because of their choice. One of the women, embarrassed, and ashamed, wondered if the local Church leaders thought she was a "bad" person. I do not know exactly what was said in the meetings between the two women and their ecclesiastical leaders, but none of the women suffered official Church sanctions or retributions because of the activity.

These women utilized agency to act in a manner that transgressed religiously prescribed norms of appropriate sexual behavior, yet they recognized the spiritual authority of the stake president. Although they didn't originally recognize they were diverging from prescribed norms, once they were so informed, they continued their original plans, mostly undeterred. In the conversations I had with several of the participants,

27. Let me clarify, the women each made one calendar consisting of twelve different pictures of themselves and gave them to their husbands. They did not exchange pictures of themselves with other women and the men did not share their calendars with each other. In this way, it was a confidential calendar.

28. For an interesting look at Mormon women's sexual agency see Jennifer Finlayson-Fife, "Female Sexual Agency in Patriarchal Culture: the Case of Mormon Women," PhD dissertation (Boston College, 2002). Finlayson-Fife argues that although Mormon women's sexual identity is formed within a patriarchal structure, the regulation of male sexuality potentially can lead to Mormon women's sexual agency by domesticating the sexual behavior of Mormon men. Another observation that Finlayson-Fife makes is that Mormon women and some men struggle with the legitimacy of sexual desire. She also links agency with freedom as she uses the radical feminist theoretical analytical category of agency as one of her frameworks.

surprisingly, I never felt that these women considered their ecclesiastical leader domineering or oppressive. I anticipated a gendered reading of the event, but none was offered. Rather, they simultaneously recognized his spiritual authority while maintaining that they were adequate judges of appropriate sexual behaviors within the bounds of their marriages. This is an example of *simultaneous agency*, which includes a negotiation between many factors. These women negotiated between a range of loyalties: self, kin, and religious community, in order to determine if they would continue with their plans to give the calendars to their husbands. Each woman negotiated this differently—as is evident from the woman who worried about what her leader thought of her, to the women who seemed unconcerned. They lived within a religious culture that acted to bind them to a set of codes that were considered appropriate behavior, and they responded by resisting certain codes—such as shooting nude photos for their husbands—while maintaining other gendered codes, such as being stay-at-home mothers and not contesting many other gender norms. By examining this event with the lens of a retooled concept of agency, particularly one that attends to its simultaneous nature, it is much more difficult to assert that the Church member's resistance was unilateral subversion to gender norms. More realistically, it is a subversion of one gendered norm while overall they maintain their deep commitments to the very system that binds them through highly distinctive gendered notions.

It would be easy to depict these women as oppressed by a patriarchal leader who was displeased with their behavior. Flexing his spiritual muscles, the stake president called them in for a "chat" and admonished them to cease with the boudoir calendars. The story could continue: the women are offended and subsequently challenge his authority by continuing with their plans. While such a reading is indeed plausible, it forecloses other facts, such as that the women did not take issue with his ecclesiastical authority, nor did they read this as gendered oppression. They never questioned that he had the right to lead them spiritually or that he had been "called of God." By assuming that resistance is embarked upon in order to subvert institutional authority due to gender differences, the complexity of human action is overlooked and the practices and beliefs of culturally specific peoples is occluded, not clarified. This example demonstrates how the LDS women I worked with used *simultaneous agency* to negotiate between their individual, marital, and ecclesiastical expectations and desires. Although an important tenet of the LDS faith is the belief in the patriarchal family, these women showed both resistance from and adherence to the patriarchal norms within the LDS faith.

Within the LDS tradition, men have the priesthood and are considered the patriarchs.[29] In this way, some men have had considerable authority within LDS marriages. Because of the historic premium placed on men's opinions within the home, a divergence from a husband's authority can be seen as transgressive, not just of the family dynamic but of the larger religious tradition. One of the questions I asked the women I worked with was a hypothetical: if you had a strong desire to do something, say, go back to college, and your husband didn't support your decision, how would you handle this? During the many interviews I conducted, most of the women answered that this would never happen, because their husbands would find a way to make it happen if it was really important to them. Secondly, the women reminded me, this was an unlikely scenario because of the premium the Church places on women's education.[30]

During an interview with Ellen, a Caucasian woman in her thirties with four children and a full-time career, I asked this question expecting the same response. I have left the dialogue in its entirety in order to be attentive to how the dialogue shaped the conversation and to allow Ellen's voice to be heard.

> Amy: Okay, this is a hypothetical: if you really wanted to go back to college, and Bob said "absolutely not, I don't want you to go back," how would you handle that?
>
> Ellen: *That did happen* . . . when we moved back here . . . I had gone to BYU for a semester, then we got married then I went to Utah Valley State for two more semesters while we lived there. So when we moved back, I was pregnant with John and I started working for my mom, just kind of part-time hours here and there, and I started realizing, wow, I kind of like this, so I told Bob, I want to go back to school. And he said "this isn't important right now" . . . and I said. . . "yeah, it is . . . it is important to me!" So we went back and forth and we went back and forth and he found things about what you know,

29. Rex Eugene Cooper, *Promises Made to the Fathers: Mormon Covenant Organization* (Salt Lake City: University of Utah Press, 1990).

30. Gordon B. Hinckley, "Inspirational Thoughts," *Ensign*, June 1999, 2.

> writings from Spencer W. Kimball saying family is the most important thing, or he would highlight all the stuff and I remember talking to Sister Clive, she was the Relief Society President at the time and I remember telling her, "you know, this just doesn't feel right because I feel like it's a good decision, I feel like it would be good for me," and so she started finding quotes . . . we were in this quote battle . . .
>
> Amy: Yeah . . . different leaders, Church leaders . . .
>
> Ellen: Yeah . . . and I had gone and prayed about it and I knew that it was a good thing—I could go back to school and so I just finally said "you know what? Whether you are going to support and help me on this . . . or you are not, this is the choice that I'm making . . . so where are you going to stand?" And he just said, "okay then, I guess I'm supporting you."[31]

Ellen's answer to my question clearly demonstrates that agency is a simultaneous negotiation. She negotiated between loyalties to her husband, who had considerable authority in the home, herself, and her religious community. She was acting within limits that suggest that women's most important role is mother, who is perpetually available for her children, and wife, who should heed her husband's counsel. However, within those limits she also found a way to fulfill her own desires by invoking prayer. Ellen relied upon her commitment to her religion, her personal relationship with deity, and the advice of certain Church leaders, in order to simultaneously negotiate gendered norms within her religious culture. In this way, she negotiated between self and community, and resistance and maintenance of religious norms, at the same time.

The primacy of education within the LDS Church is important to note in order to thicken this description. Ellen could transgress her husband's authority and the gender codes of the religion because education is seen as very important for both men and women within the LDS Church. But what if this disagreement had occurred because she wanted to have a career? Within the LDS tradition, women are expected to stay home with their children whenever it is possible.[32] Could

31. Personal interview, February 28, 2006.

32. Heaton, et al. found that Mormons disapprove at higher rates than non-Mormons of mothers working, even if it is part-time when children are under five years old. Yet, Mormon women tend to work outside of the home at close to national averages, indicating no substantial difference in practice. Tim B. Heaton,

Ellen make a claim that her decision to embark upon a career was a valid maintenance of religious beliefs? This next vignette examines this by exploring how one of the women I worked with restructured her career in order to spend more time at home with her children, while simultaneously upholding and resisting particular gender norms.

Jill, a convert, described to me her first spiritual experience after joining the Church. As a professional, Jill had previously felt uncomfortable working full-time and leaving her children in daycare, but upon converting to Mormonism her discomfort became more acute. Jill explains:

> So for me, there has been an evolution from being a full-time working mom, kids in daycare, you know, working husband, that whole thing, to joining the Church and sort of having what I consider really being sort of my first really clear experience with the Holy Ghost. Of getting this really clear message . . . but feeling sort of helpless to do anything to change it and then just having the experience of feeling so strongly like "this needs to change like immediately" and feeling really really, really clear—just super clear, super strong, "you need to reduce your hours and you need to make these changes—you need to be with your family, you need to be with your children" and this is what you know, this is very strong feeling and going home and just pretty much telling Bill you know, I mean "we need to do this, you know I need to be home with the kids—we need to make some changes" and literally sitting down that night and saying and looking at numbers and you know, going through our regular process that we always go through and it working out perfectly—if I pull the kids out here, day care here, and I reduce my hours here, we—that is a wash—we can make that work.[33]

Jill demonstrated agency by negotiating between the spiritual feelings she was having, her desire to spend more time with her children, and her love for her profession. These elements, her religious commitments, her loyalty to her kin and to herself, were each weighed carefully as she lived within a religious system that actively encourages women to be full-time mothers.

Kristen L. Goodman, Thomas B. Holman, "In Search of a Peculiar People: Are Mormon Families Really Different?" in *Contemporary Mormonism: Social Science Perspectives*, ed. Marie Cornwall, Tim B. Heaton, and Lawrence A. Young (Chicago: University of Illinois Press, 1994), 103–4.

33. Personal interview, March 8, 2006.

What is particularly interesting is that Jill interpreted her spiritual prompting to mean that she needed to reduce her hours, not to quit her job. In this way, her spiritual feelings both supported and slightly diverged from the prescribed religious ideal. Jill used agency to mediate between complex desires and loyalties. She now drops her children off at school and drives to work, ending her workday immediately prior to the end of her children's school day. Jill continues:

> I'm different than a lot of the other women in the Church, you know, and so that is sort of interesting to me. I'm not a stay-at-home-mom. I don't just stay at home, but I do, I think, a really good job of balancing those two things because my kids don't know any different. I mean I was home cleaning my house, or at work seeing patients, it doesn't matter. They are at school.[34]

This ethnographic vignette demonstrates the complexity of the women I worked with. Some of them used agency as a way to support the religious norms while still maintaining a slight distance from them. To interpret this example in a strict subversion/subordination dichotomy, Jill would have to be understood as a woman who is still finding space to subvert the patriarchal hegemonic discourse—but this would run contrary to her expressed motivations. Jill, a convert, joined the religion in her thirties. She would be unlikely to join the LDS Church simply to subvert it as an "insider." More importantly, Jill, a self-proclaimed feminist, does not speak in terms that are captured within this subversion/subordination duality. Jill finds value in spending more time with her children and has implemented a system where she can maximize her family time while still maintaining a career that brings her personal satisfaction and joy.

Simultaneous agency was used repeatedly by the LDS women I studied as a way of negotiating complex circumstances and its deployment produced various behaviors, ranging from compliance to resistance and most often, simultaneous engagement of these impulses. For many of the American LDS women I worked with, agency became infused with spiritual meaning when it was enacted after a spiritual experience. These spiritual experiences, or revelations, acted to authorize the practices the women engaged in.

---

34. Ibid.

Authorizing Agency

Within this system there are varying ways in which agency is authorized. Non-spiritual and spiritual actions are authorized by individuals, by God (vis-à-vis the individual believer through prayer, the religious leader, the patriarch of the family), and by the local community (local social pressures/cultural pressures), and are all situated, ultimately, within larger theological and cultural boundaries. Many of the women I worked with relied heavily upon a type of self-interpreted authorization. What I mean by self-interpreted authorization is that they rely on their own ability to interpret their spiritual experiences, within the boundedness of the religious tradition. Many spiritual experiences are referred to as "personal revelation" within the LDS community.

Personal revelation entails the ability to receive unsolicited or solicited spiritual guidance, through prayer, priesthood blessings, scripture reading, interactions with other people, or feelings. Although priesthood blessings are administered by men, there are other ways that God's wishes are manifested, and many do not require an individual to mediate between the believer and deity. Prayer, fasting, and reading scriptures are various ways that believers seek personal revelation and interpret revelation individually. Personal revelation includes the belief that prayer can be answered in ways that are discernible.[35] Revelation is both hierarchical and linear, in that those in authority, usually men, have the ability to receive revelation for those they oversee; and every member of the LDS Church is considered able to receive "personal revelation" that can assist him or her in making decisions for themselves and for their families.[36] Thus, while men have the ability to receive institutional revelation, which ultimately sets the larger

---

35. Terryl Givens, *By the Hand of Mormon: The American Scripture that Launched a New World Religion* (New York: Oxford University Press, 2002), 218–39.

36. Todd Compton, "Non-Hierarchical Revelation" in *Women and Authority: Re-emerging Mormon Feminism*, ed. Maxine Hanks (Salt Lake City: Signature Books, 1992). Compton argues that historically, revelation has been non-hierarchical because some revelations that are revealed to those who are not in authority manage to find their way up to those who are in authority and become legitimized. Feminists working within the LDS community have critiqued the limited institutional authority that women have within the LDS Church. See Marie Cornwall, "The Institutional Role of Mormon Women," in *Contemporary Mormonism*, ed. Cornwall, Heaton, and Young, 239–64.

parameters for what would be considered acceptable, all followers are entitled to their own unmediated personal revelation.

The women I worked with most often described personal revelation as a feeling, either of peace or confidence or sometimes discomfort (when they felt they were being spiritually discouraged from particular actions). Many of the women used prayer in order to negotiate the various commitments and loyalties within their lives. As I have shown, at times, prayer supported a counter-intuitive action, such as when Jill was not prompted to quit her job but to reduce her hours, or when Ellen was prompted to attend college despite her husband's objections. In this way, personal revelation can act as a type of self-interpreted authorization for women.

Within the LDS Church, congregants are expected to volunteer in pre-assigned "callings" in order to facilitate the functioning of the Church. At the local level, no one is monetarily compensated. The LDS Church relies on the laity to run the numerous programs that operate on a weekly, monthly, and even daily basis.[37] When a calling is extended to an individual at the ward level, a member of the bishopric asks to meet with her and asks if she will accept a particular calling. Because many congregants believe that the assignments are inspired from God, they consider turning down a calling as turning down a spiritually-prompted assignment. Despite this belief, about forty-five percent of the women I worked with had turned down callings or had requested that they be released from callings for various reasons.

Louise, a Polynesian woman in her early forties with four children, was approached by a male Church leader of her local ward who "called" her to be involved in the youth program—assisting in teaching and mentoring young girls between the ages of twelve and eighteen. Louise, who just had one of her children diagnosed with a developmental disorder, was feeling quite overwhelmed, and her initial reaction was to turn the calling down. When she called the Church leader and indicated that she could not do it, he asked her if she would be willing to pray about her decision. Louise explains:

> So that night, I prayed about it, and then of course, I had the impression to look on the internet at LDS.org. So there was an article

37. Gordon Shepherd and Gary Shepherd, "Sustaining a Lay Religion in Modern Society: The Mormon Missionary Experience," in *Contemporary Mormonism*, ed. Cornwall, Heaton, and Young, 162–81.

> there, there were two . . . and this one was right to the call. And I read it and I was just bawling because it was answering concerns I had and should I do it? You know? Here He is and basically it told me that He requires us to do our best and know that whatever you do if you can touch and help someone that would be good. And I cried and am in the shower getting ready, and I was just . . . crying . . . the ugly cry . . . you know, you are just overwhelmed and so I felt His love . . . I felt "He has a purpose for you, He loves you and you need to accept the calling." And so I called [the Church leader] that morning and said "yes." I have loved it, it has been the best calling I have ever had.[38]

Louise's initial reaction to the invitation to serve within the ward could not be considered strictly supportive of religious norms. She questioned her ability to serve in the calling, which happened to be very demanding and time consuming, and vocalized her concern to the male leader. In turn, he asked her if she would pray about it, which she did. Louise used personal revelation to help her enact agency. While her mode of agency went from resisting to supporting the religious norm, she lingered within a space where she drew upon a form of spiritual authorization to mediate along this continuum. Turning down a calling, particularly if one believes that it is inspired by God, can be quite daunting. Louise's willingness to ensure the well being of her family before accepting a Church calling shows some signs of simultaneous engagement within this fluid framework of agency. Ultimately, she resolved her doubt by determining that she would do the best she could and use Jesus as a way of making up the difference. Although Louise's experience with personal revelation involved her ecclesiastical leader, since he suggested that she seek revelation about it, most personal revelations are fairly private. Furthermore, there is a certain amount of privacy that surrounds personal revelation.

The women I worked with were very protective of personal revelations but would say things like "I prayed about it, and I feel good about it," or "I feel that this is a good decision for me and my family, and I've prayed about it." Once a person invokes personal revelation, there is a certain amount of space that is granted by other believers. It is highly unusual to question others' personal revelations. There is fluidity that comes with an open canon and the belief that every person is entitled to an individual relationship with God, or that every person may know God's wishes for him or her through

38. Personal interview, June 5, 2006.

dialogical engagements with deity.[39] This flexibility potentially results in a religious tradition that is highly individualized, although rampant relativism is tempered by the constructs that are set within a larger framework, which ultimately constitutes the sanctioned limits.[40]

One of the most disturbing situations I encountered during my ethnography was a woman, Kelly, who had been sexually abused by a male family member as a young girl. Her relative had lied about the incident, avoiding Church sanctions. Normally, he would have been excommunicated from the Church but because of his deceitfulness, he suffered no immediate religious consequences. After Kelly was molested, she told her mother about the incident. Her mother promised her daughter that she was going to demand that the family member move out of the house and, in the interim, sent her daughter to live with her grandparents for a period of several months. Upon returning home, her family was still intact. The mother brushed it off and explained to the girl that she had prayed about it, and she was doing what was right. Kelly continued to live at home and finished school, all the while living in the same house as her molester. Repeatedly, the mother told Kelly that she had prayed about it and that God had instructed her to keep their family together. As a young woman, Kelly married and had children. Safely away from her family, she began to question the validity of her mother's revelations.

Working with this woman, I was taken aback by the seemingly infinite claim to personal revelation that her mother utilized, which resulted in a life of terror and secrecy for her daughter. Because the mother also lied to other Church members, there was no one who knew the true situation of this family. Thus, there was no intervention, and Kelly, who had been sexually abused, became spiritually abused by her mother. As an adult, Kelly began to "out" her family to the community, slowly telling

---

39. Givens, *By the Hand*, 218–39.

40. As scholar Lawrence A. Young observes, their "emphasis on experience does not result in freedom of self from the community. For Mormon religious experience to be valid, it must be interpreted in ways that elevate the organization above the self." Young makes an important observation about the place of individuality within the larger Mormon construct; it is subordinate to that of the community in some ways. However, my ethnographic findings suggest that Young overstates the priority of the community over the individual, they actually act more in concert; individual and kinship responsibilities are equally important. Lawrence Young, "Confronting Turbulent Environments: Issues in the Organizational Growth and Globalization of Mormonism," in *Contemporary Mormonism*, ed. Cornwall, Heaton, and Young, 76.

one or two people what had happened. As she talked about her experience, she came to feel more confident in her knowledge that she had been duped by her mother. Upon learning of the situation, one of the highest ranking Church leaders in the area and his wife ended their long-standing friendship with Kelly's mother and began to defend Kelly.

Although Kelly still seems surprised each time someone affirms that her mother could not have possibly been told by God to forsake her daughter for the sake of keeping the family intact, this example demonstrates both the flexibility and the finitude of personal revelation. In one sense, her mother utilized this situation as a never-ending authorization for not dealing with Kelly's abuser; for her mother, the boundaries of personal revelation were limitless. But for others within the larger community, her mother's claim to this particular revelation was completely invalid. Once aware of the situation, they vehemently rejected the idea that someone could receive an authentic personal revelation to subject her daughter to the possibility of additional sexual abuse once the knowledge of any abuse had been obtained. Instead, they believed that the mother was mentally ill or lacked the courage to put her daughter's needs above her own. While some members of the community may feel that questioning any personal revelation is impious, the men and women I worked with, who knew of the situation, rejected Kelly's mother's spiritual authorization.

What I want to draw attention to is how individual spiritual feelings, or personal revelations, can act to authorize a range of behaviors within the larger religious tradition. As this vignette demonstrates, there are limits within the system, particularly surrounding issues of family and sexuality, but there is also considerable flexibility because of the belief in individual spiritual authority, where the will of God must be determined by each of His believing followers.[41]

---

41. Sara Patterson has addressed the shifts within the LDS Church regarding how institutional revelations become authorized, and argues that the early LDS Church embraced a more democratic definition of revelation. Patterson contends that by the twentieth century, the dominant form of revelation within the LDS Church is what she calls the "Moroni fideist model," where members of the LDS Church pray to determine if a revelation is true and rely on the Holy Ghost to witness to them the legitimacy of the revelation. Sara Patterson, "Divine revelations/delusions revealed: historical understandings of Revelation in debates over Mormonism," PhD diss., Claremont Graduate University, 2005.

Another example of how spiritual self-authorization within institutional limits leads to the fluidity of personal revelation also demonstrates how self-authorization allows for a response that demonstrates simultaneous agency. One of the men I interviewed, Allen, indicated that his wife, Camille, felt spiritually guided in her career, and this influenced other decisions, such as the number of children they wanted and whether to work outside of the home full-time. In this way, when she acted upon her personal revelation, by limiting family size or working outside of the home, what may appear like subversion to some was actually motivated by a personal spiritual revelation. For Camille, working full-time was an act of spiritual devotion, which was authorized by her interpretation of a personal spiritual experience. This self-interpreted authorization allowed Camille to simultaneously diverge from religious tradition while affirming her religious commitment.

The women I worked with displayed a range of behaviors and did not always measure their revelations against the institutional boundaries. This is not to say that they are resisting institutional authority, although I am sure some do. Rather, most seemed unaware that the two could come into conflict. If God told them to act a certain way, why would He tell them something in contrast to the Church guidelines? Furthermore, if their revelation did diverge from official Church policy, they often felt that they were the exception to the rule, and because of their revelation, exempt from any policy that might be contrary to their personal revelation. This was not an act of subversion, but a feeling of being "different" or "special," or a feeling that God had a particular purpose for them that could not be exactly explained or understood logically.

American Latter-day Saint women offer feminist theoreticians an instructive way of reconceptualizing agency in order to be relevant to the practices of traditional religious women. The LDS women I worked with employed agency in diverse and complex ways, but it was most often a simultaneous engagement between individual, communal, and kinship loyalties that operated within a system that allows for self-interpreted spiritual authorization.

Chapter Eleven

Patriarchy

Caroline Kline

Over the last few decades, many American denominations, including the majority of mainline Protestant churches, have made efforts to remove gender restrictions from their teachings and practices. Many of these churches now ordain women. The Church of Jesus Christ of Latter-day Saints, however, maintains a position that stands against this trend. Not only does it maintain its policy of male-only priesthood ordination, it also advocates clear gender roles for its members, with women encouraged to embrace their primary role as nurturers.

Simultaneously, however, Mormon leaders encourage women to seek after education and other opportunities. In 2007, President Gordon B. Hinckley told the young women of the Church, "The whole gamut of human endeavor is now open to women. There is not anything that you cannot do if you will set your mind to it."[1] This sense of women's empowerment, possibility, and strength, combined with the clear gender roles that limit women's participation in the Church structure, can result for some women in dissonance or ambivalence about their status as women in the Church.

Issues of priesthood are further complicated in Mormonism since all worthy males are ordained. Mormon husbands are priests within their families, as well as within the Church, and they are instructed to "preside" over their wives and children. This presiding within the home is mediated by other injunctions by Church authorities to stand as equal partners with their wives. While the emphasis on spousal equal partnership has grown throughout the last few decades within Mormon rhetoric, there paradoxically remains strong injunctions for Mormon men to preside

1. Gordon B. Hinckley, "How Can I Become the Woman of Whom I Dream?" *Ensign*, May 2001, 95.

and take special leadership within the home. Thus there are two levels of priesthood and patriarchy that Mormon women contend with: within their homes and within the institutional Church structure.

In this paper, I use the Claremont Mormon Women Oral History Collection to analyze the ways in which Mormon women internally conceive of, justify, or cope with their restricted roles and the male hierarchy and priesthood of the Church. I also analyze how the participants externally act in the face of disagreement with male leaders or with desires for expanded roles for women. I find in these oral histories that there is a wide range of internal and external strategies for dealing with patriarchy, ranging from reinterpreting the meaning of "preside" to outright defiance of Church leaders.

Internal Conceptions of Men's Priesthood Roles and Women's Roles

Affirming Priesthood

A majority of women responded positively when asked about the male priesthood in the home and in the Church. Their answers tended to focus on priesthood within the home, discussing how grateful they were for good husbands who give blessings to their families, or took initiative in leading family scripture study. They also tended to be positive about motherhood being women's primary role.

While most women avoided using terms like "patriarch" or "patriarchy," favoring instead the term "priesthood holder" or "priesthood," Roxanne does not shy away from the term. Interestingly, however, she has no difficulty coupling "patriarch" with ideas about the equality of women:

> I'm a big believer that the father is the patriarch of the home and should be the head of the home. I think women should respect that. But I also don't think that women should ever roll over and play dead or take any sort of abuse. A good, honorable priesthood holder will never hold that over his spouse's head, never laud that or assume that he is better in any way. I think that you [women] are equal. I think that the men need the priesthood. Women, by their very nature are stronger in some ways and more nurturing."[2]

2. Claremont Mormon Women's Oral History Collection, Library of the Claremont Colleges, Claremont, CA, hereafter COHC, #088 (2010), 8.

By simultaneously embracing the idea that men are the patriarchs or heads of the home with the idea that women are their equals, this woman engages in a phenomenon common in the oral histories—that of embracing the rhetoric of patriarchy and the idea that men preside, but undercutting it or nuancing it with ideas about women's equality. For this woman, patriarchy does not mean a husband ordering his wife about, or a wife submitting to her husband. She sees equality as possible, even within a context in which men preside in the home.

Other oral histories give insight into how such seemingly contradictory ideas can be maintained. We see that many women do not think of priesthood or men presiding as power over women. Rather, they see it as men being involved and present in the lives of others. To them, priesthood is not about male power—it is about male support, involvement, and service. Sarah gives a sense of this:

> I love having the priesthood power in my home and the blessings it brings. I love Fathers' blessings, healing blessings, blessings of comfort. . . . I love to see the priesthood holders use their priesthood whether it is with the sacrament, conducting a meeting, performing a baptism, or temple ordinances. The priesthood can make good men great.
>
> That said, it really bothers me when priesthood holders use their priesthood calling unrighteously. Too often I have seen a brother "pull the priesthood card" when he wants his way, or a stake president unjustly withhold a temple recommend as a personal vendetta.[3]

Sarah largely conceives of priesthood as nurturing spiritual guidance within the home and important service within the Church. However, she does acknowledge the potential abuse that can occur in this system, as men "pull the priesthood card," or declare that they are right and that a woman is wrong because men have the priesthood and she does not.

Other women embrace the rhetoric of priesthood and patriarchy, while overtly rejecting ideas of male superiority. These women see priesthood as a way to equalize men and women, since they conceive of women as being spiritually stronger. Catherine gives us a sense of this:

> I know it might look from the outside that we are a male dominant church, but to me it doesn't feel that way. I feel very strongly that men were given the priesthood because they wouldn't be able

3. COHC, #091 (2010), 12.

> to progress very far without it. After knowing enough men, it seems obvious that men are more carnal by nature than women. Men are usually spiritually weaker than women. We are more intuitive, have more depth of character, and usually we are more righteous by nature. Of course, we are still carnal and have many things to overcome, but I feel that it is often times more natural for women to just "be good." We are given the gift to be mothers. We are blessed to bring children into this world. Men do not get to do this; and I would rather be a woman and have this experience than to hold the priesthood any day! And as women we will enjoy all the blessings of the priesthood as we make temple covenants and have temple marriages. Neither of us is able to progress without the other.[4]

For women like Catherine, priesthood is a means of balancing out the deficiencies in men and making them more suitable partners for women. Catherine also emphasizes the interdependence of men and women, who in the Mormon belief system can only progress to the highest levels of heaven as married couples.

These women who are content with the language of patriarchy, priesthood, and presiding, as well as with the function of an exclusively male priesthood, tend to see these concepts as male service and nurturing involvement with others, rather than as power over others. They have little problem asserting women as equals in this system, since they have either defanged the concept of presiding to mean little more than service, involvement, and guidance,[5] or they see priesthood as raising men up to be equals with women.

---

4. COHC, #093 (2010), 13.

5. These women echo trends in the pro-egalitarian rhetoric of certain Mormon General Authorities, who strongly emphasize the importance of equal partnership of spouses, while simultaneously sustaining men's presiding role. See Bruce C. Hafen, "Crossing Thresholds and Becoming Equal Partners," *Ensign*, August 2007, 25–29. This trend to incorporate egalitarian principles with patriarchal church teachings and structures is not unique to Mormons. Evangelical Christians are likewise seeing concepts of patriarchy and male headship within the home softened in recent decades. Russell D. Moore writes, "Evangelicals maintain [male] headship in the sphere of ideas, but practical decisions are made in most evangelical homes through a process of negotiation, mutual submission, and consensus." Russell D. Moore, "After Patriarchy, What? Why Egalitarians Are Winning the Evangelical Gender Debate." Available online at www.thedivineconspiracy.org/Z5209O.pdf (accessed December 30, 2011).

The above quotes largely center on priesthood and patriarchy within the home. The remainder of the chapter focuses primarily on women and priesthood and patriarchy in the institutional LDS Church. However, the ways women conceive of and speak about priesthood in the home often mirror how these more traditional women think about priesthood in the institutional Church and women's exclusion from it. Many of the women in the oral histories speak of feeling valued in their particular church roles and callings and of feeling grateful to priesthood leaders for their time and service; they see the men and the women of the Church working together in different but important ways.

Madelyn describes this type of partnership between men and women in the Church, even though she acknowledges that it's a partnership in which women do act under the direction of men:

> I think a woman's role in the Church is a very important, supportive, and equal role. I believe that over the years, I have seen what the women of the Church can accomplish under the direction of the priesthood. . . . We have a powerful spot in establishing and helping the kingdom move along. . . . It is difficult for me to explain. It is like the priesthood has the right hand, but they need the left, too. It is an intertwining sort of thing. I think the women are very strong in the Church and they are great leaders when combined with the power of the priesthood.[6]

Note how Madelyn perceives women's role in the Church as both supportive and equal. That same sense that women can be equals while functioning under the direction of men is persistent, though her emphasis on the intertwining and co-dependent roles of men and women of the Church works to further explain her idea that women are equals to men in the Church structure.

The question of how Mormon women make sense of their own place within the institutionalized patriarchal structure of the LDS Church and within the patriarchal Mormon family is one that has interested scholars. After interviewing twenty-eight Mormon women, sociologist Lori Beaman found that Mormon women tended to fall into one of three categories as they negotiated relationships in the family, Church, and society: submissive Mormons who embraced male priesthood and equated it with women's motherhood; moderates, who saw priesthood as a means of ennobling men to be equals with natu-

6. COHC, #085 (2010), 8.

rally spiritual and good women; and feminists who saw the priesthood in terms of power.[7] Women in the Claremont Mormon Women Oral History Project likewise conceive of priesthood in these three ways, however, the categories are often less distinct in these oral histories. Women who at once celebrate the male-only priesthood and rejoice in their roles as mothers also often conceive of priesthood as an equalizing mechanism designed to raise men up to be equals with women. Thus the moderate and submissive categories Beaman notes in her interviews are far less distinct in these Claremont interviews, as women incorporate both interpretations into their conception of male priesthood. In an interesting twist, the women are often quite explicit about affirming their own equality, even as they embrace the male priesthood and presiding roles. In this way, these women are making space within the Mormon patriarchal framework for principles of women's equality—a mental exercise which more feminist Mormon women tend to reject since they see unreconcilable contradictions in these conceptions.

Downplaying Gender Distinctions

While the Mormon women above embrace language of priesthood—even at times patriarchy—and find room within those terms to assert women's equality, other women, in a slightly different vein, choose to downplay the role and rhetoric of priesthood as they consider gender roles of Mormon men and women. When asked about priesthood and men's and women's roles in Mormonism, they deemphasize gender distinctions and focus on ideas of fundamental equality that the gospel teaches.

Margaret is an example of a woman choosing to emphasize gender equality rather than gender distinctions. When asked about her conception of gender roles within Mormonism, she says:

> I cling to the quote made by President Hinckley in a lesson I taught many years ago. I have used it and have repeated it for years. He said, "The role of a woman in the Church is not to walk behind the man and not in front of the man, but by his side."[8]

---

7. Lori G. Beaman, "Molly Mormons, Mormon Feminists and Moderates: Religious Diversity and the Latter-Day Saints Church," *Sociology of Religion* 62, no. 1 (Spring 2001): 65–86.

8. COHC, #007 (2009), 19–20.

Joanne downplays gender distinctions when she states that she never saw a marked division between men and women concerning the giving of blessings. She deemphasizes the typical Mormon idea that blessings are the province of male priesthood holders when she recounts these memories from her childhood:

> When I would ask for a blessing when I was sick, it wasn't Dad calling another priesthood holder, it was Dad and Mom laying their hands on my head. I never saw it as something that only men had a part in. Mom did not invoke the priesthood—Dad was giving the blessing—those blessings were blessings of parents, not Melchizedek blessings. They were blessings of love and concern. . . . There was a feeling that the priesthood was nothing if it was not shared by women. . . . I had never seen the priesthood as exclusively male.[9]

This woman grew up seeing her mother participating in ritualized blessings in her Mormon home—an unusual experience given Church leaders' assertions during most of the twentieth century that priesthood holding men should be the ones to lay hands on to bless and heal.[10] Given her experience with this, priesthood seems to her to be something that men and women could share and use together for the blessing of their families—a conception which deemphasizes particular priestly gender roles and puts men and women on a more equal plane concerning the giving of blessings.

Belinda also emphasizes similarities between men and women when asked about gender roles, stating, "I think women's primary function is to take care of their homes and families. I think men's primary function is the same." She acknowledges some difference in Church opportunities, but downplays distinctions:

> My feeling is that LDS doctrinal guidelines do not differ for men and women. I think there are different opportunities as men hold the priesthood. There is a whole set of callings men can hold

---

9. COHC, #062 (2010), 14.

10. See Linda King Newell's seminal essay on Mormon women and ritual healing for more on the Church's evolving position that moved from embracing women as ritual healers and blessers to excluding them from the practice. Linda King Newell, "A Gift Given, A Gift Taken: Washing, Annointing, and Blessing the Sick Among Mormon Women." *Sunstone: 25th Year Silver Anniversary Edition* 22:3–4, Issue 115–16, June 1999, 30–43. Originally published in *Sunstone*, September–October, 1981.

> that women cannot hold. But the women have some of their own too. That doesn't seem doctrinal to me. Men hold the priesthood, but . . . a worthy husband and wife share the priesthood together.[11]

Belinda's assertion that men's and women's primary roles are the same—to take care of their families—is an unusual twist on a common Mormon understanding of men's and women's primary roles in life. For years, Mormon leaders and members have asserted motherhood as women's primary role and priesthood holder as men's primary role.[12] She, however, initially downplays the male priestly role and focuses instead on both men's and women's primary duties to nurture their families. She once again downplays distinctions between men's and women's roles in her final statement that husbands and wives share the priesthood together. This statement is notably different from current official rhetoric about priesthood, which emphasizes that men alone hold it, but women share in all the blessings of it. Whatever distinctions are currently present between men and women in the institutional Church, Belinda implies that such distinctions might simply be current policy.

While these women downplay gender distinctions and roles in various ways, Anne both deemphasizes the importance of sex in the eyes of God and strategically emphasizes gender difference in order to argue for greater equality in the lives of men and women in the Church structure:

> I take the scripture that God is no respecter of persons very literally. I don't think that God gives a damn whether we are male or female. I think that he sees us as individuals, not as sexed bodies. But also I think, and this is so interesting because I'm informed by the Church in this belief, that women and men are different. They [Church leaders] insist [on this]! There's no room for us to argue that. In my mind, if women and men are different inherently, then we need to have both elements in leadership in order to have a full functioning healthy body. We need it in leadership, in every aspect of the Church body.[13]

Anne envisions God caring far less about sex and gender than Church teachings often suggest, but then uses the Church teachings

11. COHC, #005 (2009), 19–20.

12. See Sonja Farnsworth's article for more on this priesthood-motherhood coupling. Sonja Farnsworth, "Mormonism's Odd Couple: The Motherhood-Priesthood Connection," ed. Maxine Hanks, *Women and Authority* (Salt Lake City: Signature Books, 1992), 299–311.

13. COHC, #026 (2010), 12.

on gender differences to argue for more equality in opportunities for service within the Church structure.

Dismissing Problematic Teachings

Another mental strategy that women use to deal with male hierarchy and gender role prescriptions is to mentally dismiss teachings or policies that are problematic to them. These women recognize the roles culture and human fallibility of Mormon leaders play in some policies and teachings from the Church, and they make their own judgements accordingly. Anne has no problem dismissing actual teachings about gender that make no sense to her. She sees fundamental contradictions in the Church's teachings on gender and chalks these contradictions up to fallible leaders:

> This is something I've never understood—how the Church out of one side of its mouth can say that gender is eternal, and then out of the other side of its mouth say that I need to teach you how to be a woman. That's just ridiculous in the extreme in my mind.[14]

Anne senses a disconnect between the doctrine that gender is eternal and the way Church leaders explicitly train men and women to fulfill certain gender expectations. In her mind, if the sexes are inherently different and men and women truly are distinct in fundamental ways, then such training would be unnecessary.

Jean sees a large shift in attitude about the fallibility of priesthood holders and is careful to make a distinction between the perfect gospel and the infallible people that function within the Church:

> My mother, to this day, states and taught that you never, ever questioned anything a priesthood holder says. Unfortunately, or fortunately, I don't share that line of thinking. I think you have to separate the gospel from the Church. The gospel is absolutely true. The Church is made up of a lot of very fine people, but we are all human and we all have our individual personalities and expectations. I have had many experiences over the years in which I have gone head to head with a priesthood holder. Many times unkind things have been said and my feelings have been hurt tremendously. I have had to stop and step back and say to myself, "Ok, that is what that person said.

14. Ibid., 7.

> That is not what the Gospel says." So far, that mentality has served me well. For the most part, I've managed to not develop too many unkind feelings. I realize that people are human. The priesthood holders are very human and they say things that are not the gospel doctrine. It is their personality and their feelings about whatever the subject is.[15]

For Jean, separating the perfect teachings of the gospel from individual priesthood leaders' opinions is essential to her psychological well-being. This ability to separate the two also demonstrates a measure of confidence in herself and her own opinions about what constitutes core doctrine and what does not. Ultimately, disagreeing with certain Church leaders on various issues does not stop her from finding meaning and spiritual insight in Mormonism as a whole.

These women who occasionally disagree with Church policy, teachings, or male leaders reconcile their disagreement by attributing these policies or teachings to human leaders who are doing their best, working according to their understanding, but falling short. There's a pragmatism at play, an understanding that the Church does not have infallible leadership. As Belinda says, "[Discrimination] happens in every church, in every culture. You can't expect leaders to be perfect."[16] We see a confidence in these women that their sense of the gospel and the rightness of certain teachings is just as valid as their leaders' sense of it.

Retreating Spiritually and Emotionally

One last internal strategy I observed in the women interviewed was to retreat emotionally and spiritually from the Church when there was a disagreement with male Church hierarchy. This seemed to happen most often when the Church was grappling with serious social issues of the day, and in the minds of some, coming up short. For one woman, it was the period in the sixties and seventies when blacks were denied the priesthood—she was deeply distressed and that nearly drove her to inactivity.[17] For others it was the women's movement in the seventies which made them fundamentally question the Church's judgment in guiding its people on these social issues.

---

15. COHC, #058 (2010), 13.
16. COHC, #005 (2009), 20.
17. COHC, #007 (2009).

Lynn describes her spiritual retreat during the Church's campaign against the Equal Rights Amendment:

> I was not happy with what the Church was doing, and I was not persuaded by the arguments or the assertions in their anti-ERA pamphlet, such that I thought, "That's it."
>
> I continued to be Mormon, but in a very different way. Whereas before when I was a child, I had questions like, "This is true—how is it true?" It basically made me say, "Wait a second. Some of it might be true, and some might not be true." I had to start thinking about every single thing. I remember talking to a woman in my ward here, and she said, "That's exhausting. Don't you think it's better to just accept it all? It's just too exhausting." I said, "I can't. Not anymore and live with any kind of integrity."[18]

In the oral histories, it was often these social issues—these times when some women believed the Church to be violating its own core teachings about equality, compassion, or agency—that were the most distressing and disillusioning.

External Action When Disagreeing With Male Leadership

In the previous section, I named several different mental strategies women used to understand or cope with Mormon male priesthood hierarchy and gender prescriptions. In this section, I turn to what the women actually do—how they act—as they navigate their membership in the Mormon patriarchal structure, particularly when they feel some tension with certain teachings about gender or when they disagree with their male priesthood leaders.

Halfway Measures

Several women described acceding to their male Church leaders in the face of disagreement with them, but doing so in a reluctant way or in a way that partly honored the men's wishes and partly honored their own. One way in which they did this was to register disagreement vocally, but to go along halfheartedly. For example, when her husband was called back into leadership, Jan recounts telling her stake president,

---

18. COHC, #030 (2009), 12.

> "My boys have just gotten their father back and you want to take him away again." [The stake president] said, "We have boys and my wife feels just like you do, but the Lord needs your husband. Can you support him in this?" "Yes," I said through my tears.[19]

Jan ultimately agrees to support her priesthood leader's decision to call her husband into another leadership calling, but she does so after having expressed her pain and unhappiness with the situation.

Another halfway measure is to split the difference in some way—to do what the leadership wants, but also to do what the individual woman wants. Some women in Hawaii did this when the Relief Society lost its financial autonomy in the 1970s. Alexandra states,

> When the announcement was made about turning all [Relief Society] accounts over to the bishop, there was great consternation. Due to [our] earnings, we had a substantial bank account, but no particular needs for it, so it just built up to a large balance. [The sisters] said, "No! That's our money. We are not going to do that!" I told them we had to turn it over. The reply: "Alright then, we'll spend it."
>
> They decided to go into Honolulu to a nice restaurant and have an expensive buffet lunch. Two sisters were appointed to look over the restaurants in Honolulu to find the best buffet with large servings. I rounded up enough faculty women with cars who were willing to drive in and eat with us. The auto trip to the city was in itself a rare treat for most of the sisters, who had no cars to take them anywhere. They dressed up in their colorful muu muu's, with large hibiscus flowers behind their ears, and draped with many strands of heavy shell leis. It was a truly great event for them.
>
> They had the time of their lives. Personally, I was embarrassed because they stacked up their plates so high that I feared the food would fall off, [but they] ate every bite. . . . They each had some of everything, spent every dollar, and were very happy.[20]

In this anecdote, the women were not able to keep the money and their account, but they did find a way to not turn the money over to the men who did nothing to earn it. Thus they found a compromise position between their own sense of fairness and what the male leadership wanted them to do.

---

19. COHC, #003 (2009), 12.

20. Ibid., 15–16. Note that oral history #003 features two narrators who were interviewed together.

Innovation, Creativity, Proactivity

Another tactic Mormon women use as they navigate teachings and policies they disagree with is to be proactive and creative in figuring out more inclusive ways to live out their Mormonism. This creativity and innovation that can arise in the face of patriarchal exclusion is well expressed by religious scholar Mary Bednarowski. In her book *The Religious Imagination of the American Woman*, Bednarowski argues that religious ambivalence—feelings of constraint or exclusion within a religious tradition, but at the same time feeling nourished and enriched by it—can be a religious virtue and a conscious choice that enlivens a person's spirituality and community:

> This is an ambivalence that requires women always to be vigilant, always to be critical of their communities' inclination toward exclusion and distortion and at the same time to be open to new possibilities to hold up and reform or transform or dig up, from wherever they have been hiding, their traditions' most liberating and healing insights.[21]

This process of digging up the best within the tradition and reforming exclusivist tendencies requires an expanse of creativity and proactivity.

A handful of more feminist women interviewed for this oral history project exhibit this willingness to innovate and be proactive in their attempts to create a more gender inclusive Mormon experience. Lynn is a woman who takes situations into her own hands by coming to her leaders with new ideas. Because she was uncomfortable with teachings about males presiding within marriage, she came up with her own plan to make her temple wedding the experience she wanted it to be. In the following anecdote, Lynn knew when she married that she didn't want the temple sealer to

> ruin my day by talking about the patriarchal order. My cousin was a sealer in the St. George temple. We decided we'd get married in St. George, and I talked to my cousin and I said, "I want a woman to speak, to be part of the ceremony." He said, "You're going to have to get the temple president's ok on that. . . ."
>
> So I went to the temple president's home and knocked on the door. He had been up since the 5:30 AM session and was in a bathrobe on the sofa. I'd interrupted his nap probably. I asked, "Would you

21. Mary Bednarowski, *The Religious Imagination of the American Woman* (Bloomington: Indiana University Press, 1999), 20.

> mind if we had a couple speak?" This was our intention—a man and a woman. The temple president's response was, "I can't see a reason why not." I mentioned my cousin, and he said to just make sure we didn't go over the time allotted. His concern was the timing in the sealing room. But [the couple I had in mind] weren't available that weekend. So I asked my friend Sharon. . . . And she agreed. So she gave the talk at my wedding and [my cousin] sealed us. I didn't have to listen to any of the patriarchal order stuff I'd long since rejected.[22]

This incident stands as an example of the good results that can occur when members take initiative, come up with a plan, and present it to their leaders. We see here that there is sometimes space available for innovation and accommodation—people simply need to actively pursue it.

Lynn again pushed for greater gender inclusion while working within the confines of Church structure when she discussed ways in which she tried to find space for herself within the ritual of her son's baptism. She recounts,

> I spoke at [my son's] baptism and then stood up while [my son and husband] went into the font. I stood next to the font as [my husband] took him down, so there was some participation [on my part]. Then I stood by his side and held my son's hand when [my husband] confirmed him. . . .
>
> We tried various things [like this] and I worked with people. I was always thinking of other ways I could make things more inclusive.[23]

In the Mormon context, the performance of ritual is almost always the exclusive domain of males.[24] However, Lynn, believing strongly in the symbolic importance of women's inclusion in these seminal rituals of Mormonism, found creative ways to insert herself into the ritual, while still staying within the prescribed boundaries of Mormon ritual action.

One interesting variation of this proactivity strategy is some women's engagement in a self-conscious finessing of their leaders as they worked for greater sensitivity to women's issues within their ward communities. Anne recounts the ways she has successfully walked the line

---

22. COHC, #030 (2009), 13.

23. Ibid., 24–25.

24. One exception is the performance of ritual washings and annointings by women in the Mormon temples.

between speaking her mind to her leaders on gender issues and being understood and embraced by her community:

> My bishop in my last ward at BYU was telling all the girls that they needed to get their educations so that if something happened to their husbands they'd be able to provide, and help kids with school work. Rather than just telling him that that's B.S., which is what I felt, I found a way to couch it in terms of spiritual gifts and God giving us abilities and God expecting us to make the most of them. I told the story of the servant who buried his talents which were taken away. So I was able to couch what I was saying about education being something that women should pursue in and of itself and as an end of itself . . . in a way that was palatable, and he was able to say, "Yeah, you're right." Whenever I've been able to do that, I've had people, usually women, thank me for doing it.[25]

With this anecdote, this woman manifests a realization that she needs to be strategic in framing her points in ways that would resonate with her bishop's understandings. This is a necessary skill for women operating within a patriarchal context who hope to convince their male leaders that a change of emphasis or practice is optimal. This woman knows that strong language or perfect frankness would likely cause her leader to become defensive, so she strategically employs language and principles that he already embraces. Appealing to Mormon ideals of personal progression was sure to resonate more with this woman's bishop than a discussion about how such rhetoric reinforces certain traditional gender roles that constrain both women and men.

Lynn likewise talks about self-consciously finessing her bishop in an attempt to get him to listen to her with an open heart and understand her struggles as a feminist Mormon. While Anne finessed through appealing to Mormon principles that she knew would resonate with her leader, Lynn uses a thoughtful gift to try to eliminate any defensiveness or animosity that might have been present in the conversation:

> When a number of those women . . . were running to the bishop to tell on me after I'd said something in Relief Society, I went to meet with the bishop. It was between General Conference sessions that were being broadcast. I thought, he'll probably be hungry, so I made

25. COHC, #026 (2010), 9.

> him a sack lunch. Because who can be mad at me if I do that? Is that manipulative? I don't know, but it was also thoughtful. . . .
>
> It did break down barriers. . . . This discussion was really honest and friendly. But the irony is that he's the one who banned me from teaching. . . . He was really apologetic about it—because of the sandwich, I guess.[26]

In a Mormon patriarchal context in which male leaders have the power to decide when and how a woman contributes to her ward community, Anne strategically attempts to soften her bishop. She describes her actions as potentially manipulative, but as feminist theorists have said, in patriarchal contexts, manipulation is one key way women attempt to control their situations, given their lack of hard power.[27] These self-conscious strategies of finessing or manipulation are one type of proactive behavior women interested in issues of gender sometimes engage in to encourage their leaders to embrace more progressive stances or to understand them better.

As mentioned in the beginning of this chapter, patriarchy is not just a concept or a practice that Mormon women navigate in the Church organization. With the Proclamation on the Family's emphasis on men presiding in the home, as well as various other teachings and scriptures that emphasize the same, patriarchy is also a concept that can have an effect on their marriages. Charlotte compensated for feelings of ambivalence with her place in the Church by taking control where she could take control—in her own home and marriage:

> I can't do much to make the Church organization and structure more inclusive, but what I can do is take control of my marriage and my life here in my house. So even though in theory [my husband] is supposed to be my presider in the home, I've made it clear that that doesn't happen. We've done our best to try to be egalitarian in all of our decision making and practices. In no sense does his opinion on any matter have more weight than mine, and he certainly does not have the final say. We reject the idea that he is in some way a mediator between myself and God.[28]

---

26. COHC, #030 (2009), 22.

27. See Sarah Hoagland, *Lesbian Ethics: Toward New Values* (Palo Alto: Institute of Lesbian Studies, 1989), 100 for more on women employing manipulation in heteropatriarchal contexts.

28. COHC, #061 (2010), 8.

Anne discusses the dynamics of her sister's marriage, highlighting her sister's forthright and assertive stances. Like the previous narrator, she has rejected the idea that her husband's opinions should carry more weight than her own:

> She [my sister] decided several years ago that she didn't like what the birth control pill did to her body, so they would use condoms. Her friends all say that their husbands would refuse to use a condom. My sister's attitude is, well, does he want to have sex? If he does, then he'll accommodate my interests and needs as well. She sticks to her guns on things like that. Her husband understands that he's not the privileged one in the relationship that gets to make such determinations.[29]

In this way, Anne is proactive in creating a home and a relationship in which the husband in no way acts as final decision maker on marital issues.

Sometimes, however, empowerment within marriage is not enough to salve the sting these women feel about their subordinate place in the Church. Thus another tactic women used to deal with their ambivalence was to proactively find and cultivate communities of likeminded Mormons who were sympathetic to their concerns. These women spoke of finding progressive or intellectual Mormon publications and groups like *Dialogue*, *Sunstone*, and *Exponent II*. As Lynn stated, "I stayed in Mormonism because of those communities, whereas I might have jettisoned completely without them. I found a space where I could talk about the things and ideas I cared about."[30] These communities that were willing to delve into questions relating to priesthood, gender, and power, actually often served to keep these women within Mormonism, as they learned from others with similar struggles how they have navigated these patriarchal waters.

Outright Rejection

One last external strategy that Mormon women engaged in when they were confronted with teachings or instructions with which they disagreed was outright protest or overt disregard. For example, Maude, a single parent, recounts,

29. COHC, #026 (2010), 9.
30. COHC, #030 (2009), 11–12.

> At certain periods of my life, if I heard that women were to stay home, I'd get up and walk out of a church service. I did not feel that that was the Church of Jesus Christ of Latter-day Saints that "spoke" to me. Families are important, but the structure of families varies, especially today.[31]

Not only did Maude internally dismiss such teachings as mistaken, she visibly acted on this belief by walking out of meetings.

In another example, Genevieve, a stake Relief Society president, recounts an incident in which she simply ignores her area authority's instructions:

> At one point, I submitted a request through the stake president, which then went to [an area authority]. I asked for Barbara Winder, the then Relief Society general president, to come to our Women's Conference and speak to our sisters. [The area authority] said, No. Then he said that [I] and Barbara Winder probably knew each other. Certainly she could not be invited because [we] probably knew each other. That didn't even make any sense to me. Anyway, I went around him and got her to come.[32]

These two women clearly feel secure enough in their own judgment and in their own sense of the gospel to ignore or protest statements that went against their understandings. They see such incidents as evidence of human fallibility and individual personality quirks making their way into leaders' judgements and statements, and so they choose instead to listen to their own intuition and act accordingly.

Conclusion

While navigating one's way in a patriarchal church can be a complicated task for some Mormon women, most of the women in this chapter manage to find an equilibrium—a way to exist in the Church, often quite happily, without being in a constant state of angst. They direct their energies to outside goals, they find solace in other communities, they choose to focus on egalitarian principles that the Church also embraces, they grow accustomed to writing off certain Church practices and ideas as unfortunate products of a traditional and patriarchal culture, and they take heart in the small victories they win as they

31. COHC, #001 (2009), 15.
32. COHC, #004 (2009), 14.

find ways to live out more gender inclusive ideals. Margaret articulates nicely what can be a rough road to peace with the Church:

> I have hammered my own way to mostly peaceful living with the Church. Though when it comes along asking us to do door to door canvassing for Prop. 8, I decline. When I get pushed like that I start getting resistant. I cherish my free agency.[33]

Margaret's juxtaposition of hammering and peace is evocative of the struggles some women experience as they navigate these waters. Like many women quoted in this paper, Margaret treasures her free agency and ultimately turns to her conscience, her judgement, and her sense of the gospel to guide her when faced with policies or teachings she finds troubling.

Others, however, have found it impossible to live with integrity and maintain activity in the Church. Lynn is now largely inactive. It is difficult for her to go to church and live with integrity when the basic structure and theological premises of the Church violate some of her core principles:

> I still love some of the people in my ward. I have very good friends there, but increasingly church is not a place that I find I am welcome. At least my ideas are not. The issue gets back to integrity and how I can be involved in a culture that demands certainty, that seems to demand devotion, when I'm increasingly at odds politically and theologically with many of the stands it takes. Also, I have trouble with the basic structure of the Church. How can I be true to my conscience and yet support a structure that's patriarchal and that excludes women? That's a huge issue for me. I know there are a number of people who just want to write me off. "Oh you're a feminist, you're just power hungry." And I think, No. It really is an issue for me. I'm not just being belligerent. I'm not just being prideful. All those things they accuse you of. I'm trying to live with integrity, and I can't fake belief. I can't fake it.[34]

As Lynn explicates, sometimes women who believe so strongly in principles of gender equality are unable to pragmatically compromise and find ways to live with integrity within the patriarchal structure of the Mormon Church. Her decision to no longer remain a fully prac-

33. COHC, #007 (2009), 13.
34. COHC, #030 (2009), 16.

ticing member of the Church is deeply tied to her sense of her own integrity, honesty, and authenticity.

This chapter highlights the words of women who are steadfast and happy Mormons, despite the occasional run in with Church hierarchy or discomfort over certain teachings, and women who have deeply struggled to come to terms with women's status in Mormon teachings and the Church structure. While these women may ultimately end up in different places—some inactive, some fully active, some semi-active—a common thread that weaves all these women together is a conviction of the importance of agency and the importance of integrity. These two concepts, so fundamentally Mormon, undergird all their various decisions to agree or disagree with leaders, and to ignore or follow Church dictates.

Chapter Twelve

Relief Society

Taunalyn Ford Rutherford

In September 2010 Julie B. Beck, general president of the Relief Society of the Church of Jesus Christ of Latter-day Saints, spoke to members of the organization—LDS women eighteen years and older. Beck declared that she and the other women in her presidency had "prayed, fasted, pondered, and counseled with prophets, seers and revelators to learn what God would have [them] do to help his daughters be strong in the face of 'the calamity which should come upon the inhabitants of the earth.'"[1] Beck then said, "An answer has come that the sisters of the Church should know and learn from the history of Relief Society." Further she explained, "Understanding the history of Relief Society strengthens the foundational identity and worth of faithful women." Beck then announced, "In consequence of this, a history of Relief Society for the Church is being completed and will be available for our use next year."[2]

In August 2011 the LDS Church began distributing to members of the Relief Society the book *Daughters in My Kingdom: The History and Work of Relief Society* in English with plans to print and distribute the book in twenty-two additional languages. Because of the diverse global nature of the Church, Beck explained, "We needed something that would have global application and be applicable into the future, something that would appeal across cultures and languages, so it needed to be more message based rather than a typical chronological historian's history."[3] Susan W. Tanner, author of the book and a former general

1. Julie B. Beck, "'Daughters in My Kingdom': The History and Work of Relief Society," *Ensign*, November 2010, 114.

2. Ibid., 114.

3. The Church of Jesus Christ of Latter-day Saints, "Diversity and Strength

Young Women president, offered the following disclaimer about her work: "This book is not necessarily meant to be a conclusive history; there are already historians who are doing that." Tanner continued, "The book needed to be something that every woman could read and understand and be invited into this work no matter where they are coming from."[4]

Beck suggested that an additional justification for the publication and wide distribution of *Daughters in My Kingdom* is the book's significance as a tool for converts to the Church, who comprise the majority of members. She said, "As the Church itself grows exponentially over the years, I think there will be great value in this book for the women who join the Church to say, here's who I am, this is what I've become part of, this is my specific identity in this Church." In summary Beck clarifies the audience and intent of *Daughters* by declaring, "We've had stories written for the historians. We've had stories written for the scholars. We've had stories written for the press. But we've never had the story written for the women themselves."[5]

Early reviews of the book by scholars and historians have generally acknowledged the stated purposes of *Daughters in My Kingdom* and avoided the temptation to hold the book up to unintended standards of balanced comprehensive historical scholarship. Harvard professor and member of the Relief Society, Laurel Thatcher Ulrich, admitted that *Daughters* is not without problems as is any historical text, but she sees three positive aspects that set the book apart from recent Church curriculum. First, since most LDS instructional manuals are organized thematically and *Daughters* is organized chronologically, "it puts history in the curriculum." Second, "By focusing on the Relief Society, it puts women in the curriculum. Like other organizations, the LDS Church has also had a problem of having 'women-less history.' This is really important. *Daughters in My Kingdom* is an entire manual on women." Third, Ulrich points out that a small difference is that, unlike most Church manuals, "it names the authors of the book."[6] Additionally,

---

of Mormon Women Highlighted in New Relief Society Book," *Newsroom*, August 19, 2011, available at http://www.mormonnewsroom.org/article/diversity-strength-mormon-women-new-relief-society-book.

4. Ibid.

5. Ibid.

6. Laurel Thatcher Ulrich, lecture, November 20, 2011. Video of lecture and

Ulrich pointed to the section on polygamy as an example of one positive element in the book.[7] She goes so far as to call the book's treatment of polygamy "path breaking as many, many manuals never mention it."[8]

A review from the blog *The Exponent* also finds positive aspects of *Daughters*. The reviewer applauds the extensive use of women's voices and the treatment of material in the first seven chapters of the book. She concedes, "While professional and amateur church historians may be underwhelmed with the history presented it is still a huge step forward as far as presenting women's history in official church publications." The positive tone of the review changes however when the final chapters are discussed. "Chapters 8–10 are mostly apologetics on the church's teachings about women and women's roles," argues the reviewer. "These three chapters, about the Priesthood, Motherhood, and 'living up to your privileges,' are the most disappointing part of the book."[9] Ulrich identifies this same weakness in the last chapters. There seems to be a lack of willingness to engage fully with controversial subject matter in the historical record from the 1970s forward. Ulrich also notes the "dismal" timeline on the last page, which shows that "the history from 1969 to the present is the history of the disappearance of the Relief Society."[10]

It is important to establish the LDS Church's intended purpose for *Daughters in My Kingdom*—to serve as an accessible history of Relief Society for a culturally, intellectually, and spiritually diverse church and "provide perspective and strength for the 21st century woman."[11] It is also important to ask how well this purpose is served. The aforementioned reviews laud *Daughters* as a history of the Relief Society when the subject matter deals with issues further removed from today. This essay builds upon the foundation laid in the current reviews and moves

---

notes are available at https://www.dialoguejournal.com/2011/laurel-thatcher-ulrich-on-daughters-in-my-kingdom/ (accessed September 1, 2012).

7. See [Susan W. Tanner], *Daughters in My Kingdom: The History and Work of Relief Society* (Salt Lake City: The Church of Jesus Christ of Latter-day Saints, 2011), 46–49.

8. Ulrich, lecture.

9. Starfoxy, "Review: Daughters in my Kingdom," *The Exponent* (blog), August 28, 2011, http://www.the-exponent.com/review-daughters-in-my-kingdom/ (accessed December 3, 2011).

10. Ulrich, lecture.

11. Julie B. Beck in LDS Newsroom's "The Diversity and Strength of Mormon Women."

beyond them to consider what can be learned about the history and work of the Relief Society today from *Daughters*. A second focus will be women's narratives, in which I address the question of what can be learned from some of the "daughters" themselves. The women considered here speak of their Relief Society experiences in the Claremont Mormon Women's Oral History Project. Their voices serve as a barometer of the usefulness and authenticity of the history and the messages in *Daughters*. Juxtaposing this institutional history with the lived experiences of Mormon women helps reveal possible explanations for the historical lapses within the final chapters of the manual.

What *Daughters in My Kingdom* Reveals about the LDS Relief Society of Today

When Julie Beck declared that her presidency had received the divine direction that the sisters of the Church should "know and learn from the history of Relief Society" she was, most likely unknowingly, confirming historian Jan Shipps' theory about Mormonism's distinctness and strength. According to Jan Shipps, Mormonism is a new religious tradition distinguishable from all other existing religious traditions because of its "foundational tripod, a metaphorical support unit composed of prophetic figure, scripture, and experience—Joseph Smith, the Book of Mormon, and the corporate life of the early Saints."[12] According to Shipps "the survival and endurance" of Mormonism depends upon the emphasis and strength of each of these legs.

The majority of Latter-day Saints understand the importance of Joseph Smith and the Book of Mormon to the integrity of the Church. However, they would be less likely to understand the importance of "the corporate life of the early Saints" or what Shipps refers to as "sacred time and space" of the foundational history.[13] In fact many women quietly expressed surprise when President Beck suggested that the solution to many of the problems facing Latter-day Saint women was to know and learn from the history of Relief Society. Shipps claims that what maintains the boundary for modern Latter-day Saints, which al-

12. Jan Shipps, *Mormonism: The Story of a New Religious Tradition* (Urbana: University of Illinois Press, 1985), xiii.

13. Ibid., 128–29.

lows them to thrive as a new religious movement, is their ability to reenter this sacred time and space:

> The reading of the history of the pioneer period, standing in Temple Square, looking up at Eagle Gate, sitting in conference when the whole community is symbolically gathered back to the center place, participating in or even simply watching the pioneer parade on 24 July each year—these are examples of customary situations that can take modern Saints back to the mythic time when the Mormon world was fresh and new. This does not happen all the time, nor does it happen to all the Saints. But the return to the uniquely sacred time . . . happens often enough to a large enough number of Latter-day Saints to guarantee that today's Saints live out their lives in a corporate community that still stands squarely and securely in the presence of the past.[14]

By providing a link to this sacred time through reading historical narrative and looking at the many pictures and paintings of this history, *Daughters in My Kingdom* is an invitation into sacred time and an assurance that even new converts feel a connection to the foundational history of the Latter-day Saints. Thus, *Daughters* reveals that the Church has grown and globalized such that the members no longer can connect to sacred time and space by physically going to the place of its occurrence. Furthermore, it reveals that the members need help to access, understand, and find meaning in the founding narratives of the Church.

Another current trend in Mormonism is revealed by a close reading of *Daughters.* Armand Mauss has identified a greater openness on the part of the Church stemming from the years of Gordon B. Hinckley's presidency. He cites a LDS Church news release about the 2009 opening of the new Church History Library, which states:

> the new Church History Library is the substance behind the growing emphasis of transparency in the Church's interaction with the public. This facility opens the door for researchers and historians of all kinds to flesh out the stories of Mormon heritage that pass through the imagination of Latter-day Saints from generation to generation. The Church cannot undertake this project on its own. . . . It is in the interests of the Church to play a constructive role in advancing the cathartic powers

14. Ibid., 29.

> of honest and accurate history. . . . A careful, yet bold presentation of Church history, which delves into the contextual subtleties and nuances characteristic of serious historical writing, has become increasingly important. If a religion cannot explain its history, it cannot explain itself.[15]

The candid discussion of polygamy, the Indian placement program, and even the acknowledgement of shortcomings in programs and people that are present in *Daughters* seem to confirm this trend. One hundred and twenty-two years after President Wilford Woodruff's Manifesto ordering the cessation of plural marriages, *Daughters* contains evidence of a greater willingness on the part of the Church to reclaim polygamy in its history to the degree that an authorized manual of the Church could say, "The women of the Church who, by revelation, embraced plural marriage and who, by revelation, later accepted the Manifesto are worthy of admiration and appreciation."[16]

One final trend that is revealed via textual analysis of *Daughters in My Kingdom* is the clear disconnect between the real and the ideal in the areas of priesthood authority and women's autonomy, as well as the defining of gender roles. I examine these issues from the presentation in *Daughters*—which tends to favor the ideal of institutionalized history. Then I juxtapose this presentation with the experiences of women from the Oral History Project narratives that favor the individual and "lived" perspectives. The disconnect is not surprising and is one that the institutional Church recognizes and anticipates as members with different circumstances all over the world seek to adapt the gospel to their everyday lives. My intention here is to demonstrate how personal narrative and institutional history can generate a dialogue that leads to further understanding and growth.

The organization of *Daughters in My Kingdom* follows a topical pattern. However, a clear chronological outline also emerges in chapters 1–7. For instance, Chapter 1, "Relief Society: A Restoration of an Ancient Pattern" deals primarily with the period of the New Testament and suggests that the Relief Society "is of ancient origin" and that Joseph Smith taught that "the same organization existed in the church

15. "'A Record Kept': Constructing Collective Memory," LDS Newsroom, as cited in Armand L. Mauss, "Rethinking Retrenchment: Course Corrections in the Ongoing Campaign for Respectability," *Dialogue: A Journal of Mormon Thought* Volume 44, no. 4 (Winter 2011): 18.

16. [Tanner], *Daughters in My Kingdom*, 48.

anciently."[17] Chapters 2–7 are each topical as well as primarily chronological as their chapter titles suggest: Chapter 2, "'Something Better': The Female Relief Society of Nauvoo"; Chapter 3, "'Cleave unto the Covenants': Exodus Migration, and Settlement"; Chapter 4, "A Wide and Extensive Sphere of Action," which covers the last half of the 19th century; Chapter 5, "Charity Never Faileth" deals with the first decades of the 20th century, the Relief Society's work during two wars, and the rise of the Relief Society Social Service Department; Chapter 6, "A Worldwide Circle of Sisterhood" covers the postwar/Cold War period and emphasizes the international growth of the Church. The text then takes a large leap to 1992, highlighting the 150th anniversary of the Relief Society; finally, Chapter 7, "'Pure Religion': Watchcare and Ministering through Visiting Teaching" is both topical and internally chronological as it treats the history of visiting teaching from its beginnings to the present.

This clear chronological pattern is important to note since it ends somewhat abruptly with chapters 8–10 and shifts to topics that have historically led to contention and division among Mormons interested in issues of gender. Perhaps a more jarring shift in this later section of the book is the lack of individual women's voices. Instead, we hear about women through the voices of Church leaders—most of them men. This trend of predominantly male authoritative voices in the concluding chapters of *Daughters* is significant, and we need to ask why authoritative women's voices are elided. Several LDS oral history repositories are emerging and we can turn to the Claremont Oral History Project to find narratives of Relief Society sisters in the decades from 1970 forward.

Chapter 8 "Blessings of the Priesthood for All: An Inseparable Connection with the Priesthood"

From the chapter's title and the cover photo of a black couple at an LDS temple, one would anticipate that this chapter would relate the story of the extension of priesthood authority to all worthy males in 1978. However, the central theme is: "All Heavenly Father's sons and daughters are equally blessed as they draw upon the power of the priesthood."[18] The phrase "equally blessed" suggests that equality is

17. Eliza R. Snow, Quoted in ibid., 7.
18. [Tanner], *Daughters in My Kingdom*, 127.

an issue that pervades discourse on priesthood. Yet there is no treatment of the history behind the priesthood being given equally to all men. Furthermore, the chapter is comprised mainly of quotes by male Church leaders or general Relief Society leaders that reflect a defensive tone. For instance, Sheri Dew states, "Sisters, some will try to persuade you that because you are not ordained to the priesthood, you have been shortchanged. They are simply wrong, and they do not understand the gospel of Jesus Christ."[19] The presence of such quotes implies that there is a need to assure LDS women that they do not need to be ordained in order to be equally blessed.

Further insight can be gleaned through a focus on the women in the Claremont oral histories. According to these women there is not unanimous understanding of priesthood and the need for a gendered division of labor. These quotes offer glimpses into individual case studies of lived religion. These narrators reveal diverse reactions and read together; they articulate a certain disconnect when it comes to understanding of priesthood.

A majority of voices in the oral histories speak of contentment with the current situation of a male-only priesthood and see LDS women as wielding power. One woman, Angela, said:

> I think women are a powerful force in the Gospel. I think sometimes people see that the Gospel is a competition between men and women. But I don't see it that way. I think our roles are complementary . . . I mean, with priesthood, maybe a woman can do it better than a man, but that is not the purpose of it. I think it is Heavenly Father who has designed it in such a way that women can do their work to bring the Church forward in a way that man cannot do. He may have the priesthood, but that's not the end of it all. Women are powerful forces. They really are. I admire that about women.[20]

Yet some of these "contented" women felt the need to stress their contentment with Relief Society's auxiliary and subordinate status to the point that they begin to sound ambivalent:

> I absolutely love Relief Society. . . . but the males—the priesthood has all the authority in everything. That doesn't bother me in the least, but I know it does some people. I think that is the divine

19. Quoted in ibid., 128.

20. Claremont Mormon Women's Oral History Collection, Library of the Claremont Colleges, Claremont, CA, hereafter COHC, #65 (2010), 13.

> way. The priesthood is the ruling power—everything comes under the priesthood it is obviously the ruling power. It's not obvious in a visual sort of way, but it is obvious in the books—even the Relief Society is under the authority of the priesthood—even though you've got a Relief Society president it is still under the authority of priesthood. It doesn't bother me in the least. My eldest daughter is horrified at that sort of thing. But I'm not. [21]

There are several who support the male priesthood but feel there is room for improvement in the distribution of leadership opportunities and a need for a better balance of men and women's voices:

> I believe and sustain the priesthood leadership in the Church and I have only ever had good experiences with it. I definitely feel it is the right structure that men and women have been given the correct roles. At times though, I do feel a longing for women to be more prominent during general conference addresses and other such occasions. I remember while on my mission, the Assistant to the President asked my companion to conduct one of the all day missionary conferences. She did as requested (and did a very good job!) however the mission president wasn't very happy. I understood why it wasn't in standing with the Church organization, but felt it was a shame that sister missionaries weren't given similar opportunities as the elders. To be honest, I wouldn't want the priesthood but would like to see women to be more visible.[22]

The oral histories reveal a broad range of experiences with authority in the Church, and some narrators, such as Erica, express outright discontent with the status quo:

> I quite frankly think that the current second-class position of women in the Church is a result of Victorian-era masculinity devices which limit women to the nature role of spiritual[ity] and men to leadership. It is worldly, sexist and false. I think these roles were constructed in an era where the roles of men and women were politically and culturally defined, and that current leadership is not confident enough to seek out real revelation in regard to the worldly positioning inherited from Joseph Smith and Queen Victoria.[23]

21. COHC, #126 (2011), 5–6.
22. COHC, #114 (2011), 9.
23. COHC, #127 (2011), 10.

Erica's view is in direct contrast to the perspective that is strongly emphasized in Chapter 8 of *Daughters in My Kingdom*, which argues that, "Men have no greater claim than women upon the blessings that issue from the Priesthood and accompany its possession." The key argument in *Daughters* is that "the priesthood is not owned by or embodied in those who hold it. It is held in a sacred trust to be used for the benefit of men, women, and children alike."[24] This argument works on the assumption that there is no benefit inherent in *giving* priesthood service but only in *receiving* it. The women of the Claremont Oral History Project, such as Susan, however, report tremendous fulfillment and blessings received from their official service in Relief Society and the other auxiliaries:

> I was Relief Society President of the Chicago Heights Stake when it was formed in 1974. I enjoyed it; I felt like I could affect change. And I felt like I had authority. And then I was the Stake Young Women President, and I initiated having a Young Women Preview. This was like when the boys get the priesthood but we had a special night for the girls who were coming into Young Women. Those callings were important to me.[25]

The operative question is this: are women given sufficient opportunities without the priesthood to, as this woman claimed, "affect change," exert authority, and truly serve? *Daughters in My Kingdom* observes that women may not be taking full advantage of their opportunities for service and influence because they fail to see Relief Society as anything more than a class to attend rather than viewing it "after the pattern of the priesthood." The argument is that "Relief Society is intended to accomplish similar purposes as Priesthood quorums that organize men in a brotherhood to give service, to learn and carry out their duties, and to study the doctrines of the gospel."[26] Lauren exhibits this lack of interest in the Relief Society and its opportunities spoken of in *Daughters*:

> If I had my way, I would not be a member of the Relief Society, but the only way to remove my membership is to remove my Church membership. That is not fair. Men have the choice of being set apart with priesthood—but I am doled Relief Society based on my sex and age.[27]

---

24. Dallin H. Oaks, Quoted in [Tanner], *Daughters in My Kingdom*, 127.
25. COHC, #115 (2011), 12.
26. Boyd K. Packer, quoted in [Tanner], *Daughters*, 138.
27. COHC, #127 (2011), 10.

Are LDS women taking full advantage of the opportunities that they have already been given in the Church? Is the lack of priesthood really the issue?

A quote by Joseph Fielding Smith in Chapter 8 of *Daughters* assures eventual power for women: "It is within the privilege of the sisters of this Church to receive exaltation in the kingdom of God and receive authority and power as queens and priestesses."[28] However the eventual priesthood power for women is not the focus of the chapter. The Claremont oral histories do reveal a current sense of empowerment felt by Mormon women in their Church callings and in interactions with priesthood leaders. These narrators confirm the words of President Gordon B. Hinckley that conclude Chapter 8: "There is strength and great capacity in the women of this church. There is leadership and direction, a certain spirit of independence, and yet great satisfaction in being a part of this, the Lord's kingdom, and of working hand in hand with the priesthood to move it forward."[29] Some of the women, such as Jena, speak mostly with fondness about their opportunities to serve in leadership positions and exert influence:

> I had been in the Church for about five years when we arrived in Saudi Arabia and they asked me to be the Relief Society president. I hadn't the merest clue what that could possibly mean. I remember that the lady who had been president before me handed me this very strange object, which you attached to your telephone and said, "You will need this." It was one of those things that allowed you to put the telephone on your shoulder and walk around all day with it. I there became aware of the great complexities of women's lives in the Church."[30]

While Jena experienced the weight of responsibility and authority as she served as Relief Society president, Lynne acknowledged her experience of powerlessness when she was summarily released from her teaching calling after her comments in opposition to Proposition 8 in California were published in a Salt Lake newspaper:

> I received a note from a woman in the ward thanking me for my fine lessons and saying that she would miss them. I called to tell her that I wasn't released. She kindly acknowledged that she might have

28. Quoted in [Tanner], *Daughters in My Kingdom*, 133.
29. Ibid., 143.
30. COHC, #80 (2010), 9.

made a mistake. It turned out that there was no mistake. I *had* been released. I was told firmly, "Yes, you were." I asked [my Church leader] why. His response was that "someone" had told him that I wasn't doing my calling. I explained that was not correct and explained that I had arranged for a substitute when I knew I would be away. I asked again why he had released me, and coldly and firmly he said, "You opposed the Church!"[31]

As we examine issues relating to priesthood authority and women's autonomy, one central question to address is this: In a history of the Relief Society why did the author feel it necessary to devote an entire chapter to the priesthood? One could also question whether the issues surrounding equality are as clear as *Daughters* makes them seem. The Claremont oral histories demonstrate a need for greater clarity on the topic of LDS women and the priesthood.

Furthermore, another important question revolves around what some scholars see as women's waning influence in the Church. As Ulrich states, "The sphere of influence of the Relief Society has slowly yet steadily been in decline for generations. [And] this book inadvertently does an excellent job of documenting that decline."[32] The voices of women in the oral histories speak both for and against this perspective. Both of the following women speak of the current status of Relief Society:

> Another change is that the Relief Society has less control over its own affairs than it once did. The Relief Society used to have its own buildings. And the Relief Society started the Church adoption agency. We were more autonomous. Relief Society sisters were encouraged to take more initiative. We paid dues of $.50 per year. We had bazaars that people really worked hard at, and we had our own funds. It was more autonomous. It changed gradually. The Church consolidated and tried to simplify, and not have members drawn in so many different directions. A lot of that was a loss for Relief Society.[33]

> I now see, as another change, a greater openness, especially toward women, as well as a greater importance given to women's leadership and presence in ward council. In my ward, the Relief Society President has much to say. Everyone listens to her. The bishop asks

31. COHC, #133 (2011), 17.
32. Ulrich, lecture.
33. COHC, #115 (2011), 10.

> her advice. . . . I remember when stake boards were a very big deal. I remember when it was a great honor to be on a stake board. . . . Almost all of that stake board organization is gone now, and all the wards and stakes have continued to function pretty well. It was very nice while it lasted, but maybe [it was] truly superfluous.[34]

Regardless of whether one's perspective is that the simplification was beneficial or that the changes robbed the Relief Society of power, these changes were not discussed in any historical detail in *Daughters in My Kingdom* except in the timeline. Thus the Claremont oral histories serve as an important resource documenting how women navigated the change.

A handful of narrators mentioned when the Relief Society lost their financial autonomy in the 1970s. While some narrators reported their Relief Society sisters resisting the idea of turning their hard-earned money over to the bishops, others were happy to have the responsibility of raising and controlling funds taken from them. Jackie remembers:

> I was president when we were required to close our bank account, and turn our funds over to the Bishop. I thought, "OK, orders are orders. But first we are going to use some of it." So we bought a few things that we wanted, some new tablecloths and a good wheat mill, and then we had a catered lunch. No one brought any food. No one did any dishes and *then* we turned over our money.[35]

On the other hand, Elaine remembers the transition positively:

> We welcomed the time that we didn't have to raise money. In Wisconsin we had bazaars and bake sales and made some money, but I don't mind not having to do that. The change is representative of the new solider footing that the Church finances are on. The Church can now pretty much finance all the things that need to be done. The turning over of the Relief Society's money to the priesthood was not a big thing where we were because we didn't have that much money to turn over. We were barely getting by. The [Relief Society] then had one less thing to be responsible for.[36]

In addition to the change in finances, the women of the oral histories also abound with opinions on how these changes in the last decades of the twentieth century influenced the curriculum of Relief Society. From

34. COHC, #5 (2009), 18–19.
35. COHC, #3 (2009), 15.
36. COHC, #4 (2009), 16.

the timeline in *Daughters* we learn that 1997 was the year that "Relief Societies, high priests groups, and elders quorums begin to study from the same curriculum on Sundays."[37] Women from the oral histories rarely point to this as a positive change. Most often there is either resentment or nostalgia for an earlier time, as was the case for Molly:

> I really dislike the current one-size-fits-all manual. There is so much that women need of their own. To have all the lesson materials go through a unisex sausage grinder puts a tremendous burden on the teachers to make lessons relevant. I really miss the fine lessons that were written individually for the Relief Society years ago.[38]

Furthermore, some, such as Rachael, mourned over the focus away from motherhood and homemaking lessons:

> I loved having lessons as I was growing up on how to raise children. The Mother Education lesson was the most important to me and it's no longer in the curriculum. I'm really disappointed in that because I feel the young women today need so much help. They have a hard time getting it. The only way they can get any education on that is through their mothers and through their peers who are having just as much trouble raising their children. Today is such a scary time to raise children that they need it more than ever.[39]

This omission of mother education does seem strange in light of the focus the next chapter of *Daughters in My Kingdom* given to this role.

Chapter 9 "Guardians of the Hearth": Establishing, Nurturing and Defending the Family

Chapter 9 begins with a historical reference to September 23, 1995, when Gordon B. Hinckley read for the first time "The Family: A Proclamation to the World" at the general Relief Society meeting. Quotes from two former members of the general Relief Society presidency follow, which express their feelings at the time the Proclamation was read. The question is then posed: "Why did the First Presidency choose to announce the proclamation on the family in a general Relief

37. [Tanner], *Daughters in My Kingdom*, 184.
38. COHC, #7 (2009), 23.
39. COHC, #14 (2009), 10.

Society meeting? After President Hinckley read it, he provided an answer to that question. 'You are the guardians of the hearth.'"[40]

Chapter 9 is also full of quotes on motherhood and nurturing from general Relief Society presidents and General Authorities, as well as a few anecdotes from nineteenth-century women. It is notable that the origin of the mother education lessons in Relief Society beginning with Sister Bathsheba W. Smith, the fourth Relief Society general president, was mentioned although the cessation of the lessons was not.[41] The chronological treatment of historical events was dropped in Chapter 9, and again we can turn to the Claremont oral histories for insight about contemporary Mormon women's views on motherhood and nurturing.

One narrator, Abby, recalls, "Growing up I thought Relief Society was called that because it offered 'relief from children' for the mothers of the Church."[42] Clearly from the emphasis on motherhood in *Daughters in My Kingdom*, this is not the case. Why the need to focus so heavily on a topical subject in a book about the history of Relief Society? Just as in the previous chapter on priesthood, this may be an indication of the author's struggles to interpret and navigate diverse ideals and realities of motherhood. The Claremont oral histories demonstrate how difficult it may be for some women to face this chapter on motherhood. For instance, Erin struggles with the common Mormon rhetoric used to appease and comfort childless women:

> I want to be a mother now, not in the next life. And if I don't get to be a mother now, I am satisfied with not being a mother in the next life. Because I know God loves me and doesn't want me to be limited. Plus, I hate the "in the next life" line. It is condescending. You would never say to a man who has a sliced off his bleeding arm that in the next life he'll have an arm. But that is what it is like when you tell a childless woman that in the next life she'll have a child. Childlessness can be "bleedingly" painful, and it is cruel to disregard, to ignore and belittle her pain and struggle by assigning it to the next life.[43]

Stacey, from Australia, acknowledges economic realities that force mothers to abandon the stay-at-home-mother role so often touted by Church leaders:

40. [Tanner], *Daughters*, 148.
41. Ibid., 153.
42. COHC, #128 (2011), 5.
43. COHC, #127 (2011), 10.

> In an ideal world, yes, it would be wonderful if women could stay home and it was Miss Patty Perfect that would often have her bread made and a perfect house, and we'd all love to be like that, but it isn't an ideal world. In Sydney, the cost of living is very high, and I think the majority of women do need to get outside and work apart from the home.[44]

The oral histories also reveal flexibility in gender roles, which are not emphasized in *Daughters*:

> When I was [the Relief Society] president, I had to attend the ward council meetings an hour before our own church started. That meant taking separate vehicles, and my husband would be the one getting our little daughters ready for church. I would hold back a little giggle when I would see them racing into the sacrament room. One would have matted hair, the other would be wearing a dress backward and running shoes. It was comic relief for a Sunday.[45]

Chapter 9 does provide examples from a variety of different family types and a variety of different nationalities. However, there is only a slight acknowledgement of diverse gender roles. The fact that historical events from the period from Equal Rights Amendment to Proposition 8 are scarce in *Daughters* could indicate a continued anxiety about gender roles and definitions of the family among Relief Society and priesthood leaders. For example Katelyn offers her frustrations: "I get really, really tired of being told that all I am supposed to do is train and learn about motherhood in Relief Society. I see Relief Society as a 'Mother's Club' and I don't want to join."[46]

The problems for some women inherent in the final chapters of *Daughters in My Kingdom* become clearer through the perspectives of "daughters" in the oral histories. Their voices confirm the value in the Relief Society's efforts to call for women "to know and learn from the history of Relief Society," as well as continuing to "add to the history of Relief Society through [their] words and actions."[47] One important question that comes from this juxtaposition of their voices and *Daughters* is how long it takes to gain enough perspective to clearly

44. COHC, #124 (2011), 6.
45. COHC, #118 (2011), 9.
46. COHC, #127 (2011), 10.
47. [Tanner], *Daughters in My Kingdom*, 114.

write history. Perhaps the events of the decades that are omitted from *Daughters* are still too fresh and the issues still too close to our lived reality for the author to treat them with the objectivity that even an institutional history requires.

While the last few chapters of *Daughters* do not always reflect the complex, nuanced lives and experiences of Mormon women, the book and the oral histories do share a conviction about the importance of women's lives and stories. Paula, whose feelings and viewpoints about family and gender do not reflect those expressed in Chapter 9 of *Daughters*, reinforces the profound importance of telling women's stories:

> My sorrow is manifest in tears every Sunday, and my anger is aimed at ignorance. What I feel is akin to mourning a death. Something precious is missing from my life: trust and belief in leadership. I take the sacrament on Sunday, even when I am away from my home. I pay tithing, pray, read scriptures, and live the teachings of Christ. . . . I'm a piece from the wrong puzzle, and yet I lay there on the table positioned face down and to the side, with the other pieces that are face up. I was not given a calling for a year. I now spend four hours a week in the Family History Center. No one released me from being a visiting teacher, so I have performed that calling faithfully. I have to keep reminding myself now that I have a hill to climb. I've had to look for something to fill in, and I'm taking a class in writing my life story. That class came about as an answer to prayer. I had been praying, "Tell me what I should be doing," and I was looking through the newspaper one day and I saw this little article titled, "Write your own History Class." It just stood out like a light. It has been a wonderful thing for this time of my life. We're all learning each other's stories. It's fantastic.[48]

Daughters in My Kingdom and the "daughters" in the Claremont oral histories demonstrate that there is power in women's narratives. There can never be just one definitive history of Relief Society for a globally diverse church. Ultimately, institutional histories like *Daughters*, oral histories, and the scholarly studies of both are only points of departure. LDS women and men need to claim and write their own personal narratives and learn from those of others.

48. COHC, #133 (2011), 17–18.

Chapter Thirteen

Heavenly Mother

David Golding

Archaeologists in 2009 announced the discovery of the oldest known depiction of the human form: a figurine of a woman carved from mammoth bone that dates to the Paleolithic Era, some thirty-five thousand to forty thousand years ago.[1] Findings like this figurine, or "Venus" as archaeologists have called this type of artifact, are nothing new. Excavations over the past century have uncovered dozens of prehistoric Venuses and most of them share characteristics like the naked and corpulent (possibly pregnant) body, the small size and fine detail, and the exaggerated female body parts.[2] This time, however, the Venus discovered at Hohle Fels Cave in Germany astonished researchers not because it exhibited the classic features of a Venus figurine but because its carbon-dating placed it almost a full five thousand years before all other similar finds. This indisputably female sculpture single-handedly pushed the envelope back on Paleolithic material history. Where archaeologists had thought early humans were barely acquiring the skills of crafting stone tools and where the art depicted only animals and plants—there she was in superb detail, the hidden mother, possibly the mother goddess of prehistoric religion.[3]

1. Nicholas J. Conrad, "A Female Figurine from the Basal Aurignacian of Hohle Fels Cave in Southwestern Germany," *Nature* 459 (May 14, 2009): 248–52.

2. Patricia Monaghan, *Encyclopedia of Goddesses and Heroines*, 2 vols. (Santa Barbara, Calif.: Greenwood Press, 2010), 1:xii–xiii.

3. The verdict is still out whether this particular Venus is a depiction of a mother goddess, a heroine, or an anonymous woman. As a whole, however, Venus figurines—which outnumber prehistoric male figurines ten to one—do provide ample support for goddess worship. See Lucy Goodison and Christine Morris, eds., *Ancient Goddesses: Myths and Evidence* (Madison: University of Wisconsin Press, 1998); James J. Preston, "Goddess Worship: An Overview" in *Encyclopedia*

Artifacts like this directly challenge the assumption that male-oriented monotheism has dominated human religiosity. Anthropologists and other scholars throughout the twentieth century focused on monotheism as a fairly ubiquitous worldview across human societies. Some even attributed monotheism to the default religious impulse of the human condition. More technical debates that recognized variants like polytheism and pantheism still operated on the basis that modern religiosity culminated in a monotheistic standard.[4] Historians often implied this standard in the case of American religious history, since the communities under discussion have generally held to a monotheism devoid of a female deity.

A norm of situating studies of religious history within the male or monotheistic frame emerged even as these same scholars continued to discover more Venuses and other goddess artifacts. Regardless of the technical arguments debated in the previous century, the material history available today suggests that goddess worship or the veneration of female divinities has had as much occurrence and salience as any other theism. And yet studies of religion that consider the context of historical goddess belief fall outside the norm.[5]

---

of Religion, 14 vols., ed. Lindsay Jones (New York: Thomson-Gale, 2005), 6:3585–86; Gary Beckman, "Goddess Worship—Ancient and Modern" in *"A Wise and Discerning Mind": Essays in Honor of Burke O. Long*, ed. Saul M. Olyan and Robert C. Culley (Providence, R.I.: Brown Judaic Studies, 2000), 11–23. For a critique against assumptions that Venus figurines constitute depictions of mother goddesses, see Naomi Hamilton, et al., "Can We Interpret Figurines?" *Cambridge Archaeological Journal* 6, no. 2 (1996): 281–307.

4. Key works that advanced the theory of prehistoric monotheism include Andrew Lang, *The Making of Religion*, 3rd ed. (New York: Longmans, Green, and Company, 1909); Wilhelm Schmidt, *Der Ursprung der Gottesidee*, 12 vols. (Münster: Aschendorff, 1912–1955). Even studies that noticed the prevalence of goddess worship in prehistory still invoked assumptions of male-oriented monotheisms or a patriarchal kind of matriarchy. Now a classic in the anthropology of goddess cultures, Erich Neumann's *The Great Mother: An Analysis of the Archetype*, trans. Ralph Mannheim (Princeton, 1955) has sustained criticism in recent years for adhering to these assumptions.

5. Rosemary Radford Ruether, *Goddesses and the Divine Feminine: A Western Religious History* (Berkeley: University of California Press, 2005) deals mainly with anthropology and feminism, but many of these same trends have also occurred in the fields of history and religious studies. See also Lotte Motz, *The Faces of the Goddess* (New York: Oxford University Press, 1997) for sustained argumentation supporting these observations; also Andrew Fleming, "The Myth

Against the backdrop of historical goddess belief and historical monotheisms, Mormonism presents a unique convergence. Here is both the belief that a goddess exists as the Heavenly Mother and the avowal of the First Commandment to have no other gods before God the Father. With their anthropomorphic concept of God-as-male, Mormons have ventured beyond Christian orthodoxy by taking male descriptors of God to a literal extreme. He not only embodies male attributes, but he is anatomically male. Such masculine literalism did not exclude the divine feminine from early Mormon thought, but rather became the impetus itself for Mormons to arrive at a belief in Heavenly Mother. This development occurred because of early Mormons' fascination with hyper-literalistic readings of scripture. They arrived at the texts of the scriptures relishing the simplicity of their meaning and purposefully eschewing "spiritualizing" (or non-commonsensical) modes of interpretation.[6] Feeling unencumbered by formal theological creeds, early Mormons projected onto the characters of the Bible, including the Godhead, a uniform humanity. God was human—just in a resurrected, immortal, and glorified state of being.

When earth functioned as a transitional (albeit essential) phase of one's eternal progression toward godhood, the human family and the heavenly family shared a physical correspondence. There are mothers on earth, so the logic went, so there must be mothers in heaven.[7] Eliza R.

---

of the Mother-Goddess," *World Archaeology* 1, no. 2 (1969): 247–61 and Peter J. Ucko, *Anthropomorphic Figurines of Predynastic Egypt and Neolithic Crete,* Royal Anthropological Occasional Paper No. 24 (London: Andrew Szmidla, 1968).

6. Parley Pratt is perhaps the most famous critic in early Mormonism of what Mormons called "spiritualizing" the Bible. "Does that need spiritualizing?" Pratt asked after quoting from the New Testament in an 1855 sermon. "Does it need some learned man from a college to tell you what that means, and give you the spiritual sense of it? It had but one sense, and that a child could understand." Statements like this are indicative of the early Mormon antipathy toward non-literalistic readings of the scriptures. Parley Pratt, October 7, 1855, in *Journal of Discourses*, 26 vols. (London and Liverpool: LDS Booksellers Depot, 1854–86), 3:129. See also Terryl L. Givens and Matthew J. Grow, *Parley P. Pratt: The Apostle Paul of Mormonism* (New York: Oxford University Press, 2011), 110–11.

7. Linda P. Wilcox provides an excellent brief history of the development of Heavenly Mother doctrine in "The Mormon Concept of a Mother in Heaven," in *Sisters in Spirit: Mormon Women in Historical and Cultural Perspective*, ed. Maureen Ursenbach Beecher and Lavina Fielding Anderson (Urbana and Chicago: University of Illinois Press, 1987), 64–77.

Snow, one of the first to give expression to a Mormon belief in Heavenly Mother, saw the doctrine as a necessary and logical corollary to this understanding of the grand cosmic narrative. "In the heav'ns are parents single?" she posed in an 1845 poem, "No, the thought makes reason stare; / Truth is reason—truth eternal / Tells me I've a mother there."[8]

As soon as the idea of a Heavenly Mother was introduced, Mormon commentators immediately set out to qualify it as a belief, not a practice of worship, saying that many exalted people in the eons of pre-existence had become gods and that current mortals could also attain to divinity. Mormons all along avoided worshipping these exalted individuals—they understood their worship to be directed only to God the Father.[9] With this new cosmology came a key distinction that would preclude goddess worship yet allow goddess belief.

An ambivalence has resulted within Mormonism over whether to extend that belief into ritualized or devotional practices. As a fully qualified goddess and the coequal spouse of God the Father, Heavenly Mother enjoys an omnipresent power only gods can have. And yet she remains, like the Venus of Hohle Fels Cave, hidden from view and just under the surface of all of God's dealings that Mormons celebrate. The degree that Mormons see her accompanying God in sacred history fluctuates. In a sense Heavenly Mother remains present and absent in all of Mormon theology about God—everywhere and nowhere. One thing is certain: belief in her existence persists to the point of a resounding affirmation.[10]

---

8. Eliza R. Snow, "Invocation, or the Eternal Father and Mother," *Times and Seasons* 6 (November 15, 1845): 1039; also Eliza R. Snow, *Eliza R. Snow: The Complete Poetry*, ed. Jill Mulvay Derr and Karen Lynn Davidson (Provo: Brigham Young University Press; Salt Lake City: University of Utah Press, 2009), 313–14. Snow's is one of the first documented expressions of Heavenly Mother belief in Mormon history, though she claimed that the idea originated with Joseph Smith who had died more than a year before this poem's publication.

9. Joseph Smith's last recorded sermon attempted to reconcile his new doctrine of deification with charges that he was teaching polytheism. He would claim a monotheistic mode of worship while affirming that the Bible itself taught a plurality of gods in its formula of Father, Son, and Holy Spirit. See Smith, Sermon, June 16, 1844, in *The Words of Joseph Smith: The Contemporary Accounts of the Nauvoo Discourses of the Prophet Joseph*, ed. Andrew F. Ehat and Lyndon W. Cook (Provo, Utah: Grandin Book Company, 1991), 378–82.

10. Margaret Merrill Toscano explores in greater detail than I will undertake

Mormon belief in a Heavenly Mother has not been lost on scholars. Excellent work in the past has focused on the contested space that such a belief has set up within Mormon culture. After all, women do not hold ecclesiastical office within the Church of Jesus Christ of Latter-day Saints and Church leaders have explicitly discouraged the practice of Heavenly Mother worship.[11] Most recently, a survey of Mormon and non-Mormon literature about Heavenly Mother has improved the historiographical discussion.[12] Scholars have yet to undertake, however, a contextual reading of Mormonism's Heavenly Mother theology that places it within the greater phenomenon of historical and prehistorical goddess worship.

The terrain shifts considerably when we navigate these waters. Here the source material abounds in oral and material history. Documentation—the staple of historians—lacks coverage of goddesses especially for the most recent age. Mormonism follows suit. We have no shortage of statements regarding the existence of a Heavenly Mother, but not much moves beyond this basic affirmation, and no qualified theological work has emerged that systematically connects Heavenly Mother to the principal theologies of Mormonism. Official statements and policies say much about the institutional level of Mormonism, but like most cultures of the world's goddess worshippers, modes of god-

here how Mormon culture and policy have contributed to a theological silencing of Heavenly Mother. See Toscano, "Is There a Place for Heavenly Mother in Mormon Theology? An Investigation into Discourses of Power," *Sunstone* 133 (2004): 14–22.

11. The most explicit statement to this effect came from Gordon B. Hinckley as a counselor in the First Presidency in his sermon "Daughters of God," *Ensign* 31 (November 1991): 97–100. While this ban on Heavenly Mother worship does not appear as official policy in administrative manuals of the Church, in one case the ban was enforced at Brigham Young University in 1996 when Assistant Professor Gail Turley Houston was effectively fired for praying to "Heavenly Mother as well as Heavenly Father." The University administrators considered Houston's prayer as constituting "a pattern of publicly contradicting fundamental Church doctrine and deliberately attacking the Church." Houston was an outspoken critic of the Church's policies toward Heavenly Mother worship prior to being denied continuing status at BYU. See Linda Ray Pratt, C. William Heywood, and Robert M. O'Neil, "Academic Freedom and Tenure: Brigham Young University," *Academe: Bulletin of the AAUP* 83, no. 5 (September–October 1997): 52–68.

12. David L. Paulsen and Martin Pulido, "'A Mother There': A Survey of Historical Teachings about Mother in Heaven," *BYU Studies* 50, no. 1 (2011): 71–97.

dess worship tend to find expression outside of institutional fixtures. Oral histories better target where these expressions thrive: in the private, familial, and extra-orthodox spaces of a culture. New sources based in oral history and material culture would provide access for drawing a more symmetrical comparison between the Heavenly Mother of Mormonism and historical goddess belief.

Thanks to the recent and growing Claremont Oral History Project containing oral histories by Mormon women, such access has become at least preliminarily available. The interview questions included specific references to Heavenly Mother belief. Comments ranged from a simple affirmation to detailed descriptions of theology and private devotional practices. Despite variations between these women on their beliefs in Heavenly Mother, several patterns emerge in the oral histories that complement and uniquely amplify historical goddess belief. This context suggests that Mormonism aligns at certain points with goddess history and diverges at others.

James J. Preston's *Mother Worship*, an important anthropological anthology on goddess history, ends with a summary of patterns that have emerged across world cultures. These patterns set apart practices and beliefs surrounding goddess worship from other religious expressions and traditions. Preston observed that worshippers have tended toward connecting goddesses to motherhood, the bearing of children, virginity, and nurturant attributes. Even those female divinities that held no expressed role as a mother-figure could serve as a nurturer in miscellaneous ways. Goddesses often imbued ambivalence by functioning as the supreme agent of such opposites as beauty and violence, love and anger, and nurturing and destroying. Other patterns included venerating the goddess as the source of fertility of crops and humans, as a mediator between humans and more distant male deities, as polymorphous and associated with nature, and as a divine receptacle for suffering.[13]

The oral histories of these Mormon women exhibit a correspondence with some of these patterns of historical goddess worship despite arising out of a Christian monotheism. Mormon women reported a strong association of Heavenly Mother with motherhood and derived a sense of their social ideals of the mother from her. They tended to

13. James J. Preston, "Conclusion: New Perspectives on Mother Worship," in *Mother Worship: Theme and Variations* (Chapel Hill, N.C.: University of North Carolina Press, 1982), 330–36.

appeal to nurturant and natural metaphors to describe how they understood Heavenly Mother's role within (or sometimes without) the Godhead. Where these Mormon women diverge from historical goddess traditions demonstrates some Mormon innovations. The oral histories show that Mormon women currently occupy the space many goddess worshippers in the past have inhabited—a space where the dominant understanding of God-as-male moves the open veneration of the Goddess to the sidelines, and yet their accepted and orthodox view of cosmology prevents them from denying her presence.[14]

What follows illustrates how Mormonism and particularly Mormon women have a place within the broad and ancient movement of goddess belief. The renaissance of goddess belief in the case of Mormonism coincides with Mormons' core goals of "restoration," or the resurrection from a primitive or primordial age a truth long obscured or a practice long dormant. Perhaps what we are observing in these oral histories is a moment within the continuing process of Mormon restoration, a process via Heavenly Mother of reclaiming and reinstituting modes of goddess awareness and communion diminished within Christianity after the rise of orthodox theologies and the rise of male monotheisms. Whether Mormons identify Heavenly Mother within their own restoration narrative, their goddess concept functions within various contexts—contexts as diverse as historical goddess traditions and idiosyncratic theologies of Mormonism.

General Patterns in the Oral Histories

Motherhood, Nurturant Attributes, and Childbearing

Many Mormon women automatically associated Heavenly Mother with motherhood; no interviewee in the oral histories indicated anything to the contrary.[15] This might seem an obvious aspect of

14. For an extended discussion on this sidelining effect in Euroamerican religious cultures, see Rosemary Radford Ruether, *Sexism and God-Talk: Towards a Feminist Theology* (London: SCM Press, 1983).

15. The oral histories referenced in this chapter are from the Claremont Mormon Women's Oral History Collection, Library of the Claremont Colleges, Claremont, CA, hereafter COHC. Oral histories that made explicit mention of the motherhood or mothering qualities of Heavenly Mother included #012, #014, #020, #021, #025, #036, #043, #044, #046, #057, #072, #076, #095, #096, #123,

Heavenly Mother belief, however in historical context, motherhood has not always been immediately associated with goddesses. In the cases of Anat of ancient Israel and the goddesses of Çatal Höyük, Crete, and Malta, worshippers venerated women deities for their divine queenship, not because they understood their goddesses as divine mothers.[16] Recent scholarship has questioned the presumption that all goddesses throughout history served a motherly role. These scholars point out that researchers with a Eurocentric perspective have brought their own cultural presuppositions to their interpretations of the evidence.[17]

A good deal of goddess worship, therefore, does not immediately include mother worship. Nevertheless, many cultures have still held to a mother-goddess cosmology. In these settings, goddess worshippers viewed their divine mothers as extensions of the earthly matriarchs.[18] By framing a Heavenly Mother belief in principally motherhood terms, Mormon women in the oral histories parallel both those historical groups that saw their goddesses as extensions of earthly matriarchs and the Euroamerican researchers that have assumed a uniform mother-goddess aspect to historical goddess traditions.

Of the ancient traditions, the West Semitic goddess Athirat most closely resembles the Heavenly Mother of Mormonism. Her proper name in the earliest sources was Ashratum-ummi, "Athirat is my mother." Later Ugaritic mythological texts depict Athirat as the mother of the other gods and the consort of Amurrum, the chief deity of the Babylonians over the western nomads. Some scholars believe that because Amurrum served as the moon god, that Athirat filled the role of a solar deity, a sun goddess governing the diurnal rhythms and giving life and beauty to nature. Athirat appeared in later Syriac and Ugaritic texts as the consort of the chief god El, the mother of all the gods, and the "Queen of Heaven." A Hittite text names her the wife of Elkunirsha, meaning "El, the owner of the earth." This matrimonial connection to El brings Athirat into an association with the God of the Torah, Elohim.[19]

---

and #132.

16. Goodison and Morris, *Ancient Goddesses*, 17, 48–49, 60, 85–88.

17. Ibid., 17; Motz, *The Faces of the Goddess*, 2–4, 18–23.

18. Goodison and Morris, *Ancient Goddesses*, 19–21.

19. Edward Lipiński, "Athirat" in *Encyclopedia of Religion*, 1:589–92; Monaghan, *Encyclopedia of Goddesses and Heroines*, 1:62–63; Goodison and Morris, *Ancient*

Exactly what Elohim meant and how the ancient Semitic concept of El changed with Israelite history remains debated among scholars.[20] Nevertheless, the vicarious presence of Athirat in the Old Testament via El connects her with Heavenly Mother in one crucial way: Heavenly Mother is conceptually possible for Mormons because of her association with God the Father, and, from as early as 1842, they have identified God the Father with the Elohim of the Old Testament.[21] While

---

Goddesses, 79. For over thirty years, scholars have debated the "Asherah problem," or the difficulty establishing exactly what Athirat and Asherah meant in their ancient source texts. The Khirbet al-Qom and Kuntillet Ajrud contain inscriptions where the phrase "Yahweh and his Asherah" appears. Two views differ over whether to interpret *ašhērāh* as the name of a goddess or as an early Hebrew word for "holy place." To avoid an overly technical discussion on the nuances of the Asherah problem, I side with Lipiński and offer Athirat as the consistent example across western Semitic traditions of ancient goddess veneration of the wife of El and the Queen of Heaven. Regardless of the verdict on pre-exilic Israelite worship of an Asherah goddess, Athirat worship has been well substantiated with evidences dating to the periods I discuss here and provides the best ancient comparison for a Heavenly Mother–type goddess. New discoveries might yield better insights into a contextual comparison between Asherah and Heavenly Mother, but for the time being, the evidence for Asherah remains suspect and prone to etymological and semantic debates over the meaning of Khirbet al-Qom and Kuntillet Ajrud. For an extended defense of Asherah as a pre-exilic Israelite goddess, see Judith M. Hadley, "The Cult of Asherah in Ancient Israel and Judah: Evidence for a Hebrew Goddess," *University of Cambridge Oriental Publications*, No. 57 (Cambridge: Cambridge University Press, 2000). See also Baruch Margalit, "The Meaning and Significance of Asherah," *Vetus Testamentum* 40, fasc. 3 (July 1990): 264–97. Lipiński's article as cited in this note remains the most recent challenge (2005) to Hadley's and Margalit's arguments.

20. M. H. Segal, "El, Elohim, and YHWH in the Bible," *Jewish Quarterly Review* 46, no. 2 (October 1955): 89–115; Patrick W. Skehan, "The Divine Name at Qumran, in the Masada Scroll, and in the Septuagint," *Bulletin of the International Organization for Septuagint and Cognate Studies* 13 (Fall 1980): 14–44; Claus Westermann, *Genesis 1–11: A Commentary*, trans. John J. Scullion (Minneapolis: Augsburg, 1984); Diana V. Edelman, ed., *The Triumph of Elohim: From Yahwisms to Judaisms* (Grand Rapids: William B. Eerdmans, 1995).

21. Joseph Smith recorded a prayer to Elohim in his journal in 1842: "O, thou who seeeth [sic], and knoweth the hearts of all men; thou eternal, omnipotent, omnicient, and omnipresent Jehovah, God; thou Eloheem, that sitteth, as sayeth the psalmist, enthroned in heaven; look down upon thy servant Joseph, at this time; and let faith on the name of thy Son Jesus Christ . . . be conferred upon him." Smith, Journal, August 23, 1842 in *Journals*, ed. Andrew H. Hedges, et al., vol. 2 of

Mormons clearly have not gone so far as to identify Heavenly Mother with Athirat, they do have in this ancient example a contextual cousin.[22] Venerating a goddess because she accompanies the chief deity as a spouse and because she serves a motherly role came naturally to Mormons and ancient western Semites alike.

---

the *Journals* series of *The Joseph Smith Papers*, ed. Dean C. Jessee, Ronald K. Esplin, and Richard Lyman Bushman (Salt Lake City: Church Historian's Press, 2011), 117. Smith also gave an exegesis of Elohim as it appeared in Genesis 1:1 in his King Follett Discourse. See Stan Larson, "The King Follett Discourse: A Newly Amalgamated Text," *BYU Studies* 18, no. 2 (1978): 202–3. Kevin L. Barney explores how Smith understood Elohim to mean the head of all the gods convening a grand council before the creation of the earth in "Joseph Smith's Emendation of Hebrew Genesis 1:1," *Dialogue: A Journal of Mormon Thought* 30 (Winter 1997): 103–35 and "Examining Six Key Concepts in Joseph Smith's Understanding of Genesis 1:1," *BYU Studies* 39, no. 3 (2000): 107–24. Barney defends Smith's exegesis of Elohim as consistent with what biblical scholars now conclude about the meaning of Elohim and the persistence of Hebrew pluralism across biblical eras. For a scholarly examination of Elohim by a Mormon scholar, see Donald W. Parry, "4QSam[a] and the Tetragrammaton," in *Current Research and Technological Developments: Proceedings of the Conference on the Judaean Desert Scrolls, Jerusalem*, April 30, 1995, ed. Donald W. Parry and Stephen D. Ricks (Leiden: E. J. Brill, 1996). Even major shifts in Mormon conceptions of godhead have not displaced their association of Elohim with God the Father. Compare David John Buerger, *The Mysteries of Godliness: A History of Mormon Temple Worship* (San Francisco: Smith Research Associates, 1994), 60, 80, 111–14; Brian W. Ricks, "James E. Talmage and the Nature of the Godhead: The Gradual Unfolding of Latter-day Saint Theology," Master's thesis, Brigham Young University, 2007; and Nate Oman, "Scripture and Interpretation: Some Thoughts Inspired by 'The Family: A Proclamation to the World,'" *Times and Seasons* (blog), February 13, 2007, http://timesandseasons.org/index.php/2007/02/scripture-and-interpretation-some-thoughts-inspired-by-the-family-a-proclamation-to-the-world (accessed July 2012).

22. Daniel C. Peterson argued that the Book of Mormon provides scriptural evidence of this connection in Nephi's account of the Tree of Life; see Peterson, "Nephi and His Asherah," *Journal of Book of Mormon Studies* 9, no. 2 (2000): 16–25. Whether or not the Book of Mormon contains traces of ancient Semitic goddess worship, the women interviewed did not mention the Book of Mormon as a source for their belief in Heavenly Mother. Peterson does provide a useful account of the ancient Israelite context of goddess worship, though it should be noted that his references of "Asherah" largely correspond to my use of "Athirat," except in some technical distinctions between the two. Recent scholarship has challenged prior associations of "Asherah" with the consort of El (see note 19 above).

One woman captured the motherhood pattern that appears in the oral histories with this wonderfully succinct statement: "I guess she would be a lot like our mothers here."[23] Her logic is instructive. First, she performs mental guesswork in answering the interview question about Heavenly Mother, and in so doing exposes the impulse to begin with herself and her own family. Many Mormon women shared this impulse throughout the oral histories; the subsequent concepts they derived from Heavenly Mother were frequently interpreted relative to their own mothering experiences. Second, for this woman, pre-mortal, mortal, and post-mortal mothers share a continuity in their motherhoods regardless of any barrier between these mortal and heavenly spheres.

Heavenly Mother's role as mother does not, however, extend into the mortal realm. Whenever the interviewees explored the motherhood of Heavenly Mother, they invoked spiritual, not physical, vocabulary. As one woman described, "I think of what my Mother in Heaven is—Mother of our spirits, the way [Heavenly Father] is the Father of us all. She is the mother of us all."[24] She left out any direct resemblance between the mortal process of childbearing and how Heavenly Mother might have conceived spirit children. Perhaps the human reproductive process is implied in associating Heavenly Mother with spirit birth, though spiritual motherhood does correspond to some ancient patterns.

A grand mother of human spirits appeared in the religious expressions of some ancient Hellenistic societies. Known as *meter* and *mater* ("mother"), this Mother of the Gods ruled the mountains and the peoples below them (*metropolis* meant a whole town built in her honor), not due to reproductive powers but because of a spiritual motherhood. For giving spiritual life to earth and her human creation, she was revered by some as the *Magna Mater*, the Great Mother/Queen.[25] No one in the oral histories described Heavenly Mother's spirit birthing with any biological reproductive terminology. They left the status of her being the mother of human spirits in the same mysterious ambiguity of the *Magna Mater*. Procreation for both Mormon women and the Hellenized traditions of the Phrygians and Romans involved strictly spiritual possibilities, nothing directly mortal or biological.

---

23. COHC, #057 (2010), 11.
24. COHC, #072 (2010), 23.
25. Motz, *The Faces of the Goddess*, 115–17.

Mormon women did use physical metaphors to insinuate that Heavenly Mother participated in something similar to the reproductive and birthing processes in bearing spirit children. Their metaphors in most cases, though, maintained rather than collapsed the separation between physical and spiritual categories. A pregnant Heavenly Mother was never described as such in the oral histories, though some women in their own pregnancies felt a spiritual connection to her as though she understood the experience of having a child. Mormon women left the biological aspects of motherhood ambiguous and resonated instead with the emotional roles mothers share in giving life to a child and nurturing that child to adulthood.[26] A mother of six mentioned, "As a mother I am cognizant that emotions are so much more magnified in a woman than they are in a man. . . . I can't imagine the sadness she feels about choices we make or things that happen to us. It must be a hundred times more for her."[27] Another woman identified both Heavenly Father and Heavenly Mother as co-nurturers, though the Mother had more involvement in giving beauty and gentleness to nature. "I totally believe that we have a Mother in Heaven [who] is the co-nurturer with Heavenly Father. . . . I think that the women in the Church are obviously the nurturers and the decorators and the ones who make things beautiful and gentle. That is our role in life."[28] Most of the interviewees generalized the nurture of a Heavenly Mother as simply love, or sometimes "unconditional love."[29]

Heavenly Mother's role as a bearer of children remains vague in the oral histories, often nothing more than assumed, most likely due to her stronger association with the spiritual and the ambiguity surrounding spirit birth. Prehistoric goddess traditions likewise left little detail about how they imagined goddesses and childbirth. Not until the Bronze Age did creation myths involving goddesses giving birth to the human family surface. One of the earliest childbearing goddesses was Inanna-Ishtar, the goddess likely to have originated in Sumeria whom Egyptian and Babylonian cultures transposed from a divine creator into a warrior goddess. For traditions like the Inanna-Ishtar culture,

26. Oral histories that mentioned the nurturing attributes of Heavenly Mother included #014, #021, #025, #063, #070, #082, #095, #112, #124, and #125.

27. COHC, #021 (2009), 8.

28. COHC, #082 (2010), 5.

29. COHC, #124 (2011), 9.

the mother-goddess conceived in her womb through intercourse with a consort or another god and then birthed life by converting her womb into the earth itself.[30]

When Mormon women identified Heavenly Mother with childbearing, they sometimes began the line of reasoning with a kind of biological assumption that could possibly mirror Bronze Age goddess traditions, but would still align with these traditions indirectly—the interviewees never suggested that Heavenly Mother birthed the world. One example is typical: "It's always made sense to me that there should be a Mother in Heaven because if family is the most important thing then everybody has a mother." She went on to reason that no one could exist without a mother, so at some point a spirit birth must have occurred, and the one doing that birthing would consequently be Heavenly Mother.[31] Another woman suspected that the physical reality of Heavenly Mother's childbirth was what led Church leaders to leave out details. "God didn't have us all by himself," she put it bluntly, suggesting that Heavenly Mother participated sexually in bearing children.[32] Though some room for a more sexual association with childbearing appears in the oral histories, by and large Mormon women did not connect Heavenly Mother with childbirth, sometimes even minimizing such a connection. For one woman, Heavenly Mother was motherly due to her service and attitude, not because she "has given birth to children."[33]

The least vague reference to childbirth in the oral histories recognized Heavenly Mother as sharing in the birth process. As a former Catholic, this woman felt a reticence to pray to or even think much about Heavenly Mother, fearing that the Mormon doctrine of plural marriage might mean that multiple Heavenly Mothers could exist, an idea she found disturbing. Still, she saw in the Mormon belief in a Heavenly Mother the eternal ideal for women to follow: "I've felt that in times of birth that there was a strong connection with a Mother who understood the power I was going through. I felt assured by that,

30. Anne Baring and Jules Cashford, *The Myth of the Goddess: Evolution of an Image* (London: Viking, 1991), 148–55; Melissa L. Meyer, *Thicker Than Water: The Origins of Blood as Symbol and Ritual* (New York: Routledge, 2005), 1, 5, 34, 37–39.

31. COHC, #036 (2009), 15.

32. COHC, #042 (2010), 14.

33. COHC, #123 (2011), 10.

and that I got a little glimpse of something eternal that I don't usually bother to think about a lot."[34]

While this woman felt a "strong connection" through childbirth, others tended to focus less on Heavenly Mother's motherhood in child-bearing terms and resonated instead with her role as a divine nurturer. The conceptions of divine motherhood in goddess traditions and Mormonism both include nurturant attributes but deviate on the stronger associations with procreation, pregnancy, and childbearing. For Mormon women, Heavenly Mother is mother because of her role in providing pre-existent spirits with life and because of her divine nurturant qualities, not because the earth sprang from her primordial womb.

Supreme Agent and Mother Nature

Among the larger patterns of historical goddess worship and belief, only scant references remain in the oral histories. Mormon women did acknowledge Heavenly Mother as a supreme agent in the ordering and government of the universe and as evident in nature, but not with as much detail as they directed to Heavenly Mother's motherhood, nurturant attributes, and associations with childbearing. Furthermore, statements that demonstrated one of these patterns tended to express opinion or admit to falling outside of the general views of most Mormons.

Those that identified Heavenly Mother as a supreme agent in the universe used qualities commonly associated with Heavenly Father to describe her glory and power.[35] "I conceive of her as the absolute equal in stature, power, and authority to God the Father," went the most concise of these descriptions.[36] Understanding the Mother and Father as two glorified people in an eternal marriage relationship led one woman to associate Heavenly Mother with supreme agency. "[My husband] and I see in that situation an eternal union, a fifty-fifty relationship. I see Heavenly Mother as someone who is so central and as one hundred percent part of godhood as Heavenly Father."[37] Marriage, though, did not immediately connote supremacy; the fundamental notion of goddesshood stood out

34. COHC, #056 (2010), 19–20.

35. Interviews that mentioned the supremacy of Heavenly Mother include #061, #072, #116, and #125.

36. COHC, #061 (2010), 17.

37. COHC, #062 (2010), 24.

for another woman as phenomenal enough to identify her with biblical motifs of God's authority. "You look at Isaiah, and you read, 'Wonderful! Counselor! The Mighty God-Goddess! The Everlasting Mother! The Author of Peace!' I think of her in those terms."[38]

The matriarchal role of the goddess in ordering the heavens is one of the longest threads connecting historical goddess belief across traditions. Not too distant from the Isaiah-esque concept of Mighty Goddess, examples abound of goddesses ruling with absolute power in the ways that Christians have ascribed to God. Venus figurines that date to the earliest epochs of human prehistory possibly suggest supreme goddesses, even a supremacy of female goddesses over male gods. Neolithic pantheons included goddesses associated with sky, earth, and the waters, and when natural catastrophe struck, these prehistoric peoples often attributed the turbulence to the behaviors of a supreme goddess. Egyptian, Babylonian, Greek, Anatolian, and Roman traditions each included goddesses who commanded veneration because of their supernatural power and often their superiority above other deities.[39]

Compared with Mormonism, these ancient traditions maintained a much stronger sense of the goddess as absolute, sovereign, and supreme. While Mormon women allowed for a Mighty Goddess, they never superordinated her above Heavenly Father. In fact, her supernatural power was possible to them because of her relationship to God the Father. Whereas Mormon women derived their concept of Heavenly Mother from their understandings of motherhood, these other ancient traditions derived their concepts of goddesshood from understandings of sovereignty, power, queenship, and matriarchal preeminence. Ideas of queenship or supremacy only supplemented Mormon women's sense of Heavenly Mother as the divine mother; for much of ancient goddess traditions, this dynamic was inverted; and motherhood only supplemented their sense of goddesshood as power and sovereignty.

Like supreme power, nature has factored significantly in historical descriptions of the goddess. Once again, Mormon women made little mention of nature in their reflections of Heavenly Mother, but

38. COHC, #072 (2010), 23.

39. Book-length studies of these traditions abound. See especially Preston, *Mother Worship*; Goodison and Morris, *Ancient Goddesses*; Baring and Cashford, *The Myth of the Goddess*; and Monaghan, *Encyclopedia of Goddesses and Heroines*, as previously cited in this chapter.

the ones who did expressed similar views. Their reasoning combined Heavenly Mother and nature through beauty: nature is evidently beautiful; women are more inherently in tune with beauty than men; thus Heavenly Mother has a divine connection with nature. The outdoors displayed Heavenly Mother's influence for one woman with a hobby for hiking and backpacking. During regular trips to national parks, she found evidence of Heavenly Mother in the scenery: "I see Mother in Heaven as a divine Mother Nature who created all that is beautiful in our natural world. I credit her for the majesty of natural wonders and the breathtaking landscapes of our earth."[40] Even landscaping arranged by human designers suggested something of Heavenly Mother's touch for another woman: "I have this window that I look out of when I sit in my office and I'm looking out of it right now. It looks out onto a golf course and it's so beautiful and serene. . . . I just think there's a woman involved in that."[41]

Only aesthetics factored into these women's concepts of Heavenly Mother as being uniquely involved in the creation of the natural world. Unlike other goddess traditions, Mormon women did not venture into any topographical associations with Heavenly Mother. For example, no one in the oral histories described making a pilgrimage to a sacred natural site or identified a mountain, ocean, river, or natural feature with Heavenly Mother herself. Heavenly Mother creates natural beauty but does not embody nature for these women—a sharp contrast from the traditions that have detailed mythic narratives of the land and sky, sun and moon, and forces of nature that locate the goddess in the natural world.[42]

40. COHC, #071 (2010), 29.

41. COHC, #082 (2010), 13.

42. African traditions provide excellent historical examples of the veneration of the goddess as nature. A classic study that some consider dated material but nevertheless one of the first important studies of African goddess worship is Joseph Boakye Danguah, *The Akan Idea of God*, 2nd ed. (London: Cass, 1968). Daniel McCall's work provides more recent contextual examples. See his chapter and bibliography in "Mother Earth: The Great Goddess of West Africa," Chapter 15 in *Mother Worship*, ed. James J. Preston (Chapel Hill: University of North Carolina Press, 1982). See also Noel Q. King, *African Cosmos: An Introduction to Religion in Africa* (Belmont, Calif.: Wadsworth, 1986); and Barbara C. Sproul, *Primal Myths: Creating the World* (San Francisco: Harper and Row, 1979), esp. Chap. 1, "African Myths." Other traditions that have earth-mother or mother-nature myths, rituals, or beliefs include some Anatolian, Vajrayana Buddhist, Native American, and

Discontinuities

Several patterns of historical goddess traditions find no traction in the oral histories and remain discontinuous in the larger Mormon culture. The goddess served as a mediator between humans and a more distant deity in many traditions; only one woman in the oral histories cast Heavenly Mother in a mediator relationship, and then reversed what would have been the typical arrangement in other goddess cultures. In this woman's view, Heavenly Father mediated her prayers and passed along only essential information to Heavenly Mother in the way that she wrote emails to her mother and let her mother pass that information along to her more distant father.[43]

No one mentioned or associated Heavenly Mother with virginity, fertility of crops or humans, polymorphism, or suffering. These patterns appear in prehistory and early human history due likely to the emergence of agriculture and the decline of nomadic societies.[44] A great deal of the human life cycle in those ages involved the diurnal and seasonal patterns cultivation brought, as opposed to strictly hunting and animal migration. Mormon belief in Heavenly Mother arose during a time of intense industrialization in the United States and Europe in which those agrarian life cycles were displaced by machinery and human labor. In the contemporary context, Mormon women of the oral histories made only passing mention to any kind of farming, and if that, never located themselves as actors within a subsistence economy. The urgency toward sustaining a close-knit family group that could till the land effectively, which likely led to worship patterns that celebrated goddesses' virginity, fertility, and powers over the land, is just not felt by these women. In this sense, their goddess belief has developed along a distinct trajectory asymmetrical from the social circumstances that informed earlier goddess traditions.

Patterns Unique to Mormonism

Some patterns that emerge in the oral histories are better contextualized by Mormon society and history than by ancient goddess tra-

---

Orisan-Indian. See Preston, "Goddess Worship," 6:3583–91.

43. COHC, #107 (2010), 17.

44. Preston, "Goddess Worship," 6:3588–91.

ditions. These patterns derive from features of Mormon theology and society that developed from an inchoate field into a distinctly Mormon system of thought. Here we might look to historical and sociological developments within the Mormon community to note influences on Heavenly Mother belief. The first expressions of Heavenly Mother belief began to appear in the mid-1840s before Mormons left Illinois for Utah. A system of church government and revelation had gained enough of a grip by then that Mormons would consider doctrine within these institutional and ecclesiastical structures. This meant that Mormons regarded "official doctrine" as coming only through certain key men of ecclesiastical authority or through official Church departments. It turned out that those men in positions to interpret or reveal Heavenly Mother doctrine neither issued any revelatory claim regarding her nor enacted any policy that restricted Latter-day Saints from worshipping her.

These theological and cultural circumstances unique to Pioneer-era and later Mormonism set the stage for five major patterns[45] to appear in the oral histories: (1) the lack of revelation regarding Heavenly Mother;[46] (2) the cultural reaction to that lack of revelation by assuming God the Father must be protecting Heavenly Mother through a kind of sacred censorship;[47] (3) the anthropological understanding of Heavenly Mother as an exalted human being;[48] (4) Heavenly Mother's relationship to the Father as his wife;[49] and (5) the possibility of mul-

---

45. I have noticed patterns similar to what Paulsen and Pulido found in their research on LDS leaders' statements on Heavenly Mother, as previously cited; their major headings have inspired some of the structure of this section on patterns unique to Mormonism.

46. Interviews that mention the lack of revelation regarding Heavenly Mother include #009, #012, #014, #018, #022, #023, #024, #035, #040, #042, #047, #051, #053, #057, #063, #072, #094, #122, #126, #134, and #138.

47. These comments included those women who expressed favor regarding this sacred censorship concept and those women who were either offended by or against it. The pro-censorship statements appear in interviews #021, #037, #046, #049, #058, #076, #102, #116, and #134. The anti-censorship statements appear in interviews #019, #061, #072, #085, #099, #107, and #119.

48. The interviews included #012, #018, #021, #026, #039, #045, #061, #062, #072, #103, #107, #116, and #133.

49. These interviews included #039, #044, #045, #046, #049, #055, #059, #062, #104, #107, #119, #122, #126, and #139. Some of these types of comments mentioned Heavenly Mother that mention the divine parent motif include

tiple Heavenly Mothers who live in a polygamous relationship with a single Heavenly Father.[50] These five patterns deviate sharply from the historical patterns of goddess belief in ways that highlight the singular aspects of a Mormon theology of Heavenly Mother. These motifs as imagined by Mormon women within the Mormon theological and cultural systems demonstrate an idiosyncratic idea of the mother goddess.

Lack of Revelation

More than any other single theme in the oral histories, Mormon women acknowledged a lack of revelation regarding Heavenly Mother by a factor of almost two to one.[51] One woman wondered why Heavenly Mother herself had chosen to remain hidden,[52] but most interviewees attributed this lack of revelation to either the scriptures, the leaders of the Church, or Heavenly Father deliberately protecting his divine wife from the ridicule of people who take his own name in vain. In all of these statements, revelation served as the primary mode for doctrine making. Even the women who lamented a lack of revelation about Heavenly Mother regarded the Mormon process of revelation as paramount for any discourse about her to thrive. Standardized revelatory procedures, or at least perceived procedures, dictated their expectations. Many women felt beholden to the system, as though they could not wonder about Heavenly Mother without facing scrutiny or censure by Church leaders. Until further revelation could come down through the

---

#055 and #061 as a divine parent while others included a reference to her direct involvement in the interviewee's life. The interviews #069, #070, #072, #085, #107, #113, and #117. Interviews that mention the involved parent motif include #021, #025, #043, #046, #068, #070, #076, #082, #117, and #133.

50. Women who mentioned a polygamous aspect to Heavenly Mother's relationship with Heavenly Father or a plurality of Heavenly Mothers usually expressed skepticism about such a possibility. Their interviews include #047, #055, #056, #104, #109, #112, #122, and #126.

51. The single most common category of Mormon-specific patterns in the oral histories was the lack of revelation; in second place were references to Heavenly Mother as wife. More precisely, the lack of revelation theme occurred 1.6 times more often than the Heavenly Mother as wife theme. If we combine the pro- and anti-censorship motifs into a single category, then the lack of revelation theme occurred only 1.4 times more often.

52. COHC, #009 (2009), 19.

authoritative channels already in place, Mormon women preferred to wait rather than rock the boat with any kind of theological activism or theorizing about Heavenly Mother in public.

The revelation issue fosters a tension in the mental world surrounding Heavenly Mother belief. One of the strongest sources of their commitment to Mormonism—ongoing revelation—is precisely what blocks further exploration of a topic for which Mormon women generally felt an affinity. This tension inculcates the two most common attitudes to emerge in the oral histories: apathy and waiting. Some women decided not to care about Heavenly Mother because no authoritative revelation existed on the topic, and others, though interested in Heavenly Mother, decided to wait it out. Regardless, both camps saw official revelation as necessary for Mormons to realize a more robust doctrine of Heavenly Mother.

The women that recognized the current lack of revelation regarding Heavenly Mother almost always had an opinion in mind for how Latter-day Saints should regard her. These reactions ranged from urging others to accept that humans would not learn much about Heavenly Mother on this mortal side of the veil to a kind of feminist incredulity toward the status quo. In an LDS Institute classroom setting, an instructor urged the class not to probe into Heavenly Mother theology on the grounds that the Latter-day Saints first needed a revelation to justify further belief; anything else would inevitably lead to speculation and folklore. "Our teacher has the courage," a student of this class reported, "to say we don't know." She saw a connection between speculating about Heavenly Mother and Jacob 4:1—"I think about [this scripture] in the Book of Mormon . . . where it talks about the Jews looking beyond the mark to their detriment." She concluded that she only needed to "work on the things that I do know" and that "part of the gospel that I understand."[53] Another woman valued the relative anonymity Heavenly Mother would enjoy as a result of an obscured theology. Part of her was "OK with not knowing." Many good women "are behind the scenes," she said, "and we don't know what they do. They're the real influence behind a man. . . . Why [Heavenly Mother]'s not mentioned, I don't know."[54] Still another woman desired to keep the doctrine closed. "The Mother in Heaven controversy is another non-issue for me. Yes, she is

53. COHC, #138 (2011), 19.
54. COHC, #018 (2009), 21.

there. Do I need to know more than that? Heavenly Father and Jesus don't seem to think so. Neither do I."[55]

Others, however, bristled at the current state of Heavenly Mother theology. They wished for further revelation and even thought the male leadership was to blame for little, if any, progress in obtaining a revelation. A former ward Relief Society president reported,

> I think we'll wait a long time if we wait for men to talk about her, officially, in the Church. But I look forward to that. One of the great promises of the Church, and again, one of the theological tenets is continuing revelation. . . . As we mature spiritually, and as we become ready for revelation, it is opened to us. . . . I think that fear drives the idea that she is too sacred to talk about or talk to. . . . Fear on the part of men losing control, of everything. Fear by women of rocking the boat.[56]

Sacred Censorship

One of the chief reasons Mormon women gave for a lack of revelation was centered on a concept of sacred censorship. Latter-day Saints already practice an esoteric liturgy in their temples in which only adult initiates who have demonstrated faithfulness and conviction are invited to participate in the ordinances of the endowment and marriage sealings. The temple has come to occupy the pinnacle of Latter-day Saints' sense of the sacred, and they maintain this sacred space by closing participation to outside observers or even members of the faith who have not received a formal, ecclesiastical recommendation. Within the culture, Latter-day Saints emphasize a sacred silencing of temple rituals and liturgy. In the interests of not casting pearls before swine or compromising the sacred integrity of temple ordinances, they have limited much of their temple discourse to the temple itself; only in the temple do many Latter-day Saints feel comfortable discussing what occurs in temple rituals. Outside of the temple, Mormons alter their temple-speak to almost a meta-temple discourse. They talk frequently and thoroughly about the temple, but never explicitly of temple practices.

---

55. COHC, #094 (2010), 6.
56. COHC, #072 (2010), 23.

By adhering to this sacred censorship pattern, Mormons feel they are preserving the sanctity of their most holy places, not practicing deception or an exclusionary elitism meant to favor temple participants. In the same ways that Mormons have prized guarding the temple from outsiders who might profane it, Mormon women in the oral histories valued a sacred censorship of Heavenly Mother. She was too holy to God the Father for Him to allow her to be profaned, and so her absence from scripture and revelation was justified as chivalrous protection. These women not only appreciated God blocking humans from knowing about Heavenly Mother, but also admired him for it. Good men who love their wives stand up to protect a woman's honor, so goes the reasoning.

Mormon women were divided over this rationale. Approximately half of the responses that mentioned censorship took a pro-censorship position while the other half argued against it. All of those that resonated with the idea of a sacred silencing considered this a protecting act on Heavenly Father's part. Many pointed out the spousal relationship the two share, as though Heavenly Father had a duty as the Mother's husband to see to it that her name not be insulted. One of the more vivid examples of this line of thinking emphasized Heavenly Father's chivalry: "I personally feel that the reason we don't read about her is that our Father in Heaven loves her so dearly that he will go to any lengths to protect her. She is so treasured by him."[57] In many cases like this, the interviewee recognized the need for a scriptural basis before speculating about Heavenly Mother, but then offered a non-scriptural justification for censorship. This incongruity of reasoning suggests that these women feel comfortable with what appears emotionally palatable, but they feel uncomfortable with an intellectual foray into Heavenly Mother theology.

Some women spotted this incongruity in other Mormons' attitudes about pro-censorship and even criticized it: "I don't believe that we don't know about her because Heavenly Father is trying to protect her. She's a God; surely she can take care of herself and whip some butt if she needs to."[58] Most women simply did not buy the idea that Heavenly Mother needed protecting. And if she were indeed so special, then shouldn't Mormon women pursue further understanding of her

57. COHC, #046 (2010), 18.
58. COHC, #107 (2010), 17.

qualities and attributes? "People would say that she is so special that we don't talk about her. I thought, 'But if I'm going to love her I've got to know her and her personality.'"[59]

Divine, Glorified Human Person

Early Mormonism of the 1830s and 1840s produced a radical reconceptualization of the nature of God, angels, and humankind tantamount to heresy for much of the Christian mainstream. Prominent Mormons like Joseph Smith, William Phelps, and Parley Pratt turned the traditional formula of divine and human nature on its head. The hierarchical distinctions between a transcendent, incomprehensible deity and mundane, earthly humans became inverted as these key Mormons projected the mortal human family arrangement and ontology onto the order of the heavens. God was human in very nature, just glorified by undergoing a process that included resurrection and exaltation. Humans superseded the angels as a species and could eventually ascend to the same glory and status as God. It was in their blood to be godly, and so their families reflected the same order as the godly family—the family that culminated in a great Chain of Belonging extending into the eternities.

Without arriving at these major innovations of divine anthropology, Latter-day Saints might not have had enough of a theological toolkit from which to fashion a belief in Heavenly Mother. As it was, Heavenly Mother belief arose out of early Mormons' conceptual network of ideas about the physical, ontological nature of God, angels, and humans. It would be this backdrop that would delimit much of the Mormon belief system surrounding Heavenly Mother.[60]

Three major threads that connect with this divine anthropology came to the surface in the oral histories. First, many women extrapolated Heavenly Mother's personality and behaviors from their imagined

---

59. COHC, #085 (2010), 9.

60. The divine anthropology of earliest Mormonism and its development is given excellent treatment in Samuel Morris Brown, *In Heaven as It Is on Earth: Joseph Smith and the Early Mormon Conquest of Death* (New York: Oxford University Press, 2012), especially Chapter 9, "Divine Anthropology: Translating the Suprahuman Chain," 248–78. See also Benjamin E. Park, "Salvation through a Tabernacle: Joseph Smith, Parley P. Pratt, and Early Mormon Theologies of Embodiment," *Dialogue: A Journal of Mormon Thought* 43, no. 2 (Summer 2010): 1–44.

sense of the divine, glorified woman. This image of the glorified woman did not imbue superhuman or transcendent characteristics, rather exemplified the fullest potential of human women. "If the temple promises to both men and women today are true," mentioned one grandmother, "then we have the potential to become as God is with our husband, and if that idea is true and if He was once as we are, then the model would include a Mother in Heaven."[61]

Second, many women located Heavenly Mother strictly in the hereafter, usually with the anticipation of meeting her after death.[62] This linear arrangement of space and time fits the Mormon narrative of eternal progression and divine anthropology. One could not skip mortality to go from an unembodied spirit to a divine exalted god. The whole purpose of earth life was to provide the conditions whereby humans could follow in the progression of their heavenly parents. It did not make sense to Mormon women to identify Heavenly Mother with mortality or with a kind of spiritual otherworld that shares the same space as earth. In this vein, a businesswoman anticipated the hereafter experience to include a reunion with Heavenly Mother. "I pray that I can be the mother in Zion that my Father in Heaven wants me to be, that my parents hoped I would become, and that I know I'm responsible for exemplifying. I look forward to being reunited with my Mother in Heaven and hopefully making her proud."[63]

Third, Heavenly Mother offered a singular model for mortal women to emulate.[64] Mormon women resonated with this option as more closely linked to their own female experience and fully emblematic of the greatest potential a human woman could realize. Some narrators identified features in Heavenly Mother that could not necessarily be demonstrated by (even glorified) men. For one grandmother, Heavenly Mother exhibited the desired image to which all mortal women should aspire. She believed that prayer and meditation involving Heavenly Mother would help "women who have felt alone in a patriarchal church," but "leaders

61. COHC, #051 (2010), 40.

62. Interviews that mentioned Heavenly Mother as present in the hereafter include #027, #039, #049, #050, #069, #078, #082, #085, #104, #114, and #118.

63. COHC, #050 (2010), 23.

64. These types of statements appear in interviews #021, #022, #026, #029, #044, #047, #051, #056, #058, #062, and #072. One interviewee disagreed with the idea that women should emulate Heavenly Mother: COHC, #042 (2010), 14.

tell us that it is not suitable for a woman to pray to her Mother in Heaven because Jesus is only recorded as having prayed to his Father." It was unfortunate for her that "authority has to come down hard on people who are feeling a need for some feminine leadership and comfort."[65] Another woman found the potential for goddesshood in herself and sought to follow Heavenly Mother's example. "I think about what my role would be as a goddess, a queen, a co-partner. I feel like there is this perfect woman whose ideal I have to live up to somehow."[66]

Wife of the Father and Involved Heavenly Parent

A number of oral histories identified Heavenly Mother as the wife of God. Just as the motherhood of Heavenly Mother followed a basic logic and seemed to most Mormon women fundamental to the very possibility of a goddess, so did her status as the wife of God seem obvious. She could not be mother without also being wife, the two identities cooperating simultaneously in the theologies of exaltation and deification. "Obviously my Father in Heaven is living a Celestial marriage," one laconic comment went.[67] Another thought the idea obvious. "Of course Heavenly Father has a partner," this woman said, almost in passing.[68] Little other details about how she behaves or functions as the divine wife appear in the oral histories.

The idea that Heavenly Mother was married to God led women to identify other traits in her as a co-creator with God, a co-framer of the Plan of Salvation, and a heavenly parent involved in the lives of Her children. She participated regularly, for one woman, in making eternal decisions in counsel with Heavenly Father. Others understood her as not only a mother of spirits but as a contributor to the ordering and creation of the universe.[69] "I do believe I have a Heavenly Mother who participates fully with Heavenly Father in overseeing this world they created," mentioned a mother of six.[70] Despite downplaying overt worship toward Heavenly Mother, another woman felt blessed by her and

65. COHC, #012 (2009), 38.
66. COHC, #056 (2010), 20.
67. COHC, #059 (2010), 14.
68. COHC, #122 (2011), 12.
69. COHC, #043 (2010), 8; #056 (2010), 19–20; #117 (2011), 13.
70. COHC, #117 (2011), 13.

that she was cognizant of everyone's feelings and challenges: "I have had experiences with my Mother in Heaven. . . . The times when I have been alone and I needed a mother's comfort, particularly at the time when I lost three of my babies, she was there. I felt comforted and I knew she was real."[71] For others, that heavenly involvement did include separation. One woman described this kind of involvement much like the way a mother stays involved with a child while that child is away on a mission. She thought that this earth life represented a profound separation between Heavenly Mother and humankind to the point that her direct presence remained distant though her concern would never waver.[72] Heavenly Mother's parental involvement helped another woman relate to marriage. "She knows everything I'm going through. She talks to [Heavenly Father] and she knows me just as I talk with my husband concerning the children."[73]

Plurality of Heavenly Mothers

Polygamy and Mormonism have become such a tired dyad that after over a century of repudiating plural marriage, Mormons still cannot shake off their reputation as polygamists.[74] Neither can Mormon women totally consider Heavenly Mother apart from the strong history and theological currency of polygamy in Mormonism. Eight women referenced or alluded to multiple heavenly mothers on the grounds that Celestial marriage as practiced in early Mormonism would mean that God enjoys a polygamous relationship with his goddess-wives. This belief did not stem from polytheistic leanings or a belief in a pantheon of goddesses like other ancient goddess traditions. These women ranged from feeling disturbed by the prospect of a plurality of mothers in heaven to accepting polygamy as a necessary condition in the heavens, even for God the Father.

---

71. COHC, #070 (2010), 12.
72. COHC, #076 (2010), 17.
73. COHC, #133 (2011), 21.
74. As of 2007, "polygamy" continued to be the first one-word association with Mormons that Americans reported when asked in a national survey. See "Public Opinion about Mormons," Pew Research Center, December 6, 2007; available online at http://pewresearch.org/pubs/648/romney-mormon.

A former Catholic felt uneasy about a polygamous Heavenly Mother arrangement to the point of angst. "That sometimes upsets me," she said, not entirely disagreeing with polygamy itself but finding the possibility of multiple mothers disturbing.[75] Such angst disappeared for one grandmother who saw in the idea of multiple heavenly mothers a useful explanation for racial diversity: "I've often thought maybe different races come from different wives. I don't know, I just know that the principles that the gospel are founded on are going to be the same in heaven as they are here." She went on to associate the responsibility to populate the earth with multiple mothers, as though reproducing on this scale could only occur in a polygamous fashion: "I used to moan and groan about various different things about women not being important. My father said to me 'Oh shucks, you won't mind there being more wives because you don't want to populate a whole earth.' I don't think I said another thing about polygamist marriage or plural wives."[76] Another woman agreed that God would need more than one wife to people earths with children: "Maybe Heavenly Father was here on this planet and brought one of the heavenly mothers here who started this half divine, half mortal race."[77] One woman regarded Heavenly Mother's polygamy as fundamental to her existence: "I think the reason that Heavenly Father doesn't talk about Heavenly Mother is because there are too many of them. He obviously has numerous wives."[78] "Isn't polygamy supposed to be rife in the Celestial Kingdom?" asked another.[79]

Attitudes toward Heavenly Mother

Beyond conceptual commentary on Heavenly Mother, the oral histories also evince several attitudes surrounding Heavenly Mother belief. The most common attitude to appear in the histories was by far apathy: most women who gave any indication of their feelings didn't care about Heavenly Mother.[80] "Does it matter?" was one woman's

75. COHC, #056 (2010), 19–20.
76. COHC, #104 (2009), 18.
77. COHC, #055 (2010), 9.
78. COHC, #109 (2010), 3.
79. COHC, #126 (2011), 8.
80. Interviews that expressed apathy included #009, #011, #012, #015, #017, #023, #032, #038, #048, #050, #054, #063, #078, #080, #081, #086, #092, #093,

response.[81] Their reasons for feeling apathetic about the topic usually followed three types: those that recognized a lack of revelation about Heavenly Mother, those that wished to avoid controversy, and those that felt exercising faith in Jesus Christ or in God the Father sufficed for their religious practice. Unless a revelation demanded their attention, many women said they would not let Heavenly Mother belief or worship crowd into their lives. These women seemed to almost scoff at other women who considered the Church's current position somehow unfair or misogynistic. "We don't know, so let it go," would be a fair characterization of these women's comments.

The sufficiency of Jesus or Heavenly Father had more coverage in the oral histories beyond just those that expressed apathy. Many women who felt a connection to Heavenly Mother nevertheless deferred that connection to God and Jesus in their daily lives. A musician in her thirties responded to feminists' critique of Heavenly Mother's invisibility in the larger Mormon culture by downplaying the importance of a model of divine femininity: "That's never been as much of a problem for me because I look at what we're told in the scriptures and in revelation, and we're told that we should be like Christ." Whether male or female, everyone could emulate Christ because "he displays characteristics and traits and actions that are appropriate for anyone regardless of their sex." To teach that Christ was the perfect example for all humankind meant that one must be "willing to acknowledge that men can be like women and women can be like men."[82] Other women thought along these same lines, which always resulted in less agitated or confused attitudes about how Mormons regard Heavenly Mother.

Many oral histories manifested more rational than emotional colors in their descriptions of belief. Such belief in Heavenly Mother was simply a matter of logic for sixteen of the women interviewed. These women adhered to a simple syllogism, described well in this interview: "If I have a mother and father here on earth, then certainly I have a mother and a father in heaven. It would be necessary. I believe heaven is gender-oriented. I think we have male and female, therefore a mother and father in heaven is logical."[83] In other words, there are mothers and

#094, #099, #109, and #114.

81. COHC, #011 (2009), 6.

82. COHC, #026 (2010), 19–20.

83. COHC, #039 (2009), 12.

fathers on earth, the society in heaven mirrors human families; therefore there are mothers and fathers in heaven.

Few women gave any indication that they felt free to worship Heavenly Mother, and those that did admitted to disguising their worship in front of other Mormons. The most detailed statement describing an open worship attitude about Heavenly Mother began by asking how anyone opening oneself up to the divine could offend God or be immoral. "So I think about [Heavenly Mother] and I want to include her in my language." She acknowledged the controversy such open worship would likely bring in a Mormon setting, so by referencing Heavenly Parents, she could include Heavenly Mother in her worship without offending others. "I use the term God in church because in my mind I'm defining God as both of them—God the Mother and God the Father. So whenever possible I pray to God." She didn't feel right excluding Heavenly Mother from prayer.[84]

While this woman implied a sense of pressure that would preclude Heavenly Mother worship, other women made explicit mention of social pressures. These types of statements denoted feelings of stress, frustration, confusion, disturbance, or ambiguity. A district Relief Society president experienced public gossip in her Mormon congregation for having discussed Heavenly Mother at church.[85] Only one woman reported having a negative encounter with her local Church leaders over publicly acknowledging Heavenly Mother, which resulted in her feeling scared enough about her membership that she began to censor herself in public. She admitted that she might risk excommunication to include Heavenly Mother more openly in her worship.[86] Some histories reported negative emotions or attitudes about the doctrine or its surrounding Mormon culture.[87] On the contrary, others mentioned not feeling worried about the doctrine or the social environment.[88]

---

84. COHC, #061 (2010), 17.

85. COHC, #060 (2010), 17.

86. COHC, #119 (2011), 23–24.

87. The interviews that expressed social pressure included #012, #029, #034, #060, #119, and #121; Oral History (OH) #019 expressed confusion; OH #060 and #115 expressed frustration; and OH #074 and #124 expressed feeling disturbed or anxiety.

88. COHC, #018, #020, #027, and #048.

Finally, two exceptions emerge among the oral histories in which Mormon women admitted to having little or no concept of a Mother in Heaven. Though in the minority, these women suggested that Heavenly Mother belief does not immediately attend Mormon belief or practice. Even so, these women did not repudiate the existence of Heavenly Mother outright; she was not seen as incompatible with their Mormonism as they understood and practiced it. One woman put it this way: "It makes sense that I have a Mother in Heaven, but I have no real conception of her. My own mother is in heaven as well. Still, I feel like a motherless child."[89] The other described her concept of Heavenly Mother as "sketchy": "I believe there is a Mother and that she is very important and sacred, but other than this, I have no other beliefs or thoughts."[90]

Conclusion

This survey of Heavenly Mother belief includes three major contexts: the historical range of goddess belief and practice, the uniquely Mormon theological and social spaces, and the emotional attitudes Mormon women conveyed in their reflections on Heavenly Mother. Together these contextual analyses describe an idiosyncratic goddess belief among Mormon women. True, these women have not formed many of their beliefs from official Latter-day Saint theology, but they have maintained a concept of Heavenly Mother that, when compared with other goddess traditions, deserves recognition as a legitimate version of historical goddess veneration. Heavenly Mother occupies a supreme yet hazy location in their expansive Mormon cosmology. She inhabits this status through the systematic reasoning and spiritual attunement of these Mormon women.

The Heavenly Mother of the oral histories is foremost a divine mother who arrived at that matriarchal role as a human being who had once participated in a mortal life. She progressed to the point of glory and resides in the hereafter, ready to reunite with her daughters and sons. In these oral histories, Mormon women's feelings about Heavenly Mother range from apathy to careful consideration. Where she is present in the hearts and minds of these Mormon women, she exudes sovereignty, nurture, involvement, and creative power. Where

89. COHC, #069 (2010), 16.
90. COHC, #114 (2011), 11.

she is absent or little-known, her daughters wait for further revelation, still regarding her existence and still calling her their divine mother. For some, Heavenly Mother is more than one, the collective array of wives all sealed to God the Father—a vestige of the early Mormon family that knew what it felt like to call more than one woman "mother."

The goddess of the oral histories shares some qualities with Anat, Inanna-Ishtar, and still other goddesses like Athirat and Cybele: she is queenly, a sovereign agent in the married godhead; she is motherly, a creator and (in some mysterious fashion) a birther of spirits; she is more than a consort, the very wife of the male god, the father of creation. The patterns of goddess worship that cut across these very different human cultures speak to the complexity of goddess traditions. Mormon women have a place in that discussion and a tradition that offers intriguing congruities with other, even prehistoric, settings. Above all, Heavenly Mother decidedly occupies a place in the consciousness and spirituality of contemporary Mormon women.

Chapter Fourteen

Proposition 8

Anna Terry Rolapp

The involvement of the Church of Jesus Christ of Latter-day Saints in California's Prop. 8 confrontation brought out passionate defense of the proposition as well as equally passionate criticism. Some women saw themselves forced to choose between two options—belief in obedience to prophetic authority weighed against belief in the civil right of citizens to marry those of the same sex. Of the one hundred twenty-eight women interviewed for the Claremont Oral History Project as of summer 2011, almost one-fourth commented on the proposition—even though many respondents were not living in California and the topic was not originally on the list of suggested interview questions.[1] These women reported either their support or opposition to LDS Church involvement in this widely publicized political issue. Many women interviewed for this project had strong feelings about the topic.

Background on Defense of Marriage Propositions

Prior to 1977, California law was somewhat ambiguous as to who could legally marry whom. At that time, it was "not clear whether partners of the same sex [could] get married."[2] The legislature amended the legal definition of marriage in California to being a "civil contract between a man and a woman."[3] This legislation left a potential loophole that allowed the state of California to recognize same-sex mar-

---

1. The question was added to the oral history questionnaire in March 2011.
2. California Assembly Committee on the Judiciary, Bill Digest for A.B. 607 (1977) as quoted in "California, Proposition 22 (2000)," *Wikipedia*, http://en.wikipedia.org/wiki/Prop_22 (accessed April 25, 2011).
3. California Family Code, Section 300, as quoted in ibid.

riages performed elsewhere. As a result of the passing of Proposition 22 in 2000, California only recognized marriages between opposite-sex couples.[4] Prop. 22 resulted from California's unique initiative process allowing citizens to exercise direct democracy (as opposed to legislative or judicial actions) by placing proposed legislation directly on the ballot.

Prop. 22 remained in effect for seven and one half years until it was deemed unconstitutional by the California Supreme Court in May 2008. Following this decision to overturn the ban on gay marriage in California, both the LDS Church and the Catholic Archdiocese in San Francisco released statements about the decision, reiterating their respective theologies on homosexuality and their disappointment in the decision.[5] Proposition 8 was a response to this May 2008 judicial ruling by the California Supreme Court.

Subsequently, "a broad-based coalition of churches and other organizations"[6] placed Proposition 8 on the California ballot in 2008 to re-affirm heterosexual marriage as the only legal form of marriage in California. The First Presidency of the LDS Church released a letter to be read to all congregations on Sunday, June 29th defining its position on family and marriage:

> The Church's teachings and position on this moral issue are unequivocal. Marriage between a man and woman is ordained of God, and the formation of families is central to the Creator's plan for His children. Children are entitled to be born within this bond of marriage.[7]

The LDS Church joined the coalition after being "approached by the Roman Catholic" church. The *New York Times* reported that the Mormons played an "extraordinary role" in passing Prop. 8 "with money, institutional support and dedicated volunteers."[8] The proposition was

---

4. Ibid. Proposition 22 passed with 61% voting 'yes' with a 54% voter turnout. Proposition 8 passed with 52% voting 'yes' with a 79% voter turnout.

5. Carrie A. Moore, "LDS Church Expresses Disappointment in California Gay Marriage Decision," *Deseret News*, May 16, 2008, http://www.deseretnews.com/article/700226242/LDS-Church-expresses-disappointment-in-California-gay-marriage-decision.html?pg=all (accessed August 23, 2012).

6. "California and Same-Sex Marriage," *LDS Newsroom*, June 30, 2008, http://newsroom.lds.org/article/california-and-same-sex-marriage (accessed January 3, 2012).

7. Ibid.

8. Jesse McKinley and Kirk Johnson, "Mormons Tipped Scale on Ban on Gay

passed on November 4, 2008, after substantial controversy and international press coverage. Same-sex marriages performed in California between May and November 2008 remained valid.[9] Prop. 8 added a new provision to the California Constitution stating, "only marriage between a man and a woman is valid or recognized in California."[10]

Proponents of Prop. 8, according to the California General Election Voter Information pamphlet dated November 4, 2008, stated "that exclusively heterosexual marriage was an essential institution of society, that leaving the constitution unchanged would result in public schools teaching our kids that gay marriage is okay, and that gays . . . do not have the right to redefine marriage for everyone else."[11] Proponents, including LDS attorneys who spoke eloquently to congregations in 2008, argued that if Prop. 8 should pass, churches could lose their tax-exempt status if they refused to allow same-sex marriage and that religious adoption agencies, such as Catholic Charities, would lose their ability to place kids only in opposite gender families.[12]

The same voter pamphlet described opponents of Prop. 8 as believing that "the freedom to marry is fundamental to our society, that the California constitution should guarantee the same freedom and right to everyone and that the proposition mandates one set of rules for gay and lesbian couples and another set for everyone else."[13] Latter-day Saint opponents of Prop. 8 further argued that Church involvement in politics violated its own 1907 First Presidency statement stating:

> The Church of Jesus Christ of Latter-day Saints holds to the doctrine of the separation of church and state; the non-interference of church authority in political matters; and the absolute freedom and independence of the individual in the performance of his politi-

---

Marriage," *New York Times*, Nov. 14, 2008, http://www.nytimes.com/2008/11/15/us/politics/15marriage.html?pagewanted=all (accessed August 23, 2012).

9. "California Proposition 8," *Wikipedia*, http://en.wikipedia.org/wiki/California_Proposition_8_(2008) (accessed April 25, 2011).

10. "Text of Proposed Laws" *Official Voter Information Guide*, State of California, p. 128. Available at http://vig.cdn.sos.ca.gov/2008/general/text-proposed-laws/text-of-proposed-laws.pdf#prop8 (accessed September 2, 2012.)

11. "California Proposition 8."

12. "Six Consequences the Coalition Has Identified if Proposition Fails," (Anonymous). Directive read by LDS attorneys/leaders and distributed in LDS congregations in California, 2008. Copy of directive in possession of author.

13. "California Proposition 8."

> cal duties. If at any time there has been conduct at variance with this doctrine, it has been in violation of the well-settled principles and policy of the Church.[14]

In August of 2008, the LDS Church leaders released a six-page statement on why the faith is opposed to same-sex marriage and asked the membership for "donations of time and money in support of Proposition 8"[15] and to "do all they can to support the proposed constitutional amendment."[16] The California Proposition ultimately passed with a 79% voter turnout, with 52% voting in favor. The election was followed by protests across the country with many attacks directed at the LDS Church. Thousands of people marched through the streets in San Francisco while "more than 1,000 people protested at a Mormon temple in Los Angeles, shutting down traffic and leading to several arrests."[17] Additionally, "protesters marched around the headquarters of the Mormon Church [in Salt Lake City] . . . criticizing the church's support for [California's constitutional amendment]." In New York City, "thousands of people gathered in front of the Upper West Side [LDS Temple] to protest the Mormon Church's support for Proposition 8."[18]

Kevin Hamilton, an LDS Public Relations representative in southern California responded to the protesters and defended the work done by Latter-day Saints in California by circulating an email outlining twelve "facts" to justify the LDS Church's involvement in the "aftermath of the recent election." He stated that LDS parishioners found themselves "oddly on the defensive regarding . . . support for the Yes on Proposition 8 cause." His correspondence reiterated that Mormons did nothing wrong but only acted as "civic minded American[s]." He

---

14. Joseph F. Smith, *Teachings of the Presidents of the Church: Joseph F. Smith* (Salt Lake City: The Church of Jesus Christ of Latter-day Saints, 1998), 125.

15. Carrie A. Moore, "LDS Church Issues Statement on Same-Sex Marriage," *Deseret News*, Sept. 10, 2008, http://www.deseretnews.com/article/700257603/LDS-Church-issues-statement-on-same-sex-marriage.html?pg=all (accessed August 23, 2012).

16. "The Divine Institution of Marriage," *LDS Newsroom*, August 13, 2008, http://newsroom.lds.org/article/the-divine-institure-of-marriage (accessed Jan. 3, 2012).

17. "Protesting Ban on Gay Marriage," *New York Times*, Nov. 8, 2008, http://www.nytimes.com/2008/11/08/us/08protest.html (accessed August 23, 2012).

18. Colin Moynihan, "At Mormon Temple, a Protest Over Prop 8," *New York Times*, Nov. 13, 2008, http://cityroom.blogs.nytimes.com/2008/11/13/at-mormon-temple-thousands-protest-prop-8 (accessed Jan. 3, 2012).

concluded, "Mormons make up less than 2% of the population of California," and "were less than 5% of the yes vote." Further, he emphasized that the LDS Church "donated no money to the . . . campaign" but that "individual members were encouraged to support the . . . efforts." Interestingly, he pointed out that the supposedly wealthy "Yes on 8" campaign actually raised less money than the "No on 8" campaign. He defended the advertising campaign of "Yes on 8" as being "based on case law and real-life situations." He quoted statistics showing that African Americans and Latinos voted overwhelmingly in favor of Prop. 8 and that the "Yes on 8 coalition was a broad spectrum of religious organizations [including] Catholics, Evangelicals, Protestants, Orthodox Jew, [and] Muslims." Further, Hamilton emphasized that Mormons were not told how to vote and were "free to choose for him or her self." He stated that the Church did not violate the ubiquitous principle of "separation of church and state," but rather that the LDS Church occasionally "chooses to support causes that it feels to be of a moral nature." And finally, Hamilton argued that Mormons "did what Americans do. We spoke up, we campaigned, and we voted."[19]

In August 2010, Chief Judge Vaughn Walker ruled that Prop. 8 was unconstitutional in that it violated the Fourteenth Amendment of the United States Constitution. The judge maintained that Prop. 8 denied Due Process and Equal Protection to some citizens. The Ninth Circuit Court of Appeals (Northern District of California) upheld this ruling on February 7, 2012. The current decision is that Prop. 8 is in violation of the United States Constitution. It is assumed that the United States Supreme Court will hear this landmark case in 2013.

Respondents from Oral Histories

Thirty-one women in the Claremont Oral History Project commented on Prop. 8. Fourteen of the respondents supported the proposition and the Church's involvement in varying degrees. Sixteen respondents recorded their opposition to Prop. 8 and specifically disliked the LDS Church's involvement. One respondent spoke exten-

19. Kevin Hamilton, email to Karen Palfi, November 6, 2008. To see the text of this letter, see http://www.nauvoo.com/mormontimes/columns/2008-11-13.html (accessed August 23, 2012).

sively of her justification for not supporting or opposing Prop. 8. This paper will discuss these three categories.

Yes on Proposition 8

The fourteen supporters of Prop. 8 ranged from those who reluctantly voted for it to those who fervently supported it and were involved and committed to its passage. Four supporters of Prop. 8 were either disinterested or voted reluctantly for the proposition. Their comments included: "I don't know if there's any conflict between church and politics because I don't pay enough attention. I don't follow politics."[20] Another respondent weighed her personal beliefs on gay marriage against what she was being taught in church:

> Prop 8 was very hard for me . . . because I am not committed to it. I have a really hard time with it. But I have faith in the Priesthood and I think it's one of those things that I just have to trust the Lord on. I hope to heaven that our prophet is following the Lord. I know he's still a man and he's not infallible. So I have to just trust that I'll be blessed for being obedient.[21]

Another called the Prop. 8 campaign a "devastating [and] very difficult experience":

> I put a sign in my yard even though I've never been involved in politics before. It was hard for me to do, to put this sign up, just because I don't like to offend anybody. But I put it up and I made some donations and I made a lot of phone calls.[22]

These last two women supported Prop. 8 with reluctance. Other respondents favored the proposition reluctantly because of people they knew who were gay. They expressed tolerance as well as sympathy. Others indicated admiration of so-called gay characteristics and felt sorrow that their support of Prop. 8 would offend their gay friends:

> Homosexuality exists and it is real. I think it's very important to accept that. How it comes about? I don't know and I don't think anyone

20. Claremont Mormon Women's Oral History Collection, Library of the Claremont Colleges, Claremont, CA, hereafter referred to as COHC, #020 (2009), 8.

21. COHC, #018 (2009), 19.

22. COHC, #017 (2009), 28.

that is not gay can fully understand a gay person. We need to be tolerant of all law-abiding citizens, as we want them to be tolerant of us.[23]

Another said, "I feel sorry for gays, but I don't agree with gay marriage."[24]

One woman who was previously married to a gay man, spoke of his characteristics that she said should have "pointed to his being gay": "He was very good with his patients and their families. He was a compassionate doctor. I think gay individuals are generally very artistic and usually outgoing."[25] These women spoke positively of gay individuals but remained opposed to gay marriage.

Another woman described a gay couple that was very friendly with her straight daughter:

> [They] live in a beautiful home. One of them is an excellent cook, and takes pride in inventing new dishes to serve. They're very kind, they make a lot of money, and they give generously to charities. My daughter thinks they should be able to get married. I am equally firm in believing that marriage is between a man and a woman. Marriage is sacred. One very good reason for its existence is to raise a family with a female and a male parent.[26]

These women, like the one above, often felt that they were on opposite sides of the Prop. 8 debate than other family members. Some women reported that family and friends were offended by their support of the proposition:

> I have a really good friend at school [who] is a lesbian. She got married over the summer and found out about my support [of Prop. 8 and] it pretty much destroyed our friendship. We'd been really good friends for about fifteen years. We are collegial now, but we're not friends anymore. That was very painful for both of us. She just can't understand how I could belong to a church that hates her. That's how she sees it.[27]

Other women reported that they were happy to be very involved in the Prop. 8 campaign. They made phone calls, went door to door, made

23. COHC, #024 (2009), 14.
24. COHC, #022 (2009), 28.
25. COHC, #001 (2009), 5,12.
26. COHC, #065 (2010), 17.
27. COHC, #017 (2009), 28.

posters, and participated in demonstrations. Many expressed tremendous support for the Church and its courage in backing the initiative. One respondent spoke of her work as a zip code coordinator and her sadness that she is now on gay hate sites on the Internet. She eloquently expressed her opposition to gay marriage:

> When you put a man and a woman together into a home, you have united the two most opposite things there can be. If they can learn to love each other, their children will see someone who is like them and someone who is not like them, disagreeing, making compromises, loving each other, tolerating each other. They can learn tolerance through the diversity of their own parents. They can learn to accept what they are and to love what they are not. I think loving the "other" begins at home. If we start saying that it's okay to not have a woman in a marriage, or it's okay to not have a man in a marriage, then we are saying, at some level, that men don't matter or women don't matter. Although the general attitude is that a move toward the legalization of gay marriage is a move towards greater tolerance and diversity, I think actually the opposite is true. Tolerance and diversity begins with the respect and love of a man and a woman who have created a family.[28]

While this respondent was clear in her interpretation of marriage and fully supported Prop. 8, others were asked to attend demonstrations but did so reluctantly:

> It was very difficult for me to put myself out there to others and say it is wrong for society to break down these barriers. I made phone calls and talked to a number of people about Prop 8. One day our ward . . . got together to carry signs and [held] a rally at a major intersection. I was very embarrassed to do that but I gained courage as I saw how people driving by cheered for us.[29]

Despite the difficulties, one woman thought the entire campaign was a positive experience:

> I think people appreciated our being organized and willing to . . . take the position we did and be seen and heard. It is interesting that [everyone] seemed to think [Prop. 8] passed because of the Mormons. Well, there were a whole lot of people that voted on that proposition other than just Mormons. It wasn't just us, but for some

28. COHC, #022 (2009), 28.
29. COHC, #049 (2010), 14.

reason we were targeted. I think it was probably a positive thing for the Church because it makes people ask questions. I think people admire Mormons because they take a stand on what they believe, whether it is a popular stand or not. Proposition 8 was a good thing.[30]

Several women supported the proposition because of their belief in strong, traditional family values. For example, the woman divorced from a gay man frankly stated, "Marriage is between a man and a woman, period. [Gays] should have federal rights, but . . . many of them want the word 'marriage.'"[31] Some referred to the 1995 LDS directive "The Family: A Proclamation to the World" as justification for their values. The 1995 Proclamation is considered by many Latter-day Saints to be revelation even though it is not canonized LDS scripture. The Proclamation is a defense of traditional marriage, stating that the LDS Church "solemnly proclaim[s] that marriage between a man and a woman is ordained of God and that the family is central to the Creator's plan for the eternal destiny of His children." It further outlines specific responsibilities of fathers and mothers and declares this type of traditional family "as the fundamental unit of society."[32]

Two women affirmed their positions based on the 1995 Proclamation:

> I was asked to give a talk on the Family Proclamation about five years ago . . . and gained a testimony of [it] and consider it scripture. When I gained that testimony, I could truly move forward confidently helping Proposition 8. We tried to emphasize that the proposition was "pro-marriage" and not "anti-gay." It was a difficult time for . . . me and many others who were heavily involved [in the campaign].[33]

Like others, she admitted the difficulty and divisiveness of the LDS Church's support of Prop. 8, but she was able to be more active with her own support because of the Proclamation. Another respondent similarly affirmed that the Proclamation "became much more than just a statement of what [she] already believed in" when she became involved in supporting Prop. 8:

---

30. COHC, #083 (2010), 14.
31. COHC, #001 (2009), 20.
32. "The Family: A Proclamation to the World," available at https://www.lds.org/topics/family-proclamation (accessed August 23, 2012).
33. COHC, #046 (2010), 19.

> If the Proclamation on the Family didn't exist . . . I might not really care that much if gay couples were married legally. My first reaction is that I don't really care what they do if it doesn't affect me. But because there is a Proclamation . . . that is modern day revelation and therefore a commandment, I have to dig down and find my courage and actually take a stand for something I really do believe in.[34]

The fourteen respondents in favor of Prop. 8 responded with a variety of levels of commitment. They ranged from supporting Prop. 8 because their leaders advised it to those who believe they were supporting a divinely inspired mandate.

No on Prop 8

More respondents in the Claremont Oral History Project spoke out against Prop. 8 than those that spoke for it. Their responses can be categorized three ways. Some, who viewed the situation from outside California, felt that an objective view required a negative response. Others felt that the LDS Church should follow its own declaration of avoiding political issues, several of them seeing parallels with the Equal Rights Amendment campaigns. A third group opposed Prop. 8 because of personal experiences that led them to have compassion and tolerance for gay individuals.

Some respondents stated emphatically that they were happy to avoid involvement in California's Prop. 8 by not living in the state. One simply said, "I have been very glad that I have not lived in California during this whole Prop. 8 issue."[35] A former resident of California took this even further, saying "I [was] incredibly grateful not to have been living in San Francisco in the Prop. 8 era. I would have had to move as I would not have wanted to campaign."[36] Another questioned the Church's involvement: "And what were we doing in California with Proposition 8?"[37]

Another woman who had recently moved to California compared attitudes that she saw in Washington, DC with those she viewed in California:

34. COHC, #093 (2010), 11.
35. COHC, #033 (2009), 11.
36. COHC, #080 (2009), 18.
37. COHC, #060 (2009), 15.

Proposition 8 was bad. I left D.C. in July [of 2008] and they had literally just read the letter over the pulpit in my sacrament meeting there saying [that the] elections are coming up in the fall. We do not hand out the ward list and we do not get involved. This is D.C. Then I showed up [in California] and they [were] reading over the pulpit the letter from the First Presidency saying [that we] must get involved in [our communities] to help pass Prop. 8. And I'm thinking, wait a minute; these [statements] don't match.

I wouldn't [sign up to help], in part because I have friends who are gay and I couldn't make it work in my head. Well, one day in Sunday School class this woman stood up, and while getting prepared to hand out the sign-up sheet, [she] bore her testimony and cried for over fifteen minutes, and I am not exaggerating because again I was sitting there thinking, how much longer do I have to sit here before I can actually get up and leave because I can't breathe? I was basically having an anxiety attack. I had to leave the room.[38]

Others declared their angst over Church involvement in politics. One said, "I am more impressed all the time that the center of the gospel is simply love. [The gospel is] being decimated right now by certain political factions."[39] Others saw parallels between the Prop. 8 campaign and the Equal Rights Amendment of the 1970s.

I . . . think it [is] politics once again. I don't know why the Church [says it] chooses to stay out of politics and then makes a statement both on the ERA and the proposition regarding marriage.[40]

[The Church says it doesn't] get involved in political issues but they were definitely involved in [the ERA] and I felt at the time the way I did about Proposition 8—that they should have backed off and told people to vote their conscience rather than telling us [how to vote].[41]

The proposition 8 campaigns in California . . . mirrored some of the problems of the ERA battle. Mormons were pulled into political activity. Church buildings were used for political purposes. Heavy preaching supported a definition of marriage as between a man and a woman, therefore against any marriage between two people of the

38. COHC, #008 (2009), 16.
39. COHC, #009 (2009), 22.
40. COHC, #033 (2009), 11–12.
41. COHC, #099 (2010), 18.

> same gender. Those unwilling to join the battle were considered to have failed a religious test.[42]

These women were very clear in their belief that the LDS Church should stay out of politics.

Some felt increasingly on the outside of LDS Church policies and felt a conflict between the Church's involvement in politics and their personal compassion for and love of gay individuals. For example, one woman thought that gay marriage should be allowed:

> Politically, I'm liberal. I tend to end up on the other side of every major issue the Church takes a stand on. The whole Prop. 8 thing has taken a huge toll on me. I [was] very active in the "No on 8" campaign. [I] still am. I'm part of an equality team that [comes here] to make calls to voters in Maine encouraging them to support their legislature in validating gay marriage there. Ironically they went through the legislative process. It wasn't some "activist judge" (I hate that term) who decided it. It was the legislature and the governor. I'm very active in those sorts of things.[43]

This same respondent also opposed Prop. 8 because of its divisiveness. She reported a discussion with her bishop when they spent "half the time discussing homosexuality":

> We talked about how we could make the homosexuals in the ward feel more welcome. Parts of West Hollywood [California] are in our ward boundaries. We talked about how we could be a good and supportive and loving congregation for gay people.[44]

Several others also spoke about their compassion and tolerance for gay marriage. They felt that those who desired marriage should have that right and that God would want people to have loving, monogamous partnerships. One woman spoke of marriage as a human right:

> The LDS Church cannot deny that it had a strong influence on Proposition 8. Their involvement in the creation of the Christian Coalition and their trial run in Hawaii helped guide and direct them through this extremely publicized proposition. As a result, it tore our family apart through a series of email, phone calls, and [dinners]. I respect and sustain an institution's right to support politics, but I do

42. COHC, #012 (2009), 37.
43. COHC, #030 (2009), 16.
44. Ibid., 21–22.

> not think they thought . . . enough about the repercussions of such a public war for their interpretation of a "family." I do not understand how allowing two people of the same sex to have a human right will tear apart the foundations of the LDS Church. The idea of free agency contradicts the Church's actions.[45]

Others emphasized compassion and tolerance in opposing Prop. 8:

> I've been raised to be very tolerant of other people. I also expect others to be tolerant of me. I guess what I believe the definition of marriage is might not be the same as what somebody else thinks. I was disappointed to see the contentiousness that developed in certain groups and individuals over the issue . . . that was a very difficult time.[46]
>
> I would like to see that people [would not] be afraid if someone in their family is gay and that [the gay person] will not be afraid of remaining in the Church.[47]

Time and time again compassion and tolerance were mentioned. A wife of a bishop chose acceptance of gay rights after her husband had counseled a young gay man:

> I was not actively involved in working on passing or defeating the legislation. I did not want a sign put up in front of my house. I [feel] that being loved by someone and loving someone is the most important thing in your life. I just have a hard time denying that to people for whatever reason.[48]

These women spoke decisively of their reasons for opposing Prop. 8. Their reasons ranged from LDS involvement in political issues to reasons of compassion and tolerance. Some were angry and considered leaving the Church. Those who were most disturbed left their congregations temporarily or permanently. One woman recalled attended the funeral of a gay second cousin who had committed suicide. She was encouraged to find the family was "openly sympathetic and understanding rather than embarrassed and closeted as it might have been many years ago. More and more families include a child who is gay." She added that she feels like walking out when she hears prejudicial comments against gays in church settings.[49]

---

45. COHC, #128 (2011), 8.
46. COHC, #036 (2009), 19.
47. COHC, #062 (2010), 25.
48. COHC, #011 (2009), 7.
49. COHC, #069 (2010), 17.

Another woman, a teacher, said that she disliked the Church's strong stance in support of Prop. 8. One of her students has two mothers married in the First Congregational Church. When the proposition passed, the student was "crying and crying." The teacher said that the student felt that "her family [was] not as valuable" as a heterosexual family. Because of this, she struggled with her regularly activity in the Church:

> At church there were a few times when I almost walked out of Sacrament Meeting. Afterwards I felt that I had been a coward to stay. It was especially hard for my two daughters-in-law who were working for AIDS Project LA at the time. I don't believe that being gay is a life style choice that people are making . . . I think the Church's position makes it particularly hard. [Utah has] the highest rate of suicide of young men between 18 and 24. There are so many families struggling with this.[50]

One respondent found temporary refuge in attending an entirely different church, the United Church of Christ, during what she called the "Prop. 8 crisis":

> I've had quite a bit of interaction with another church. During Prop. 8 . . . the Mormon Church mobilized to promote [the] proposition [that] would prevent gay marriage. This was an extremely painful moment for me in my history as a Mormon; because I saw . . . good people . . . mobilize to do something that I felt was really at heart un-Christian and unkind. People want to marry. How is that a bad thing? We should be affirming this in every way!
>
> At first I went to church every week, valiantly wearing my little rainbow ribbon pinned to my shirt. Eventually, I couldn't continue going to church because it seemed that every Sunday there were talks over the pulpit about it or there would be announcements . . . or comment[s]

---

50. COHC, #040 (2010), 11. Utah leads the nation for suicide among males fifteen to twenty-four; researchers have also found that there is a powerful relationship between family rejection of youths' gay identities and high suicide rates. See Lucinda Dillon Kinkead and Dennis Romboy, "Deadly taboo: Youth suicide an epidemic that many in Utah prefer to ignore," *Deseret News*, April, 24, 2006, http://www.deseretnews.com/article/635201873/Deadly-taboo-Youth-suicide-an-epidemic-that-many-in-Utah-prefer-to-ignore.html (accessed September 2, 2012) and Robert A. Rees and William S. Bradshaw, "Guidance for LDS families with LGBT children," *The Salt Lake Tribune*, December 11, 2010, http://www.sltrib.com/sltrib/opinion/50842640-82/family-families-lgbhttp:/www.sltrib.com/sltrib/opinion/50842640-82/family-families-lgbt-acceptance.html.csp (accessed September 2, 2012).

in Sunday school. Perhaps the breaking point came when a fellow ward member referred to Mormons who didn't support Prop 8 as "tares" that needed to be separated from the wheat. So I was a tare, huh? I couldn't handle it anymore. I retreated and found my refuge at the [United Church of Christ]. They are an open and affirming congregation. The pastor is gay and has a lifelong partner. He's wonderful. A large segment of the congregation is gay and they are just such good people. I loved their services and their sermons and their music. I felt a real connection with the people there and they were good to me. I had a wonderful experience with the UCC and I'll always be grateful to them for being that refuge when I needed them during the Prop. 8 crisis.[51]

Another woman left Church activity as a result of what she described as "the Church leaders' treatment of homosexuals" leading to several suicides.[52] She began her remarks on Prop. 8 by discounting Old Testament passages traditionally interpreted as being against homosexuality. She then recounted personal experiences of her wonderful friendships with gay men. One had been her stake president:

> Our former Stake President . . . was excommunicated when he acknowledged he was gay. My husband was a high-councilman in the stake with him and we both admired [him] so much for his compassion and understanding.
>
> If we try to put the words of Jesus alongside the words and actions of the LDS leaders today they are not in accord [however] I was deeply touched by the recent story of how the Church Historian, Marlin K. Jensen, shed tears of sympathy [for LGBT people] when he spoke of California's Prop. 8.[53]

Neither Yes Nor No on Prop 8

One woman wrote extensively about being an LDS mother with a gay, now adult, son and the struggles and divisions her family endured during the two California same-sex initiatives. She refused to be involved in "defense of marriage" campaigns but continues to value her LDS Church membership:

51. COHC, #061 (2010), 14.
52. COHC, #096 (2010), 4.
53. Ibid., 5.

Difficulties arose as we had to endure California's Propositions 22 & 8 in recent years. As an active LDS family, we found the Church's involvement to be difficult and challenging for our family. Prop. 22 nearly tore our family apart. I had chosen not to be involved in the campaign at all and respectfully told my ecclesiastical leaders that I would not participate. My husband was a member of the High Council at the time, and he decided he would not be visibly involved but would allow his offices to be used for phone campaigning. When [our son, who is gay,] later found out about his [dad's passive] involvement, he was extremely hurt. He chose not to discuss his anger with us but mostly kept it to himself for several years. We eventually had to discuss his hurt and apologize and repent for it. I swore I would never let anything be so divisive in our family again.[54]

She then recounted how her family approached Prop. 8:

When Prop. 8 rolled around, my husband and I both very kindly told our bishop and stake president that we would not be involved on any level. I explained to them some of the problems that our family had had during and after Prop 22, and how we had decided never to let anything like that divide our family again. We gained the full support of our Priesthood leaders in not being involved [in Prop. 8] even though I was the Relief Society president at the time and [my husband] was on the High Council. We felt that [our leaders] had empathy for our situation. However, Proposition 8 left [our son] with definite scars and anger against the LDS Church at a level I don't think he had felt prior to Prop. 8. That has been very hard for our family. How could something we love so much, the Gospel, continue to cause deep pain for our son?[55]

She also spoke of her son's recent marriage to his gay partner and her family's involvement in the festivities. An interesting meeting in Salt Lake City preceded the wedding:

A week before our son was married [to his long-term gay partner], my husband and I happened to be in Salt Lake City donating a family Bible . . . to the Church. We had a wonderful meeting with [a general authority and others]. After the meeting, [the general authority] called me aside and said, "Tell me about your family." I was a little surprised at his interest but decided to tell him about the upcoming

54. COHC, #071 (2010), 18.

55. Ibid., 18.

> wedding [of our gay son]. I also gave him a hint of the difficulties that the various "defense of marriage" propositions had caused our family. I said that we had decided that the family does come before the Church and we felt it correct to give [our son] our full support in marrying [his gay partner]. I explained [to the general authority] that we feel it important to keep our family intact by extending our love and support for our son as family over-rides everything else. [The general authority] looked me right in the eye and said, "You have made the right decision." It was very gratifying to leave for [our son's] wedding the week after talking to [the general authority].[56]

She added that she did not have to choose between supporting her gay son and staying active in the Church:

> I often don't know which side of the [gay marriage] debate I am on. [On the one hand], I believe that our son's marriage will be good for him and good for society. His marriage will in no way undermine my marriage . . . or male-female marriage in general. On the other hand, I believe that a prophet stands at the head of our church that has spoken out against same-sex marriage. It's a good thing I have two hands!"[57]

Final Words

The Claremont Oral History Project will continue to collect histories that will shed further light on women's opinions on both defense of marriage initiatives in California and other states and whether or not the LDS Church should continue its involvement. The current state of marriage was a major discussion at the time the interviews were done. LDS women, with strong opinions on this theme, chose to respond to a topic that was not initially included on the list of suggested interview questions, even though many of them resided in states that were not actively involved in Propositions 22 and 8. Subsequent oral histories will no doubt offer further insight of women's opinions and other volatile topics.

56. Ibid., 20–21.
57. Ibid., 23–24.

Contributors

Claudia L. Bushman, an American, women's, and Mormon studies scholar, holds degrees from Wellesley College, Brigham Young University, and Boston University. She has written and edited a dozen books. She is retired from many years of teaching, most recently at Columbia University and Claremont Graduate University. She plans to spend the rest of her future recording the present.

Lisa Thomas Clayton is a graduate student at Claremont Graduate University in the history of religion. Her emphasis is LDS women's experiences from the late twentieth-century to the present. As the current director of the Howard W. Hunter Mormon Studies Oral History Project, she works with volunteers to gather Mormon women's histories. She is semi-retired from her thirty-year primary career as mother of four daughters and a son. She relishes grandmothering.

Pamela Lindsay Everson received her BA degree from UC Irvine and her MA from Chapman University, majoring in English literature. She is interested in the English and American novels of the nineteenth-century as well as the Mormon female writings of the nineteenth and twentieth centuries. She has studied under Claudia Bushman at Claremont Graduate University and is an active participant in the Claremont Oral History Project.

Sherrie L. M. Gavin is in pursuit of a PhD in history at the University of Queensland. Her academic interests are in Australian Federation and international Mormon history with an emphasis on masculinity studies. Sherrie has been published in the *Journal of Mormon History* and is a regular contributor to *The Exponent* blog.

David Golding is a PhD candidate in the history of Christianity and religions of North America at Claremont Graduate University. His research has focused on missionary history and the intercultural tensions and exchanges that have resulted from Christian missions. He has formatted and digitized the archives for this oral history project.

Amy Hoyt is a scholar of gender and religion, with particular emphasis on religions in North America. Amy teaches at University of the Pacific in the Religious and Classical Studies department. She received her PhD from Claremont Graduate University, where she helped found the Mormon Studies Council. Amy's current research interests include reconceptualizing feminist theory, masculinity within Mormonism, and examining the rituals of parenting as a religious expression.

Allison E. Keeney is a lifelong California resident. She received her BS from California Polytechnic University at San Luis Obispo. She ran a landscaping and design business for thirteen years in Los Angeles before becoming a stay-at-home mom. Allison lives with her husband and two teenage daughters in South Pasadena, California.

Caroline Kline is completing the coursework for a PhD in religion with a focus on women's studies in religion at Claremont Graduate University. Her areas of interest revolve around the intersections of Mormon and feminist theology and the study of contemporary Mormon feminist communities. She is the co-founder of the Mormon feminist blog, *The Exponent.*

Elizabeth J. Mott is completing coursework for a PhD in religion with a focus on American religious history at Claremont Graduate University. She received a master's degree in mass communications from Brigham Young University before moving to Claremont to study religion. Her interests include the role of communications in religious change, gender, theology, and lived religion.

Elisa Eastwood Pulido is a PhD candidate in religions of North America at Claremont Graduate University. She holds an MFA in writing from the School of the Art Institute of Chicago, and a BA in German from Brigham Young University. Her research interests include religion in Latin America, religious myths of origin, and the indigenization of Mormonism. She is also a poet, published in literary journals in the US and the UK.

Susan Robison attended Brigham Young University (1961–1963) and The University of California at Los Angeles (1964–1966). She received her BA in English literature from Columbia University (2003). Susan is a homemaker and has volunteered in her community. She and her husband, Ronald E. Robison, have been married for forty-nine years. They have four children and fourteen grandchildren.

Anna Terry Rolapp is pursuing an MA in the history of textiles with an emphasis on quilt studies from the University of Nebraska. She has a passion for traditional and historic quilt making, producing quilts that portray historic events or tell stories. She and her husband Frank divide their time between Southern California and Utah.

Taunalyn Ford Rutherford is a PhD student at Claremont Graduate University in the history of Christianity and religions of North America. She received her BA in history and MA in humanities with a minor in Church history and doctrine at Brigham Young University. Her research interests center on Mormon studies particularly in relation to world religions. She served an LDS mission to Sweden and is also interested in the study of modern LDS women in Sweden.

Susan H. Woster grew up in San Pedro, California. She received her BA in English at Brigham Young University. She has been a technical communicator since 1985, and currently works as principal technical writer for a well-known internet company. She and her sister, Allison E. Keeney, are best friends and share many mutual interests. She lives in Pasadena, California.

Women's Lives, Women's Voices: Selected Reading

Mabel Finlayson Allred. *Plural Wife: The Life Story of Mabel Finlayson Allred.* Edited by Martha Sonntag Bradley, 2012.

Martha Toronto Anderson. *A Cherry Tree Behind the Iron Curtain: The Autobiography of Martha Toronto Anderson*, 1977.

Patience Loader Rozsa Archer. *Recollections of Past Days: The Autobiography of Patience Loader Rozsa Archer*. Edited by Sandra Ailey Petree, 2006.

Emily Austin. *Mormonism, or Life among the Mormons. . . .Being an Autobiographical Sketch; Including an Experience of Fourteen Years of Mormon Life*, 1882, 1988, 2010.

Elna Baker. *The New York Regional Mormon Singles Halloween Dance: A Memoir*, 2010.

Phyllis Barber. *How I Got Cultured: A Nevada Memoir*, 1992, 1994.

______. *Raw Edges: A Memoir*, 2012.

Mary Batchelor, Marianne Watson, and Anne Wilde. *Voices in Harmony: Contemporary Women Celebrate Plural Marriage*, 2000.

Elouise Bell. *Only When I Laugh*, 1990.

Frances Bennett. *Glimpses of a Mormon Family*, 1968.

Joanna Brooks. *The Book of Mormon Girl: A Memoir of an American Faith*, 2012.

Juanita Brooks. *Quicksand and Cactus: A Memoir of the Southern Mormon Frontier*, 1982.

Laura Bush. *Faithful Transgressions in the American West: Six Twentieth-Century Mormon Women's Autobiographical Acts*, 2004.

Olga Kovarova Campora. *Saint Behind Enemy Lines*, 1997.

Effie Marquess Carmack. *Out of the Black Patch: The Autobiography of Effie Marquess Carmack, Folk Musician, Artist, and Writer*. Edited by Noel A. Carmack and Karen Lynn Davidson, 1999.

Hannah Cornaby. *Autobiography and Poems*, 1881, 2007.

Caroline Barnes Crosby. *No Place to Call Home: The 1807–1857 Life Writings of Caroline Barnes Crosby, Chronicler of Outlying Mormon Communities*. Edited by Edward Leo Lyman, Susan Ward Payne, and George S. Ellsworth, 2005.

Karen Lynn Davidson. *Thriving on our Differences: A Book for LDS Women Who Feel Like Outsiders*, 1990.

Mary Sturlaugson Eyer. *A Soul So Rebellious*, 1980.

______. *He Restoreth My Soul*, 1982.

______. *Reflection of a Soul*, 1985.

Moneta Johnson Fillerup. *My Treasure Trove of Memories*, 2004.

Margaret Gordon. *Pansy's History: The Autobiography of Margaret E. P. Gordon, 1866–1966*. Edited by Claudia L. Bushman, 2011.

LeRoy and Ann Hafen. *The Joyous Journey of LeRoy R. and Ann W. Hafen: An Autobiography*, 1973.

Mary Ann Hafen. *Recollections of a Handcart Pioneer of 1860: A Woman's Life on the Mormon Frontier*. Edited by Donna Toland Smart, 1983, 2004.

Martha Spence Heywood. *Not by Bread Alone: The Journal of Martha Spence Heywood, 1850-56*. Edited by Juanita Brooks, 1978.

Rodello Hunter. *A Daughter of Zion: About Being a Mormon, a Personal Story of Life Among the Latter-Day Saints*, 1972, 1999.

Carolyn Jessop and Laura Palmer. *Escape*, 2008.

Sonia Johnson. *From Housewife to Heretic*, 1981.

Journey to Zion: Voices from the Mormon Trail. Edited by Carol Cornwall Madsen, 1997.

Elizabeth Wood Kane. *Twelve Mormon Homes: Visited in Succession on a Journey through Utah to Arizona*, 1974.

______. *A Gentile Account of Life in Utah's Dixie, 1872-73*, 1995.

Ardeth Greene Kapp. *Echoes From My Prairie*, 1979.

Mary Lightner. *The Life and Testimony of Mary Lightner*, 1982.

Wynetta Willis Martin. *Black Mormon Tells Her Story*, 1972.

Melissa Merrill. *Polygamist's Wife: The True Story of One Woman's Struggle with Modern-Day Polygamy*, 1975, 1979.

Mary Lois Walker Morris. *Before the Manifesto: The Life Writings of Mary Lois Walker Morris*. Edited by Melissa L. Milewski, 2007.

Stephanie Nielson. *Heaven is Here: An Incredible Story of Hope, Struggle, and Everyday Joy*, 2012.

Chieko Okazaki. *Lighten Up!*, 1993.

______. *Cat's Cradle*, 1994.

______. *Shared Motherhood*, 1994.

______. *Aloha!*, 1995.

______. *Sanctuary*, 1997.

______. *Disciples*, 1998.

______. *Being Enough*, 2002.

______. *What a Friend We Have in Jesus*, 2008.

Carol Lynn Pearson. *Goodbye, I Love You*, 1986.

Louisa Barnes Pratt. *The History of Louisa Barnes Pratt: The Autobiography of a Mormon Missionary Widow and Pioneer*. Edited by S. George Ellsworth, 1998.

Mary Haskin Parker Richards. *Winter Quarters: The 1846-1848 Life Writings of Mary Haskin Parker Richards*. Edited by Maurine Carr Ward, 1996.

Helen Sekaquaptewa. *Me and Mine: The Life Story of Helen Sekaquaptewa*, 1969.

Patty Sessions. *Mormon Midwife: The 1846-1888 Diaries of Patty Bartlett Sessions*. Edited by Donna Smart, 1999.

Ellis Reynolds Shipp. *While Others Slept: Autobiography and Journal of Ellis Reynolds Shipp*, 1985.

Barbara Smith. *A Fruitful Season: Reflection on the Challenging Years of the Relief Society, 1974–1984*, 1988.

Lucy Mack Smith. *Lucy Mack Smith—Her Story: Biographical Sketches of Joseph Smith, the Prophet, and His Progenitors for Many Generations by Lucy Mack Smith, Mother of the Prophet*, Lucy Mack Smith and Orson Pratt, 1880. Also published as:

______. *History of Joseph Smith By His Mother Lucy Mack Smith*. Edited by Preston Nibley, 1954.

______. *History of Joseph Smith by His Mother Lucy Mack Smith: The Unabridged Original Version*, compiled by R. Virnon Ingleton, 2005.

______. *History of Joseph Smith by His Mother: Revised and Enhanced*. Edited by Scott F. Proctor, Maurine J. Proctor, 1996.

______. *Lucy's Book: Critical Edition of Lucy Mack Smith's Family Memoir.* Edited by Lavina Fielding Anderson and Irene M. Bates, 2001.

Eliza R. Snow. *The Personal Writings of Eliza Roxcy Snow*. Edited by Maureen Ursenbach Beecher, 1995.

Virginia Sorensen. *Where Nothing is Long Ago: Memories of a Mormon Childhood*, 1963, 1999.

Fanny Stenhouse. *Exposé of Polygamy: A Lady's Life Among the Mormons*. Edited by Linda DeSimone, 2008.

Susan Buhler Taber. *Mormon Lives: A Year in the Elkton Ward*, 1993.

Annie Clark Tanner. *A Mormon Mother: An Autobiography*, 1969.

Alison Comish Thorne. *Leave the Dishes in the Sink: Adventures of an Activist in Conservative Utah*, 2002.

Edward W. Tullidge, *The Women of Mormondom*, 1877, 1997.

Laurel Thatcher Ulrich and Emma Lou Thayne. *All God's Critters Got a Place in the Choir*, 1995.

Jean Westwood. *Madame Chair: The Political Autobiography of an Unintentional Pioneer*, 2007.

Helen Mar Kimball Whitney. *A Widow's Tale: The 1884–1896 Diary of Helen Mar Kimball Whitney*. Edited by Charles M. Hatch and Todd Compton, 2003.

Terry Tempest Williams. *Refuge: An Unnatural History of Family and Place*, 1992, 2000.

Women of Faith in the Latter Days. Edited by Richard E. Turley, Jr. and Brittany A. Chapman, 2011.

Women's Voices: An Untold History of the Latter-day Saints, 1830–1900. Edited by Kenneth W. Godfrey, Audrey M. Godfrey, and Jill Mulvay Derr, 2002.

Helen, Owen, and Avery Woodruff. *Post-Manifesto Polygamy: The 1899–1904 Correspondence of Helen, Owen, and Avery Woodruff.* Edited by LuAnn Faylor Snyder and Phillip A. Snyder, 2009.

Index

G–L

M–O

P–R

S–W

Also available from

GREG KOFFORD BOOKS

"Swell Suffering": A Biography of Maurine Whipple

Veda Tebbs Hale

Paperback, ISBN: 978-1-58958-124-1
Hardcover, ISBN: 978-1-58958-122-7

Maurine Whipple, author of what some critics consider Mormonism's greatest novel, *The Giant Joshua,* is an enigma. Her prize-winning novel has never been out of print, and its portrayal of the founding of St. George draws on her own family history to produce its unforgettable and candid portrait of plural marriage's challenges. Yet Maurine's life is full of contradictions and unanswered questions. Veda Tebbs Hale, a personal friend of the paradoxical novelist, answers these questions with sympathy and tact, nailing each insight down with thorough research in Whipple's vast but under-utilized collected papers.

Praise for *"Swell Suffering"*:

"Hale achieves an admirable balance of compassion and objectivity toward an author who seemed fated to offend those who offered to love or befriend her. . . . Readers of this biography will be reminded that Whipple was a full peer of such Utah writers as Virginia Sorensen, Fawn Brodie, and Juanita Brooks, all of whom achieved national fame for their literary and historical works during the mid-twentieth century"

—Levi S. Peterson, author of *The Backslider* and *Juanita Brooks: Mormon Historian*

War & Peace in Our Time: Mormon Perspectives

Edited by Patrick Q. Mason, J. David Pulsipher, and Richard L. Bushman

Paperback, ISBN: 978-1-58958-099-2

"This provocative and thoughtful book is sure both to infuriate and to delight. . . . The essays demonstrate that exegesis of distinctly Latter-day Saint scriptures can yield a wealth of disputation, the equal of any rabbinical quarrel or Jesuitical casuistry. This volume provides a fitting springboard for robust and lively debates within the Mormon scholarly and lay community on how to think about the pressing issues of war and peace." - Robert S. Wood, Dean Emeritus, Center for Naval Warfare Studies, Chester W. Nimitz Chair Emeritus, U.S. Naval War College

"This is an extraordinary collection of essays on a topic of extraordinary importance. . . .Whatever your current opinion on the topic, this book will challenge you to reflect more deeply and thoroughly on what it means to be a disciple of Christ, the Prince of Peace, in an era of massive military budgets, lethal technologies, and widespread war." - Grant Hardy, Professor of History and Religious Studies, University of North Carolina, Asheville, Author, *Understanding the Book of Mormon: A Reader's Guide*

"Mormons take their morality seriously. They are also patriotic. Tragically, the second trait can undermine the first. When calls for war are on the horizon, it is possible for well-intended Saints to be too sure of our selective application of scripture to contemporary matters of life and death, too sure that we can overcome evil by force, that we can control the results of military conflict, that war is the only option for patriots. Yet pacifism has its own critics. This collection of differing views by thoughtful scholars comprises a debate. Reading it may save us in the future from enacting more harm than good in the name of God, country, or presumption." - Philip Barlow, Arrington Chair of Mormon History and Culture, Utah State University, Author, *Mormons and the Bible: The Place of the Latter-day Saints in American Religion*

Latter-Day Dissent: At the Crossroads of Intellectual Inquiry and Ecclesiastical Authority

Philip Lindholm

Paperback, ISBN: 978-1-58958-128-9

This volume collects, for the first time in book form, stories from the "September Six," a group of intellectuals officially excommunicated or disfellowshipped from the LDS Church in September of 1993 on charges of "apostasy" or "conduct unbecoming" Church members. Their experiences are significant and yet are largely unknown outside of scholarly or more liberal Mormon circles, which is surprising given that their story was immediately propelled onto screens and cover pages across the Western world.

Interviews by Dr. Philip Lindholm (Ph.D. Theology, University of Oxford) include those of the "September Six," Lynne Kanavel Whitesides, Paul James Toscano, Maxine Hanks, Lavina Fielding Anderson, and D. Michael Quinn; as well as Janice Merrill Allred, Margaret Merrill Toscano, Thomas W. Murphy, and former employee of the LDS Church's Public Affairs Department, Donald B. Jessee.

Each interview illustrates the tension that often exists between the Church and its intellectual critics, and highlights the difficulty of accommodating congregational diversity while maintaining doctrinal unity—a difficulty hearkening back to the very heart of ancient Christianity.

Rube Goldberg Machines: Essays in Mormon Theology

Adam S. Miller

Paperback, ISBN: 978-1-58958-193-7

"Adam Miller is the most original and provocative Latter-day Saint theologian practicing today."

—Richard Bushman, author of *Joseph Smith: Rough Stone Rolling*

"As a stylist, Miller gives Nietzsche a run for his money. As a believer, Miller is as submissive as Augustine hearing a child's voice in the garden. Miller is a theologian of the ordinary, thinking about our ordinary beliefs in very non-ordinary ways while never insisting that the ordinary become extra-ordinary."

—James Faulconer, Richard L. Evans Chair of Religious Understanding,Brigham Young University

"Miller's language is both recognizably Mormon and startlingly original. . . . The whole is an essay worthy of the name, inviting the reader to try ideas, following the philosopher pilgrim's intellectual progress through tangled brambles and into broad fields, fruitful orchards, and perhaps a sacred grove or two."

—Kristine Haglund, editor of *Dialogue: A Journal of Mormon Thought*

"Miller's Rube Goldberg theology is nothing like anything done in the Mormon tradition before."

—Blake Ostler, author of the Exploring Mormon Thought series

"The value of Miller's writings is in the modesty he both exhibits and projects onto the theological enterprise, even while showing its joyfully disruptive potential. Conventional Mormon minds may not resonate with every line of poetry and provocation—but Miller surely afflicts the comfortable, which is the theologian's highest end."

—Terryl Givens, author of *By the Hand of Mormon: The American Scripture that Launched a New World Religion*

On the Road with Joseph Smith: An Author's Diary

Richard L. Bushman

Paperback, ISBN 978-1-58958-102-9

After living with Joseph Smith for seven years and delivering the final proofs of his landmark study, *Joseph Smith: Rough Stone Rolling* to Knopf in July 2005, biographer Richard Lyman Bushman went "on the road" for a year, crisscrossing the country from coast to coast, delivering addresses on Joseph Smith and attending book-signings for the new biography.

Bushman confesses to hope and humility as he awaits reviews. He frets at the polarization that dismissed the book as either too hard on Joseph Smith or too easy. He yields to a very human compulsion to check sales figures on Amazon.com, but partway through the process stepped back with the recognition, "The book seems to be cutting its own path now, just as [I] hoped."

For readers coming to grips with the ongoing puzzle of the Prophet and the troublesome dimensions of their own faith, Richard Bushman, openly but not insistently presents himself as a believer. "I believe enough to take Joseph Smith seriously," he says. He draws comfort both from what he calls his "mantra" ("Today I will be a follower of Jesus Christ") and also from ongoing engagement with the intellectual challenges of explaining Joseph Smith.

Praise for *On the Road With Joseph Smith*:

"The diary is possibly unparalleled—an author of a recent book candidly dissecting his experiences with both Mormon and non-Mormon audiences . . . certainly deserves wider distribution—in part because it shows a talented historian laying open his vulnerabilities, and also because it shows how much any historian lays on the line when he writes about Joseph Smith."

-Dennis Lythgoe, *Deseret News*

"By turns humorous and poignant, this behind-the-scenes look at Richard Bushman's public and private ruminations about Joseph Smith reveals a great deal—not only about the inner life of one of our greatest scholars, but about Mormonism at the dawn of the 21st century."

-Jana Riess, co-author of *Mormonism for Dummies*

Mormon Polygamous Families: Life in the Principle

Jessie L. Embry

Paperback, ISBN: 978-1-58958-098-5
Hardcover, ISBN: 978-1-58958-114-2

Mormons and non-Mormons all have their views about how polygamy was practiced in the Church of Jesus Christ of Latter-day Saints during the late nineteenth and early twentieth centuries. Embry has examined the participants themselves in order to understand how men and women living a nineteenth-century Victorian lifestyle adapted to polygamy. Based on records and oral histories with husbands, wives, and children who lived in Mormon polygamous households, this study explores the diverse experiences of individual families and stereotypes about polygamy. The interviews are in some cases the only sources of primary information on how plural families were organized. In addition, children from monogamous families who grew up during the same period were interviewed to form a comparison group. When carefully examined, most of the stereotypes about polygamous marriages do not hold true. In this work it becomes clear that Mormon polygamous families were not much different from Mormon monogamous families and non-Mormon families of the same era. Embry offers a new perspective on the Mormon practice of polygamy that enables readers to gain better understanding of Mormonism historically.

Saints of Valor: Mormon Medal of Honor Recipients

Sherman L. Fleek

Hardcover, ISBN: 978-1-58958-171-5

Since 1861 when the US Congress approved the concept of a Medal of Honor for combat valor, 3,457 individuals have received this highest military decoration that the nation can bestow. Nine of those have been Latter-day Saints. The military and personal stories of these LDS recipients are compelling, inspiring, and tragic. The men who appear in this book are tied by two common threads: the Medal of Honor and their Mormon heritage.

The purpose of this book is to highlight the valor of a special class of LDS servicemen who served and sacrificed "above and beyond the call of duty." Four of these nine Mormons gave their "last full measure" for their country, never seeing the high award they richly deserved. All four branches of the service are represented: five were Army (one was a pilot with the Army Air Forces during WWII), two Navy, and one each of the Marine Corps and Air Force. Four were military professionals who made the service their careers; five were not career-minded; three died at an early age and never married. This book captures these harrowing historical narratives from personal accounts.

The Gift and Power: Translating the Book of Mormon

Brant A. Gardner

Hardcover, ISBN: 978-1-58958-131-9

From Brant A. Gardner, the author of the highly praised *Second Witness* commentaries on the Book of Mormon, comes *The Gift and Power: Translating the Book of Mormon*. In this first book-length treatment of the translation process, Gardner closely examines the accounts surrounding Joseph Smith's translation of the Book of Mormon to answer a wide spectrum of questions about the process, including: Did the Prophet use seerstones common to folk magicians of his time? How did he use them? And, what is the relationship to the golden plates and the printed text?

Approaching the topic in three sections, part 1 examines the stories told about Joseph, folk magic, and the translation. Part 2 examines the available evidence to determine how closely the English text replicates the original plate text. And part 3 seeks to explain how seer stones worked, why they no longer work, and how Joseph Smith could have produced a translation with them.

Fire and Sword: A History of the Latter-day Saints in Northern Missouri, 1836-39

Leland Homer Gentry and
Todd M. Compton

Hardcover, ISBN: 978-1-58958-103-6

Many Mormon dreams flourished in Missouri. So did many Mormon nightmares.

The Missouri period—especially from the summer of 1838 when Joseph took over vigorous, personal direction of this new Zion until the spring of 1839 when he escaped after five months of imprisonment—represents a moment of intense crisis in Mormon history. Representing the greatest extremes of devotion and violence, commitment and intolerance, physical suffering and terror—mobbings, battles, massacres, and political "knockdowns"—it shadowed the Mormon psyche for a century.

Leland Gentry was the first to step beyond this disturbing period as a one-sided symbol of religious persecution and move toward understanding it with careful documentation and evenhanded analysis. In Fire and Sword, Todd Compton collaborates with Gentry to update this foundational work with four decades of new scholarship, more insightful critical theory, and the wealth of resources that have become electronically available in the last few years.

Compton gives full credit to Leland Gentry's extraordinary achievement, particularly in documenting the existence of Danites and in attempting to tell the Missourians' side of the story; but he also goes far beyond it, gracefully drawing into the dialogue signal interpretations written since Gentry and introducing the raw urgency of personal writings, eyewitness journalists, and bemused politicians seesawing between human compassion and partisan harshness. In the lush Missouri landscape of the Mormon imagination where Adam and Eve had walked out of the garden and where Adam would return to preside over his posterity, the towering religious creativity of Joseph Smith and clash of religious stereotypes created a swift and traumatic frontier drama that changed the Church.

"This is My Doctrine": The Development of Mormon Theology

Charles R. Harrell

Hardcover, ISBN: 978-1-58958-103-6

The principal doctrines defining Mormonism today often bear little resemblance to those it started out with in the early 1830s. This book shows that these doctrines did not originate in a vacuum but were rather prompted and informed by the religious culture from which Mormonism arose. Early Mormons, like their early Christian and even earlier Israelite predecessors, brought with them their own varied culturally conditioned theological presuppositions (a process of convergence) and only later acquired a more distinctive theological outlook (a process of differentiation).

In this first-of-its-kind comprehensive treatment of the development of Mormon theology, Charles Harrell traces the history of Latter-day Saint doctrines from the times of the Old Testament to the present. He describes how Mormonism has carried on the tradition of the biblical authors, early Christians, and later Protestants in reinterpreting scripture to accommodate new theological ideas while attempting to uphold the integrity and authority of the scriptures. In the process, he probes three questions: How did Mormon doctrines develop? What are the scriptural underpinnings of these doctrines? And what do critical scholars make of these same scriptures? In this enlightening study, Harrell systematically peels back the doctrinal accretions of time to provide a fresh new look at Mormon theology.

"This Is My Doctrine" will provide those already versed in Mormonism's theological tradition with a new and richer perspective of Mormon theology. Those unacquainted with Mormonism will gain an appreciation for how Mormon theology fits into the larger Jewish and Christian theological traditions.

Parallels and Convergences: Mormon Thought and Engineering Vision

Edited by A. Scott Howe and Richard L. Bushman

Paperback, ISBN: 978-1-58958-187-6

If there is "no such thing as immaterial matter," and "all spirit is matter," then what are the implications for such standard theological principles as creation, human progression, free will, transfiguration, resurrection, and immortality? In eleven stimulating essays, Mormon engineers probe gospel possibilities and future vistas dealing with human nature, divine progression, and the earth's future. Richard Bushman poses a vision-expanding proposal: "The end point of engineering knowledge may be divine knowledge. Mormon theology permits us to think of God and humans as collaborators in bringing to pass the immortality and eternal life of man. Engineers may be preparing the way for humans to act more like gods in managing the world."

From the foreword by Richard L. Bushman:

Mormon theology leads us to see eternal implications in engineering. Engineers enable us to make the world more comfortable and to perform incredible feats of movement and communication. But their work may go beyond the amelioration of the human condition. The end point of engineering knowledge may be divine knowledge. Mormon theology permits us to think of God and humans as collaborators in bringing to pass the immortality and eternal life of man. Engineers may be preparing the way for humans to act more like gods in managing the world.

Kindliness, wise parenting, righteousness, and service are probably more fundamental in leading humans toward eternal life. But improving our physical world fits serves divine purposes, too. In constructing better worlds, engineers may be learning godly skills. From a Latter-day Saint perspective, they may be incipient creators.

The papers in this volume capture the thought of a group of LDS engineers exploring the interactions of their work and their belief at the beginning of the twenty-first century. Ideally these essays will launch a discussion that will continue for many years to come.

Villages on Wheels: A Social History of the Gathering to Zion

Stanley B. Kimball and Violet T. Kimball

ISBN: 978-1-58958-119-7

The enduring saga of Mormonism is its great trek across the plains, and understanding that trek was the life work of Stanley B. Kimball, master of Mormon trails. This final work, a collaboration he began and which was completed after his death in 2003 by his photographer-writer wife, Violet, explores that movement westward as a social history, with the Mormons moving as "villages on wheels."

Set in the broader context of transcontinental migration to Oregon and California, the Mormon trek spanned twenty-two years, moved approximately 54,700 individuals, many of them in family groups, and left about 7,000 graves at the trailside.

Like a true social history, this fascinating account in fourteen chapters explores both the routines of the trail—cooking, cleaning, laundry, dealing with bodily functions—and the dramatic moments: encountering Indians and stampeding buffalo, giving birth, losing loved ones to death, dealing with rage and injustice, but also offering succor, kindliness, and faith. Religious observances were simultaneously an important part of creating and maintaining group cohesiveness, but working them into the fabric of the grueling day-to-day routine resulted in adaptation, including a "sliding Sabbath." The role played by children and teens receives careful scrutiny; not only did children grow up quickly on the trail, but the gender boundaries guarding their "separate spheres" blurred under the erosion of concentrating on tasks that had to be done regardless of the age or sex of those available to do them. Unexpected attention is given to African Americans who were part of this westering experience, and Violet also gives due credit to the "four-legged heroes" who hauled the wagons westward.

Discourses in Mormon Theology: Philosophical and Theological Possibilities

Edited by
James M. McLachlan and Loyd Ericson

Hardcover, ISBN: 978-1-58958-103-6

A mere two hundred years old, Mormonism is still in its infancy compared to other theological disciplines (Judaism, Catholicism, Buddhism, etc.). This volume will introduce its reader to the rich blend of theological viewpoints that exist within Mormonism. The essays break new ground in Mormon studies by exploring the vast expanse of philosophical territory left largely untouched by traditional approaches to Mormon theology. It presents philosophical and theological essays by many of the finest minds associated with Mormonism in an organized and easy-to-understand manner and provides the reader with a window into the fascinating diversity amongst Mormon philosophers. Open-minded students of pure religion will appreciate this volume's thoughtful inquiries.

These essays were delivered at the first conference of the Society for Mormon Philosophy and Theology. Authors include Grant Underwood, Blake T. Ostler, Dennis Potter, Margaret Merrill Toscano, James E. Faulconer, and Robert L. Millet

Praise for *Discourses in Mormon Theology*:

"In short, *Discourses in Mormon Theology* is an excellent compilation of essays that are sure to feed both the mind and soul. It reminds all of us that beyond the white shirts and ties there exists a universe of theological and moral sensitivity that cries out for study and acclamation."

-Jeff Needle, Association for Mormon Letters

The Man behind the Discourse: A Biography of King Follett

Joann Follett Mortensen

ISBN: 978-1-58958-036-7

Who was King Follett? When he was fatally injured digging a well in Nauvoo in March 1844, why did Joseph Smith use his death to deliver the monumental doctrinal sermon now known as the King Follett Discourse? Much has been written about the sermon, but little about King.

Although King left no personal writings, Joann Follett Mortensen, King's third great-granddaughter, draws on more than thirty years of research in civic and Church records and in the journals and letters of King's peers to piece together King's story from his birth in New Hampshire and moves westward where, in Ohio, he and his wife, Louisa, made the life-shifting decision to accept the new Mormon religion.

From that point, this humble, hospitable, and hardworking family followed the Church into Missouri where their devotion to Joseph Smith was refined and burnished. King was the last Mormon prisoner in Missouri to be released from jail. According to family lore, King was one of the Prophet's bodyguards. He was also a Danite, a Mason, and an officer in the Nauvoo Legion. After his death, Louisa and their children settled in Iowa where some associated with the Cutlerities and the RLDS Church; others moved on to California. One son joined the Mormon Battalion and helped found Mormon communities in Utah, Idaho, and Arizona.

While King would have died virtually unknown had his name not been attached to the discourse, his life story reflects the reality of all those whose faith became the foundation for a new religion. His biography is more than one man's life story. It is the history of the early Restoration itself.

Tiki and Temple:
The Mormon Mission in New Zealand, 1854–1958

Marjorie Newton

Paperback, ISBN: 978-1-58958-121-0

From the arrival of the first Mormon missionaries in New Zealand in 1854 until stakehood and the dedication of the Hamilton New Zealand Temple in 1958, Tiki and Temple tells the enthralling story of Mormonism's encounter with the genuinely different but surprisingly harmonious Maori culture.

Mormon interest in the Maori can be documented to 1832, soon after Joseph Smith organized the Church of Jesus Christ of Latter-day Saints in America. Under his successor Brigham Young, Mormon missionaries arrived in New Zealand in 1854, but another three decades passed before they began sustained proselytising among the Maori people—living in Maori pa, eating eels and potatoes with their fingers from communal dishes, learning to speak the language, and establishing schools. They grew to love—and were loved by—their Maori converts, whose numbers mushroomed until by 1898, when the Australasian Mission was divided, the New Zealand Mission was ten times larger than the parent Australian Mission.

The New Zealand Mission of the Mormon Church was virtually two missions—one to the English-speaking immigrants and their descendants, and one to the tangata whenua—"people of the land." The difficulties this dichotomy caused, as both leaders and converts struggled with cultural differences and their isolation from Church headquarters, make a fascinating story. Drawing on hitherto untapped sources, including missionary journals and letters and government documents, this absorbing book is the fullest narrative available of Mormonism's flourishing in New Zealand.

Although written primarily for a Latter-day Saint audience, this book fills a gap for anyone interested in an accurate and coherent account of the growth of Mormonism in New Zealand.

CPSIA information can be obtained at www.ICGtesting.com
Printed in the USA
BVOW07s1709240714

360144BV00001B/9/P